Job Savvy

Fifth Edition

How to Be a Success at Work

LaVerne L. Ludden, Ed.D.

jist
Works
America's Career Publisher

Job Savvy, Fifth Edition

How to Be a Success at Work

© 2012 by JIST Publishing

Published by JIST Works, an imprint of JIST Publishing
875 Montreal Way
St. Paul, MN 55102

E-mail: info@jist.com   Web site: www.jist.com

> **Note to instructors.** This book has substantial support materials, including a thorough *Instructor's Resources CD-ROM* with PowerPoints and videos. Visit www.jist.com for details.
>
> **About career materials published by JIST.** Our materials encourage people to be self-directed and to take control of their destinies. We work hard to provide excellent content, solid advice, and techniques that get results. If you have questions about this book or other JIST products, visit www.jist.com.
>
> **Visit www.jist.com.** Find out about our products, get free tables of contents and sample pages, order a free catalog, and link to other career-related sites. You can also learn more about JIST authors and JIST training available to professionals.

Acquisitions Editor: Susan Pines
Development Editor: Grant E. Mabie
Production Editor: Jeanne Clark
Cover and Interior Designers: Aleata Halbig, Julie Johnston, Timothy W. Larson
Proofreader: Chuck Hutchinson
Indexer: Cheryl Ann Lenser

Printed in the United States of America

18 17 16 15 14 13   9 8 7 6 5 4 3

We have been careful to provide accurate information throughout this book, but it is possible that errors and omissions have been introduced. Please consider this in making any career plans or other important decisions. Trust your own judgment above all else and in all things.

Trademarks: All brand names and product names used in this book are trade names, service marks, trademarks, or registered trademarks of their respective owners.

ISBN 978-1-59357-914-2

About This Book

This is a book to help people keep a job and advance their careers. Based on research into what employers actually look for in the people who succeed or fail, *Job Savvy* is designed to help develop critical job-survival skills, increase productivity, and improve job satisfaction and success. Using a workbook approach, many in-the-book activities are provided to reinforce key points and develop new job-survival skills and plans. The narrative is easy to read and informative, and features good graphic design, many examples, checklists, case studies, and section summaries.

This is the fifth edition of this book. Everything that made the first four editions so popular remains, so you get the best of the previous editions along with many improvements. This edition draws on more recent research about job skills. It also presents the changes that have occurred in the workplace since the fourth edition and reviews their implications.

Why People Need to Improve Their Basic Job Skills

The United States—indeed, much of the world—is in one of the largest economic downturns since the early 1980s. As this book goes to press, unemployment remains at a rate the country has not seen in almost 30 years. The need for a person to be competitive to find and keep a job is critical. Yet, the years ahead are projected to be a time of labor market opportunity as well as challenge for most workers. Some of these challenges and opportunities include the following:

- People will work in more varied ways as permanent employees, temporary employees, and independent contractors.

- Increasing competition among businesses around the globe will require changes in operations, thus requiring more flexibility in workers.

- Information technology will continue to change the way we work, and people must adapt to these changes.

- Many new and existing jobs will require higher levels of technical skills.

(continued)

(continued)

- The amount of education and training required for jobs will increase.
- Employers will expect their employees to be more productive and obtain better results in more complex jobs.

We also know that people frequently change jobs. The Bureau of Labor Statistics reported the people now ages 47–54 held an average of about 11 jobs from the ages of 18 to 44 (about 60 percent of the jobs were held in the first nine years of their work life). Many labor experts predict the rate people change jobs will increase.

Workforce trends as well as individual changes in jobs will require people who are better prepared than most workers have been in the past. The biggest need, according to most employers and labor market experts, is for employees to have good "basic" skills. These include having basic academic skills and the ability to communicate, adapt to new situations, and solve problems. Although these and other related skills are not technical skills in the traditional sense, they have everything to do with long-term success on the job. And that is what this book is about.

A Different Point of View

You will find numerous references in *Job Savvy* to the studies and research of psychologists, sociologists, economists, and other labor market professionals, yet this is *not* an academic book. Instead, this information has been used to form the basis for a practical and useful handbook for a working person—or one who soon plans to enter the world of work. Many employers have asked for such a book to give them a tool to encourage their new workers to succeed on the job. And because the author has been both an employer and a trainer of new employees, he brings a unique and helpful point of view that will bridge the gap between an employer's and an employee's expectations. The result of this is increased job savvy where, we believe, both will win.

A Parable

An explorer was once asked what he most disliked about the wilderness. "Is it the wolves?"

"No," he replied. "It's the mosquitoes."

In a similar way, many people fail on the job as a result of the little problems, not the big ones. This book will help you identify and avoid both so that you can be the best employee you can be.

Contents

Your Employment Relationship

Did you know that most of us spend almost 95,000 hours of our lives working? Work is how we earn the money to pay for our material needs. Work satisfies many of our psychological needs. And work fulfills our needs for human interaction and friendship. Because work is such a major part of our lives, it's important to have a basic understanding about work in today's society. *Seven seconds to form an opinion*

Knowing more about diversity in the labor force will help you appreciate your coworkers. This diversity extends to gender, ethnicity, and age.

Many workers are also looking for more flexible work, such as part-time, job sharing, on-call, temporary, and contract jobs. In addition, people are working at home for an employer or starting home-based businesses.[1]

This chapter looks at the labor force, occupations, the workplace, and the structure of work. It also examines what employers expect when they hire someone in the workforce and what you should expect from your employer.

"Hop out. We're replacing you with temps."

The Changing 21st-Century Labor Force

The term *labor force* refers to the people who are available and want to work. Anyone who is looking for a job or working at a job is a member of the labor force. You'll be a more effective worker if you understand some of the changes that are occurring in the labor force:[2]

1. **The labor force is growing more slowly than before.** The labor force grew 13.2 percent from 1988 to 1998 and 12.1 percent from 1998 to 2008. It is only expected to grow 8.2 percent from 2008 to 2018. This slowdown in growth is expected to continue during the second decade of the 21st century through 2018, with a projected growth of less than 1 percent a year.

   Slower growth of the labor force combined with average economic expansion has created a demand for more workers in many occupations and businesses. Businesses are having difficulty finding workers for minimum-wage jobs. This has improved the opportunities for many people to get jobs. Numerous businesses now recruit 14- and 15-year-olds because the teens are willing to work for the minimum wage. About one-third of all 14-to-16-year-olds work during the school year.

   During the first part of the 21st century, there probably won't be much competition for jobs that require little education and offer low wages. This demand for new workers might also result in more job opportunities for people with disabilities.

2. **More women are entering the workforce.** Women now account for more than 46 percent of workers in the labor force. This is a dramatic change from the end of World War II, when only 28 percent of the workforce was female. Women's participation in the workforce has had a great impact on businesses. Employers have become more concerned about child care, family leave, flexible schedules, job sharing, sexual harassment, and other issues that are relevant to women.

   The changing view of women in the workplace also has changed how many organizations view men's roles within the family. Both female and male workers are demanding "family-friendly" employment practices. Many positive changes in the workplace have resulted from the increased participation of women, and this trend is likely to continue.

3. **The labor force is aging.** The baby boom generation—people born between 1946 and 1964—makes up almost half of the labor force. By 2018, this group will be 54 to 72 years old. The 55-plus age group will grow five times faster than any other age group in the labor force. The graying of the workforce likely will force businesses to rethink retirement policies and to find new ways to use workers regardless of age. The fact that this generation will be the healthiest and most vital group of older workers in history might also alter views about changing careers later in

life and about how long people should work. This trend became apparent in 2008 when the 55-plus age group was the only age group with an increase in its workforce participation rate. At the same time the baby boom generation is aging, the labor force participation rate of individuals aged 16–24 continues to trend downward because of an increase in the number of young people completing high school and attending college.

4. **The workforce is showing greater ethnic diversity.** The face of the workforce is changing and becoming more diverse. In 1980, whites made up 81.9 percent of the workforce; this number will decline to 79.4 percent by 2018. The ethnic composition of the U.S. workforce in 2018 is expected to be 17.6 percent Hispanic, 12.1 percent African American, and 5.6 percent Asian. Other ethnic groups such as Native Americans will comprise 2.9 percent. Companies have responded to this trend by creating ethnic diversity programs to help workers understand and appreciate their cultural differences. This mix of cultures in the workplace will bring new perspectives to solving business problems. You can be a more effective (and valuable) employee if you can work in a diverse workforce.

The workforce of the future will represent a broad range of gender, age, and ethnic differences. It's important for people entering the workforce to be aware of these changes and of the need to work with all different kinds of people. Learning to appreciate differences isn't just a nicety anymore—it's a workplace necessity.

WHAT DOES YOUR WORKPLACE LOOK LIKE?

Following are descriptions of people in the workforce. Check all of the boxes that apply to people you currently work with. In the line after each group, write the number of people in your workplace who fall into that category.

Age

❑ 14 to 15 years old_____   ❑ 16 to 19 years old_____

❑ 20 to 24 years old_____   ❑ 25 to 34 years old_____

❑ 35 to 44 years old_____   ❑ 45 to 54 years old_____

❑ 55 to 64 years old_____   ❑ 65 and over _____

Gender

❑ Male _____   ❑ Female _____

(continued)

(continued)

Ethnic Group

❑ White
    (non-Hispanic origin)_____

❑ Black _____

❑ Hispanic _____

❑ Asian _____

❑ Native American _____

How would you rate diversity in your workplace?

    ❑ Low   ❑ Medium   ❑ High

Organizations and Work

In the U.S. economy, most workers—78.2 percent, in fact—are employed by service-producing organizations.[3] As the following table shows, service organizations include a wide variety of businesses—not just fast-food franchises, which is many people's first thought when they hear the words "service economy." The major areas of the service industry are in the following table. The type of service industry is in the first column. The second column shows the percentage of workers employed by each industry group in 2008. The third column shows the projected employment for 2018.

Type of Service Industry	Percentage of 2008 Employment	Projected Percentage of 2018 Employment
Wholesale and retail trade	14.2%	14.0%
Federal, state, and local government	14.9%	14.1%
Educational, health care, and social assistance	12.5%	14.1%
Professional and business services	11.8%	13.2%
Leisure and hospitality	8.9%	8.8%
Information and financial activities	7.4%	7.1%
Transporting and warehousing	5.0%	4.9%
Other	4.2%	4.3%

The remaining portion of the workforce (the other 21.8 percent) is employed in goods-producing organizations, agriculture, and self-employment. This economic sector's share of employment has declined for the past several decades, and continued decline is expected. The following table shows current and projected employment for these businesses.

Type of Business	Percentage of 2008 Employment	Projected Percentage of 2018 Employment
Goods production (manufacturing, etc.)	14.2%	12.9%
Agriculture	1.4%	1.2%
Self-employment	6.2%	6.0%

Most workers are employed in service-producing fields, and more than 50 percent work for smaller organizations—organizations with fewer than 500 employees.[4] A decline in an industry doesn't mean you can't find a good job in that sector. But working in an industry with declining employment means you must continually develop your skills. And, to be safe, you also should develop skills that will help you get a job in another industry if it becomes necessary. Many people learned this lesson as a result of corporate restructuring that has been a significant part of business in the last 30 years.

Smaller organizations are less likely than larger ones to provide their workers with training. This means that most workers must assess their own training needs and take control of their training and education. In other words, you are responsible for your own employability and competitiveness in today's work-force.

WHAT KIND OF ORGANIZATION DO YOU WORK FOR?

Do you work for a service-producing or a goods-producing organization?

_____

How big is the organization you work for?

_____

What skills do people need to work in this organization?

_____

_____

What skills do people need to advance in this organization?

_____

_____

What other industries interest you?

_____

_____

What skills do you have that can be used in other organizations and other industries?

_____

_____

Occupational Trends

Jobs that require education beyond high school form the fastest-growing segment of the job market. Jobs requiring an associate degree or higher account for 12 of the 20 fastest-growing jobs in the U.S. economy.[5]

Education and Earnings

This occupational trend helps explain why a worker's level of education has such a dramatic effect on the person's earnings. The following table illustrates the relationship between education and earnings.[6] The third column shows how much more workers with additional education can earn, on average, in comparison to high school graduates.

Level of Education	Average Annual Earnings	Percentage of High School Graduate's Earnings
No high school diploma	$21,268	71%
High school diploma	$32,522	100%
Some college, no degree	$37,024	114%
Associate degree	$39,884	123%
Bachelor's degree	$53,976	166%
Master's degree	$66,144	203%
Doctoral degree	$80,600	248%
Professional degree	$83,270	257%

The difference in earnings over a lifetime is staggering. Take the example of a high school graduate who begins working full-time at 19 and retires 51 years later at age 70. Compare that person with a college graduate who begins working at age 25 and retires at age 70. The college graduate would earn about $769,000—almost three-quarters of a million dollars—more in a lifetime. Earnings and employment opportunities for less-educated workers declined significantly in the last decade. That trend is likely to continue. There's truth to the adage "education pays."

Training and Continuing Education

It's also important—in fact, in today's economy, it's necessary—to continue learning once you're on the job. Although many businesses provide training, it's up to you to take charge of your continuing education. (Chapter 6 examines this topic.)

THINKING ABOUT YOUR EDUCATION

What education is required for your job? _____

How much do you earn in a year? (If you're not sure, multiply your hourly wage by 2,080 if you work full-time. If you work part-time, multiply your hourly wage by the number of hours you work in an average week and multiply that by 52 weeks.)

_____

How do your education and earnings compare with the national average for your occupation? (You can find this information in the *Occupational Outlook Handbook [OOH]* or online at www.bls.gov/oco.)

_____

Are you planning to get a job in another occupation? _____

What are the educational requirements and average earnings for this occupation? (Again, you can find this information in the *OOH* or online.)

_____

What kind of training does your current job offer?

_____

How can this training help you advance in your current job?

_____

_____

How can the training help prepare you for a future occupation?

_____

_____

Write some ways you can keep your education current and get the skills you need to be successful.

_____

_____

The Structure of Work

The structure of work is changing, and that affects the way jobs are organized. Most organizations recognize the need to have a flexible workforce. This flexibility allows a business to keep its workforce as small as possible, thus saving money. Organizations use a combination of core employees and nontraditional workers to increase efficiency. People engaged in what the U.S. Department of Labor identifies as "nontraditional work arrangements" help core employees achieve organizational goals. The following are explanations of the various work arrangements:

- **Core employees:** People with a traditional employment arrangement. Companies hire these full-time workers on a permanent basis—meaning that there is no planned end to the job. Core employees typically have some loyalty to the organization and understand both its short-term and long-term goals. They usually are provided with benefits such as vacation time, holiday pay, and health insurance. Core employees often coordinate or lead projects for an organization.

- **Independent contractors:** Self-employed individuals who provide services to an organization based on a contract signed by the employer and contractor. The service they provide might be computer programming, management consulting, cleaning, maintenance, payroll, accounting, security, telecommunications, editing, or printing. Contractors are paid a fee for completion of a task, rather than a wage.

- **Contract firms:** Organizations that typically supply entry-level workers to an organization. The work is typically done at the employer's site. For example, electrical component assemblers might be employed by a contract firm rather than by the manufacturer. The manufacturer doesn't have to be concerned about performing all the management and administrative support functions involved in employing a large group of workers.

- **On-call workers:** Workers who are called to work when they are needed. They are paid for work only when they are called to perform a task. Employers might use this type of arrangement if they need workers to repair specialized manufacturing equipment, computers, or telecommunications equipment, or to install equipment when ordered.

- **Temporary workers:** Workers who are hired by an organization for a short time or whose services are obtained through a temporary employment service. Many organizations prefer to use a "temp service" because it reduces their paperwork, administrative tasks, and recruitment efforts. If temporary workers are hired to work on a specific project, their employment ends when the project ends. Temporary workers might be hired when an organization's workload increases beyond the capacity of its core employees. In that case, there might be no specific date when the work ends. Rather, the organization will stop using the workers' services when the workload decreases. Temporary employees often do not have benefits—unless they are provided by the temp service—and their work can be terminated without advance notice.

Contingent Workforce

The contingent workforce is made up of individuals who are part-time workers, self-employed people working as independent contractors for organizations, workers hired for short periods of time, on-call workers, and workers who are employed through temporary employment firms. The most frequently cited reason for using contingent workers is to complete a project that has a set life span.

So what does all this mean for you? It means that you are responsible for your own career. In today's economy, you simply cannot rely on an employer to provide a "permanent" job. When one job ends, you must be prepared to find another. It's important to develop as many skills as possible so that you can adapt to new tasks and projects, and to be prepared to work either as a core employee or contingent worker. Adaptability and a willingness to work in any structure allow you to take charge of your own career.

How Job Savvy Are You?

Alisha is a computer repair technician for a company with about 100 employees. She is paid by a temporary-service firm. Alisha earned her associate degree from a community college three years ago. She earns about $600 a week but has no benefits.

1. What kind of worker is Alisha?

   _____

   _____

2. If you were Alisha, would you continue to work for this company? Give a reason for your answer.

   _____

   _____

3. What could Alisha do to increase her opportunities to work as a core employee?

   _____

   _____

Jamal is employed full-time as an orderly in a hospital and receives several benefits, such as paid holidays, paid vacation time, and health insurance. He earns about $350 per week. Jamal enjoys working in a medical environment but thinks he needs to earn more money. He graduated from high school, but he didn't like school and he doesn't want to go to college.

1. What kind of worker is Jamal?

   _____

   _____

2. Would you be satisfied working in this situation? Explain your answer.

   _____

3. What do you think Jamal could do to improve his salary and his work situation?

   _____

   _____

Herschel is self-employed, so he pays for his own benefits. He spends most of his time working for a large corporation, processing payroll checks for the company's employees, keeping time records, and filing employment-tax reports. Herschel has a bachelor's degree in accounting. His business earns about $45,000 a year, but he would like to earn much more money.

1. What kind of worker is Herschel?

   _____

   _____

2. Would you be satisfied with a work situation like Herschel's?

   _____

   _____

(continued)

3. What do you think Herschel can do to make more money?

_____

_____

YOUR WORK EXPERIENCE

In the following space, briefly describe your last three jobs. Were you employed full-time or part-time? Did the company hire you, or were you assigned by a temporary agency? How large was the company in terms of numbers of employees and customers, amount of sales, and locations? What types of technology did you use on the job?

1. _____

_____

_____

2. _____

_____

_____

3. _____

_____

_____

21st-Century Skills

Many studies provide insight into the skills that employers expect their workers to have to succeed on the job. Having a better understanding of what it takes to do well on a job will help you achieve personal success. This book can help you acquire many of the basic skills you need to do well at any occupation. Probably the most interesting aspect of studies about workplace skills is that their results have been consistent during the past 30 years. However, they have become even more important during the 21st century as workers in the United States are competing with workers around the world.

Workplace Basics

The U.S. Secretary of Labor created a commission to "define the know-how needed in the workplace." The Secretary's Commission on Achieving Necessary Skills (SCANS) was made up of people from business, education, and government who identified the skills needed to succeed in high-skilled, high-paid jobs.

They listed three foundational skills and five workplace competencies.[7] The foundation skills include the following:

1. **Basic skills,** including reading, writing, mathematics, speaking, and listening

2. **Thinking skills,** including the ability to learn, reason, think creatively, make decisions, and solve problems

3. **Personal qualities,** including individual responsibility, self-esteem, self-management, sociability, and integrity

Workplace competencies are the skills workers need to be productive. The commission listed five of these:

1. **Resources,** including the ability to allocate time, money, materials, space, and staff

2. **Interpersonal skills,** including the ability to work on teams, teach others, and serve customers, as well as to lead, negotiate with, and work with people from diverse cultural backgrounds

3. **Information,** including the ability to acquire and evaluate data, organize and maintain files, interpret and communicate information, and use computers to process information

4. **Systems,** including the ability to understand social, organizational, and technological systems; monitor and correct performance; and design or improve systems

5. **Technology,** including the ability to select equipment and tools, apply technology to specific tasks, and maintain and troubleshoot equipment

The SCANS report demonstrates an important fact: Different, higher-level skills are needed in today's labor market as compared to the skills required 20 years ago. This report is supported by the Workplace Basics study, which was conducted by the American Society for Training and Development (ASTD).[8]

ASTD asked employers throughout the United States what basic skills their employees need. The study found that most employers want their employees to possess the workplace basics, including these skills:

1. **Knowing how to learn:** The concept of lifelong learning is common in the business community. Employees who don't have good learning skills will be unable to take advantage of training and might soon find their skills obsolete.

2. **Reading, writing, and computation:** People who are weak in these skills will have trouble in most jobs. The average education required for jobs in the early part of the 21st century is approximately 13.5 years.

3. **Listening and oral communication:** The average person spends 8.4 percent of communication time writing, 13.3 percent reading, 23 percent speaking, and 55 percent listening. Communication is as critical to success on the job as the three *R*s.

4. **Adaptability:** Organizations must be flexible to adapt and keep pace with advances in technology, changes in the marketplace, and new management practices. Employees who are creative problem solvers are essential to today's businesses.

5. **Personal management:** This category covers self-esteem, goal setting and motivation, and personal and career development. For businesses to succeed, employees must take pride in their work and be able to formulate and achieve goals. Finally, employees must know how to advance within an organization and how to transfer skills to another business. As more businesses engage in participative management, these skills will become increasingly necessary.

6. **Group effectiveness:** Individualism is a thing of the past in most jobs. It is far more important that workers understand and practice teamwork, negotiation, and interpersonal skills. People who understand how to work effectively in groups are the foundations of successful enterprises.

7. **Influence:** Each employee must establish his or her own influence in order to successfully contribute ideas to an organization. Employees must understand the organizational structure and informal networks in order to implement new ideas or to complete some tasks.

Who Needs These Skills?

In 2006, the ASTD conducted an online survey that asked its members to identify the skills most lacking by employees in their organizations.[9] Because employees lack these skills, the organizations end up with the responsibility of developing these skills in their employees. The results of this survey show the following skills and the percent of training-and-development professionals that think these skills are most needed in their organizations.

Skill	Percent That Say It's Most Needed
Managerial/supervisory	55
Communication/interpersonal	51
Leadership	45
Process and project management	27
Technical/systems	24
Customer service	20
Professional or industry specific	19
Sales	17

It is interesting that employers considered many "basic skills" to be more important than technical skills needed for a job. This is different from the perception most people have. That might be why job seekers promoting their abilities often overlook and downplay their more basic skills. It is also a reason to use this book to develop these skills.

The Public's View About 21st-Century Skills

In 2010, the Partnership for 21st Century Skills—a group of major corporate and educational organizations—cooperated with the American Management Association and surveyed more than 2,100 managers and executives on their attitudes about the most important skills needed to succeed in the modern workforce.[10]

The survey defined the four skills as

- **Critical thinking and problem solving:** The ability to make decisions, solve problems, and take action as appropriate
- **Effective communication:** The ability to synthesize and transmit your ideas both in written and oral formats
- **Collaboration and team building:** The ability to work effectively with others, including those from diverse groups and with opposing points of view
- **Creativity and innovation:** The ability to see what's *not* there and make something happen

Managers and executives were asked how they believed the four skills would be viewed by their organization in the next three to five years. They responded in the following way.

Statement About Skills	Percentage Agreeing with Statement
They will become more important.	75.7%
They will remain the same.	22.5%
They will become less important.	0.6%
No opinion.	1.1%

Almost 98 percent of executives and managers indicated that critical thinking, effective communication, team building, and creativity will remain or become more important skills for workers in their organization.

Best Jobs for the 21st-Century Skills

There is another perspective for determining which skills are important to succeed in the today's workforce. This view examines the jobs that are the best in the U.S. economy and then considers the skills that are most important in performing those jobs. The U.S. Department of Labor has collected a database, called O*NET (www.onetcenter.org), of information about the major occupations in the labor market. The data presented in this section comes from the O*NET and is based on projections for occupations in 2018.

The top 20 best jobs in the U.S. economy that do not require a bachelor's degree—based on job growth, annual number of job openings, and earnings—are the following, listed according to their ranking:

1. Registered nurses
2. Dental hygienists
3. Sales representatives, services

4. Computer support specialists
5. Paralegals and legal assistants
6. Radiologic technologists and technicians
7. Computer specialists, all other
8. Sales representatives, wholesale and manufacturing, technical and scientific products
9. Sales representatives, wholesale and manufacturing, except technical and scientific products
10. Fire fighters
11. Police and sheriff's patrol officers
12. Cost estimators
13. Self-enrichment education teachers
14. Plumbers, pipefitters, and steamfitters
15. Claims adjusters, examiners, and investigators
16. Diagnostic medical sonographers
17. Licensed practical and licensed vocational nurses
18. Managers, all other
19. Respiratory therapists
20. First-line supervisors/managers of construction trades

Each occupation was analyzed to identify the five most important skills for that job. The skills listed for each job were then sorted to identify skills that occupations held in common. In other words, the point was to discover skills that occurred repeatedly among the top 20 occupations. For example, social skills was found in 16 of the 20 occupations; it appears on our list of most critical skills to succeed in the best jobs. The skills that appear most frequently among the top 20 jobs are listed in the following table.

Key Occupational Skill	Number of Occurrences Among Top 20 Best Jobs
Social skills	16
Thought-processing skills	16
Communications skills	14
Management skills	11
Technology analysis skills	10

The O*NET groups more specific skills into the general skills listed in the preceding table. These skills are defined more specifically by the O*NET and are described here in more detail:

- **Social skills** include social perceptiveness, coordination, persuasion, negotiation, instructing, and service orientation.
- **Thought-processing skills** include critical thinking, active learning, learning strategies, monitoring, complex problem solving, and judgment and decision making.

- **Communications skills** include reading comprehension, active listening, writing, and speaking.
- **Management skills** include time management, management of financial resources, management of material resources, and management of personnel resources.
- **Technology analysis skills** include operations analysis, technology design, and equipment selection.

To help you better understand some of these key skills, each chapter focuses on a specific skill. The chapters and the skill featured in each are the following:

- Chapter 2, "Avoiding the New Job Blues": Active listening
- Chapter 3, "Making a Good Impression": Speaking
- Chapter 4, "Being There…On Time!": Time management
- Chapter 5, "Communicating in the Workplace": Writing
- Chapter 6, "Learning—What It's All About": Active learning
- Chapter 7, "Knowing Yourself": Monitoring
- Chapter 8, "Getting Along with Your Supervisor": Social perceptiveness
- Chapter 9, "Getting Along with Other Workers": Persuasion
- Chapter 10, "Meeting the Customer's Expectations": Service orientation
- Chapter 11, "Problem-Solving Skills": Complex problem solving
- Chapter 12, "Doing the Right Thing": Critical thinking
- Chapter 13, "Getting Ahead on the Job": Negotiation

This book helps you be better prepared for the workforce by focusing on most of the essential skills. It also helps you understand how to learn and apply these skills in an effective manner in the workplace.

SKILLS CHECKLIST

Look at the following checklist and rank in order from 1 (most important) to 12 (least important) the employee skills that are most important to the success of your organization.

Active listening _____

Speaking _____

Time management _____

Writing _____

Active learning _____

Monitoring _____

Social perceptiveness _____

Persuasion _____

(continued)

(continued)

Service orientation	_____
Complex problem solving	_____
Critical thinking	_____
Negotiation	_____

Dependability vs. Responsibility

The dictionary definitions of these words are similar. But when they are used in the world of work, they have slightly different meanings. Dependability means being on time and at work every day and notifying your supervisor when you are unable to be there. Responsibility means following through with a job. When the boss asks you to do a job, you prove your responsibility by completing the assigned task and then looking for other things to do. Both of these skills fall into the general area of personal management skills; but employers often cite them as the most essential skills employees need.

SKILLS EXAMPLES

The following are the same skills you ranked earlier. In the spaces after each skill, explain why this skill is important in making an organization work. Give an example of how each skill is used in the workplace.

Active listening

_____

_____

Speaking

_____

_____

Time management

_____

_____

Writing

_____

_____

Active learning

_____

_____

Monitoring

_____

_____

Social perceptiveness

_____

_____

Persuasion

_____

_____

Service orientation

_____

_____

Complex problem solving

_____

_____

Critical thinking

_____

_____

Negotiation

_____

_____

How Your Skills Help Your Employer

In the first exercise, you listed the things that an employer needs to run a productive and efficient organization. Three essentials you might have included on your list are the following:

1. **Provide a product or service of high quality.** Consumers want quality in whatever they buy. Today, organizations place great emphasis on quality. The U.S. government even recognizes companies for their emphasis on quality with the Malcolm Baldrige National Quality Award.

2. **Satisfy the customer's needs and wants.** An organization depends on the goodwill of its customers. If customers are pleased with products they've purchased or services they've received, they will continue to do business with an organization and even recommend it to friends. Conversely, people talk about a bad experience with friends, family members, acquaintances, coworkers, and even complete strangers.

3. **Make a profit.** Product quality and customer satisfaction have to be provided at a cost that allows a business to make a profit. There's no reason for the owners or stockholders to continue the business if they could invest their money elsewhere and receive a higher rate of return.

An employer expects all employees to help the organization accomplish the three essentials of a successful operation. Employees are expected to work hard, help when asked, please customers, and do it for a wage that allows the organization to make a profit and stay in business.

Profit

The money an organization earns through sales or services is income. All bills the organization pays are expenses. Profit is the amount of money an organization has left after paying all its expenses. Profit belongs to the owners, partners, or stockholders of an organization; profit is the compensation business owners receive for risking their money in a commercial venture. Often owners take money from their profit and reinvest it in the organization by buying new equipment, opening new facilities, or hiring new workers. This creates a healthy economy. Some business owners have profit-sharing programs that distribute a share of the profit to all employees as a reward for their hard work.

Even government and nonprofit agencies must stay within a budget. Nonprofit agencies must earn enough money to pay all their expenses. And, although they can't distribute earnings greater than their expenses to stockholders, government and nonprofit agencies are expected to operate as efficiently as profit-making businesses.

Employers' Skill Expectations

Employers want employees who have more than just the skills needed to do a specific job. They look for employees with a broader base of *adaptive* or *self-management skills*, which help employees adjust to the workplace. For example, getting along with coworkers and listening to a supervisor's instructions are adaptive skills. These skills are explored more fully in Chapter 8.

The University of Baltimore surveyed employers to identify the most important training needs of their workers[11]—what skills employers expected their workers to possess. The following are the expectations 80 percent or more of the survey respondents cited:

1. Concern for improved productivity
2. Technical skills
3. Interpersonal skills, to promote teamwork and responsibility
4. An understanding of the importance of competition with other businesses
5. Improved employee attitudes and work habits
6. Employee personal and career development
7. Skills needed for new technology adopted by the business
8. Reading, communication, and calculation
9. Following instructions
10. Life skills, attendance, punctuality, and courtesy

Ask yourself how many of these skills you have demonstrated in the past. Think of ways you can practice these skills in your work. Remember, your employer hired you for your skills. Your value in the company increases when you apply these skills on the job.

How Job Savvy Are You?

Tom takes orders at a fast-food restaurant. He has worked at the restaurant for three weeks and believes that he deserves a raise. After his shift, Tom talks with his supervisor, Janet, and tells her that he feels he deserves a raise.

1. If you were Janet, what would you tell Tom?

_____

_____

2. Why?

_____

_____

You are a supervisor in a large insurance company. This morning, you asked Angel, a file clerk, to go to the supply room for a box of new file folders. Later, you found Angel sitting at her desk, filing her nails. When you asked, "Why aren't you working?" Angel replied, "I ran out of file folders."

1. What would you say to Angel?

_____

_____

2. What skill(s) does she need to improve?

_____

_____

Your Reasons for Working

You can't expect every job to satisfy all of your expectations and values. Many people work at jobs they don't want until they can get the education or experience necessary to start the career they do want. Sometimes you have to make sacrifices while you work toward the job you want. You must determine your most important expectations and values and then evaluate what each job offers.

Many studies have asked what American workers consider their most important job values and expectations. A study conducted by Career Systems International asked people what reasons were most important in staying at a job.[12] The table on page 20 shows the top 10 reasons people gave for staying at their job.

Reason for Staying at a Job
Exciting work and challenge
Career growth, learning, and development
Working with great people and relationships
Fair pay
Supportive management/great boss
Being recognized, valued, and respected
Benefits
Meaningful work; making a contribution
Pride in organization, its mission, and its product
Great work environment/culture

To a large degree, *you* are responsible for how satisfied you feel about a job. Select a job that will fulfill most of your expectations, but accept that no job can fulfill all your expectations. Then work with your supervisor and coworkers to make the job an even more pleasant experience. You can increase your job satisfaction even more by focusing on internal rewards—positive thoughts and compliments that you give yourself.

WHAT SHOULD YOU EXPECT?

Most of us have several reasons for working. Your motivation and interest in a job depend on your reasons for working and how well the job satisfies your needs.

1. List your reasons for working. You might think of money first. That's fine, but also think of the other reasons you work.

   _____

   _____

   _____

2. Think about the jobs you've had. What did you like about each job? What did you dislike?

   _____

   _____

   _____

3. How do you expect an employer to treat you? What are things you want in return for the work you do?

   _____

   _____

Resolving Employee Rights Issues

It's important to know your rights as an employee. Your rights are based on three factors:

1. **Federal and state employment laws:** The federal government and state governments place certain restrictions and requirements on all employers. The U.S. Department of Labor contains an *Employment Law Guide* that can be found at www.dol.gov/elaws/elg. In addition to federal employment laws, there are local laws. Local employment laws vary from one location to another and are impossible to summarize here. The U.S. Department of Labor has summarized these under an option labeled "State Offices/State Labor Laws." However, to better understand labor laws for your state, contact your local state labor office.

2. **Personnel policies:** Some organizations have personnel policies that describe the behavior expected from an employee, as well as employee rights. Courts consider personnel policies to be a formal contract between an employer and employees.

3. **Union contract:** An employer might sign a contract with a labor union. The contract might describe some personnel policies. Employees are expected to follow all of these policies; the employer must do likewise.

Understand that an organization or supervisor might not follow all laws and policies. Employees might be unhappy with these circumstances. A disagreement with an employer caused by a violation of a law or policy is called a *grievance*.

You might want to file a grievance with a supervisor. However, decide how important a problem is before you discuss it with your supervisor. Employees who question possible violations of laws, policies, and procedures might be viewed as troublemakers. If the problem is serious and you do decide to pursue the matter, follow these guidelines:

1. **Discuss the problem with your supervisor and ask him or her to correct the situation.** Approach the conversation in a calm and respectful manner. Keep in mind that you might not correctly understand the situation. Give your supervisor an opportunity to explain why the problem might not be as serious as you think.

2. **If the supervisor doesn't correct the problem or you feel the explanation is inadequate, contact the personnel office or the organization's owner.** Personnel handbooks usually describe the process you should follow when appealing a supervisor's actions. Discuss your concerns and how they can be satisfied. Always do this in a polite and nonthreatening manner. Be aware that your relationship with your supervisor might be negatively affected by this action.

3. **If the company doesn't correct the problem, you can contact the government agency responsible for seeing that a law is enforced.** An employer might fire you for this action unless a specific law protects you.

When you approach a government agency to file a complaint, you'll find that the follow-through—such as finding the right person to talk to, meeting with government officials to explain the problem, documenting your claims— requires a great deal of time. You might be required to testify at formal hearings. It's important to weigh the time requirements and pressures that are a part of such formal complaints against the benefits of having an employer change its illegal practices. Also, consider the fact that if you apply at another job and an employer discovers that you reported another employer to a government agency, the organization might be reluctant to hire you.

How Job Savvy Are You?

Kim works for a manufacturing company. The wages the company pays are not as high as those at similar companies in the area. The other workers are friendly and helpful. When someone has a problem, everyone helps out. Kim's supervisor is a hard worker and pushes everyone to produce a high-quality product as quickly as possible. The supervisor is easy to talk to and will listen to questions and complaints from employees. Kim is often asked to work overtime. It is not unusual for her to work six days a week.

1. What is positive in Kim's situation?

    gives her hours + great coworkers

2. What is negative?

    low pay

3. How likely would you be to continue working at this job?

    continue until better work coms

Jackson is a hospital nurse. His pay and benefits are good, but the hospital often changes procedures without informing the staff first. Sometimes, Jackson doesn't find out about changes until they are to be put into practice. Jackson reports to a supervisor who is not very friendly. Other workers are cooperative, but they do not get together outside of work.

1. What is positive in Jackson's situation?

    great pay

2. What is negative?

    bad communication

3. How likely would you be to continue working at this job?

    unlikely

Summing Up

The labor force, workplaces, and the structure of jobs are changing. The U.S. labor force is more diverse than ever before, with the addition of more women, people from ethnic groups, older workers, and people with disabilities.

Most organizations provide customer services, and many service-related jobs require a high level of skill. Employers are restructuring jobs so that they can be done not only by traditional workers but also by contingent workers.

These changes demand a higher level of skill. Workers need more education than ever before. Employers expect employees to have the technical skills for a specific job, but they consider basic skills to be even more important.

Employers have expectations of employees. Workers also have expectations of their employers. Your relationship with an employer is built on three important points of understanding:

- Understand that the employer is in business to make a profit, and not just to provide you with a job.

- If you understand the reasons you want to work and look for things in your job that satisfy these reasons, you will be happier and do a better job.

- You must maintain a relationship of mutual respect. Laws, policies, or contracts require employers to behave toward employees in certain ways. Many employers want to do much more. Respect your employer's reasons for making policies and decisions that affect you. Always try to resolve misunderstandings in a positive manner.

CHAPTER 2

Avoiding the New Job Blues

The impression you make on your supervisor and coworkers your first day on the job affects your future relationship with them. The first day can be confusing and difficult because you have a great deal to remember. This confusion can make it tough to create a positive first impression. But you can reduce the confusion by knowing what to expect on the first day and being prepared.

"Oh, dear. You were supposed to bring a machete to hack your way to the women's room."

Your first day on a job obviously will differ from one organization to another, but some things are the same. Here are some typical first-day activities you could expect:

- **Reporting to work:** In large organizations, you probably will report to the personnel or human resources office. Smaller companies might have you report to the office manager or directly to your new supervisor.

- **Orientation:** Organizations usually provide orientation training for new employees to introduce them to the organization, take care of necessary paperwork, and review policies and benefits. Organizations provide new-employee orientation training more often than they do any other type of training.[1]

- **Job introduction and workplace tour:** A supervisor will probably introduce you to the job that you have been hired to do. Frequently, the supervisor also will show you around the work area and other parts of the facility. During this tour, you will be introduced to people who are important to know in order to work effectively.

This chapter reviews what you can expect during each of these first-day activities.

Reporting to Work

It is important to make a good impression your first day on the job. Contacting your new supervisor a day or two before you are scheduled to start helps make the transition to the new job easier. Ask the supervisor about topics that require your attention before you arrive at the new job. You might ask these questions:

- What is appropriate clothing to wear for this job?
- When I arrive, where should I go and whom should I contact?
- Should I bring identification or any other documents?
- Are there tools, equipment, or other items that I am expected to furnish?

The following sections contain some checklists to help you prepare for your first day at work. Get the information you need to complete the checklists by asking the personnel department or your supervisor.

Dress Appropriately

It's embarrassing to show up for work dressed the wrong way. You stand out like a sore thumb, and people remember you for weeks (or even months) because of how you looked that first day. You should ask your supervisor what type of clothing is suitable or required for the job. Think about any special dress situations that might be necessary for your job.

Your employer might require you to wear a uniform. If so, find out whether it is issued on your first day or if you are to arrive in uniform on the first day.

You also should ask whether you are expected to buy the uniform or if the company provides it.

Certain jobs require special safety clothing. Working with chemicals demands a variety of clothing, depending on how toxic the chemicals are. Hardhats and steel-toed safety shoes are required on some jobs to avoid injury. If you work near machinery, you might need to avoid wearing jewelry or loose clothing that could get caught in mechanical parts. Be aware of your organization's safety requirements and obey them. (See Chapter 3 for a more thorough discussion of employer policies regarding safety clothing and equipment.)

Organizations for which no special clothing is required still have expectations about the way that you dress. When you visit an organization for interviews, notice how the workers dress. After you are hired, ask your supervisor to advise you about what is appropriate to wear on your first day at work.

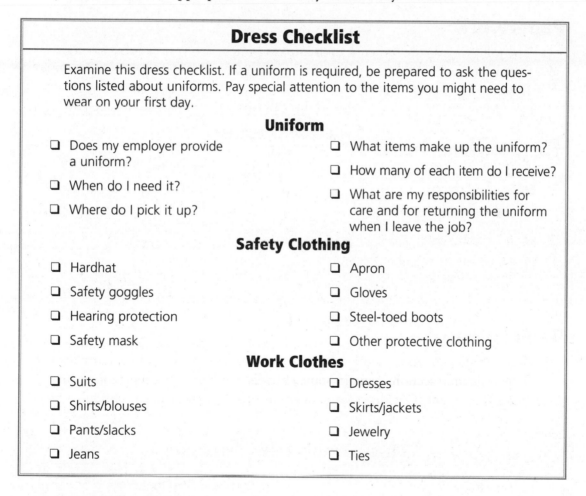

Dress Checklist

Examine this dress checklist. If a uniform is required, be prepared to ask the questions listed about uniforms. Pay special attention to the items you might need to wear on your first day.

Uniform

❑ Does my employer provide a uniform?

❑ When do I need it?

❑ Where do I pick it up?

❑ What items make up the uniform?

❑ How many of each item do I receive?

❑ What are my responsibilities for care and for returning the uniform when I leave the job?

Safety Clothing

❑ Hardhat

❑ Safety goggles

❑ Hearing protection

❑ Safety mask

❑ Apron

❑ Gloves

❑ Steel-toed boots

❑ Other protective clothing

Work Clothes

❑ Suits

❑ Shirts/blouses

❑ Pants/slacks

❑ Jeans

❑ Dresses

❑ Skirts/jackets

❑ Jewelry

❑ Ties

Starting the Day

Talk with your supervisor or the personnel department before your first day on the job and ask exactly when you should arrive, where you should go, and whom you should contact. At some companies, you report on the first workday at a different time and location than you do on other workdays.

FIRST-DAY CHECKLIST

Check off each item as you answer the question.

☐ What time should I arrive? _____

☐ Where should I report? _____

☐ To whom should I report? _____

☐ What documentation should I bring? _____

☐ What special equipment do I need? _____

☐ What will I be expected to do? _____

☐ What do people usually do for lunch? _____

Paperwork

The following are documents your employer might ask you to bring on your first day of work. Find out which documents you will need and check them off as you collect them.

PAPERWORK CHECKLIST

☐ Birth certificate

☐ Driver's license

☐ Social Security card

☐ Work permit (for workers under 18)

☐ Immigrant work authorization (for noncitizens)

☐ Medical records (physical exam results)

☐ Occupational license (realtor's, truck driver's, bartender's, or other)

☐ Other documents

_____

Be Prepared

Some employers expect workers to furnish tools, equipment, or other items. This isn't common, but you should determine whether this expectation exists. Items that might be required are shown in the following list.

MISCELLANEOUS ITEMS CHECKLIST

☐ Construction tools

☐ Electronic diagnostic equipment

☐ Electronic repair tools

☐ Excavation tools

☐ Flashlight

☐ Mechanical tools

☐ Notebook and pen/pencil

☐ Padlock for locker

☐ Reference books

☐ Weapons

Orientation

Many employers conduct orientation training for new employees. In some organizations, this is the responsibility of the personnel department; in others, the supervisor conducts orientation. Several important issues might be discussed during orientation, including these:

- **Introduction:** You need to know what the organization does, how it is structured, and who the key people are.
- **Personnel information:** You must also provide proof that you are a U.S. citizen. If you are an immigrant, you must prove that you can legally work in this country. Be prepared to provide this information when asked.
- **Payroll information:** You need to complete certain forms for payroll withholdings.
- **Benefits and services review:** You should have company benefits explained to you and be given a chance to discuss them.
- **Policies and practices review:** You should be informed about your employer's important policies and practices. This includes information about vacations, holidays, and other days approved for excused absences.
- **Employer expectations review:** You should be told what the employer expects. Many of the points reviewed in Chapter 1 will be discussed at this time.

The following sections explain common benefits and personnel policies.[2] Although not all organizations offer the same benefits or follow the same procedures, the explanations here might help you more fully understand the orientation process in general.

Personnel Information

Most employers need certain documents and tests to verify information about new employees. In most cases, you must provide these documents on or before your first day of work. This information frequently falls into five categories:

- **Verification of citizenship/immigration:** Federal law requires employers to demonstrate that all workers are legally entitled to work in the United States. They must have proof of citizenship or an immigrant work authorization permit for each employee. You will be asked to fill out Section 1 of Form I-9 and provide documentation of your eligibility to work. A copy of your birth certificate and your driver's license usually are enough to document your citizenship. If you are not a U.S. citizen, check the acceptable documents listed in the example of Form I-9 at the end of this section.
- **Social Security number:** Employers need this information to withhold taxes.
- **Licenses:** Some occupations require a license issued by the state government. If this is the case in your occupation, your employer will need to see the license and keep a copy for company records. Applying and paying for such a license are usually the worker's responsibility.

■ **Health forms:** Your employer might require you to have a physical exam. Most employers pay for the exam, and the results go directly to them. However, you might be asked to bring the results when you report to work.

■ **Drug testing:** Studies reveal that employees who abuse drugs have a tremendously harmful effect on the workplace—they are more likely to have extended absences from work, show up late, be involved in workplace accidents, and file workers' compensation claims.[3] Consequently, your employer might require you to take a drug test. If you are taking prescription medication, you should notify the people administering the drug test. If you test positive but have not been taking drugs, you should ask to be retested.

How Job Savvy Are You?

Chad arrived at Merlin Controls at 6:45 a.m., ready for his first day at work. He was stopped at the guard's gate because he didn't have an identification badge, which was needed to enter the plant. Chad explained to the guard that it was his first day and gave her the name of his supervisor, Linda. The guard called Linda and asked Chad to wait until she came to escort him into the plant. Linda arrived at the gate 45 minutes later. She apologized for not coming sooner, but said she had problems to take care of first. Linda then told Chad that he should report to the personnel office when it opened at 8 a.m. Chad waited in the reception area until the office opened.

1. How would you feel if you were Chad?

   _____

   _____

2. How could Chad have avoided this situation?

   _____

   _____

Felicia was excited about her first day as a claims processor trainee at Adams National Insurance Company, and she wanted to make a good first impression. She even took an early bus to make sure she arrived on time. When Felicia got to work, she was asked to show her Social Security card and driver's license for identification purposes. Felicia did not have them. The personnel officer told her that she could start training that day, but she would have to bring the documents tomorrow.

1. If you were Felicia, how would this make you feel?

   _____

   _____

2. How could Felicia have avoided this situation?

   _____

   _____

Following is the Immigration and Naturalization Service Form I-9 Employment Eligibility Verification. Employers must keep this form on file for every employee. Practice by completing section 1, Employee Information and Verification. The employer is required to fill out the remainder of the form.

OMB No. 1615-0047; Expires 08/31/12

Department of Homeland Security
U.S. Citizenship and Immigration Services

**Form I-9, Employment
Eligibility Verification**

Read instructions carefully before completing this form. The instructions must be available during completion of this form.

ANTI-DISCRIMINATION NOTICE: It is illegal to discriminate against work-authorized individuals. Employers CANNOT specify which document(s) they will accept from an employee. The refusal to hire an individual because the documents have a future expiration date may also constitute illegal discrimination.

Section 1. Employee Information and Verification *(To be completed and signed by employee at the time employment begins.)*

Print Name: Last	First	Middle Initial	Maiden Name

Address *(Street Name and Number)*	Apt. #	Date of Birth *(month/day/year)*

City	State	Zip Code	Social Security #

I am aware that federal law provides for imprisonment and/or fines for false statements or use of false documents in connection with the completion of this form.

I attest, under penalty of perjury, that I am (check one of the following):

☐ A citizen of the United States
☐ A noncitizen national of the United States (see instructions)
☐ A lawful permanent resident (Alien #) _____
☐ An alien authorized to work (Alien # or Admission #) _____
until (expiration date, if applicable - *month/day/year*) _____

Employee's Signature	Date *(month/day/year)*

Preparer and/or Translator Certification *(To be completed and signed if Section 1 is prepared by a person other than the employee.)* I attest, under penalty of perjury, that I have assisted in the completion of this form and that to the best of my knowledge the information is true and correct.

Preparer's/Translator's Signature	Print Name

Address *(Street Name and Number, City, State, Zip Code)*	Date *(month/day/year)*

Section 2. Employer Review and Verification *(To be completed and signed by employer. Examine one document from List A OR examine one document from List B and one from List C, as listed on the reverse of this form, and record the title, number, and expiration date, if any, of the document(s).)*

	List A	OR	List B	AND	List C
Document title:					
Issuing authority:					
Document #:					
Expiration Date *(if any):*					
Document #:					
Expiration Date *(if any):*					

CERTIFICATION: I attest, under penalty of perjury, that I have examined the document(s) presented by the above-named employee, that the above-listed document(s) appear to be genuine and to relate to the employee named, that the employee began employment on *(month/day/year)* _____ and that to the best of my knowledge the employee is authorized to work in the United States. (State employment agencies may omit the date the employee began employment.)

Signature of Employer or Authorized Representative	Print Name	Title

Business or Organization Name and Address *(Street Name and Number, City, State, Zip Code)*	Date *(month/day/year)*

Section 3. Updating and Reverification *(To be completed and signed by employer.)*

A. New Name *(if applicable)*	B. Date of Rehire *(month/day/year)* *(if applicable)*

C. If employee's previous grant of work authorization has expired, provide the information below for the document that establishes current employment authorization.

Document Title:	Document #:	Expiration Date *(if any):*

I attest, under penalty of perjury, that to the best of my knowledge, this employee is authorized to work in the United States, and if the employee presented document(s), the document(s) I have examined appear to be genuine and to relate to the individual.

Signature of Employer or Authorized Representative	Date *(month/day/year)*

Form I-9 (Rev. 08/07/09) Y Page 4

LISTS OF ACCEPTABLE DOCUMENTS
All documents must be unexpired

LIST A		LIST B		LIST C
Documents that Establish Both Identity and Employment Authorization	**OR**	**Documents that Establish Identity**	**AND**	**Documents that Establish Employment Authorization**

LIST A	LIST B	LIST C
1. U.S. Passport or U.S. Passport Card	1. Driver's license or ID card issued by a State or outlying possession of the United States provided it contains a photograph or information such as name, date of birth, gender, height, eye color, and address	1. Social Security Account Number card other than one that specifies on the face that the issuance of the card does not authorize employment in the United States
2. Permanent Resident Card or Alien Registration Receipt Card (Form I-551)		
3. Foreign passport that contains a temporary I-551 stamp or temporary I-551 printed notation on a machine-readable immigrant visa	2. ID card issued by federal, state or local government agencies or entities, provided it contains a photograph or information such as name, date of birth, gender, height, eye color, and address	2. Certification of Birth Abroad issued by the Department of State (Form FS-545)
4. Employment Authorization Document that contains a photograph (Form I-766)	3. School ID card with a photograph	3. Certification of Report of Birth issued by the Department of State (Form DS-1350)
	4. Voter's registration card	4. Original or certified copy of birth certificate issued by a State, county, municipal authority, or territory of the United States bearing an official seal
5. In the case of a nonimmigrant alien authorized to work for a specific employer incident to status, a foreign passport with Form I-94 or Form I-94A bearing the same name as the passport and containing an endorsement of the alien's nonimmigrant status, as long as the period of endorsement has not yet expired and the proposed employment is not in conflict with any restrictions or limitations identified on the form	5. U.S. Military card or draft record	
	6. Military dependent's ID card	
	7. U.S. Coast Guard Merchant Mariner Card	5. Native American tribal document
	8. Native American tribal document	
	9. Driver's license issued by a Canadian government authority	6. U.S. Citizen ID Card (Form I-197)
	For persons under age 18 who are unable to present a document listed above:	7. Identification Card for Use of Resident Citizen in the United States (Form I-179)
6. Passport from the Federated States of Micronesia (FSM) or the Republic of the Marshall Islands (RMI) with Form I-94 or Form I-94A indicating nonimmigrant admission under the Compact of Free Association Between the United States and the FSM or RMI	10. School record or report card	8. Employment authorization document issued by the Department of Homeland Security
	11. Clinic, doctor, or hospital record	
	12. Day-care or nursery school record	

Illustrations of many of these documents appear in Part 8 of the Handbook for Employers (M-274)

Form I-9 (Rev. 08/07/09) Y Page 5

Payroll Information and Enrollment

Most employers will ask you to complete payroll information on your first day at work. This section explains what information your employer will require and why.

Withholding Taxes

In addition to Form I-9, all new employees typically must complete two tax forms before they can be added to the payroll: a W-4 form for federal withholding taxes and a state tax withholding form. The tax-withholding forms are used for the following purposes:

- **Federal income taxes:** Your employer will automatically withhold federal income taxes from your paycheck. The amount of taxes withheld is based on the number of personal allowances you claim. All taxpayers automatically get one personal allowance. You may claim more than one personal allowance if others are dependent on your income. Or you can claim zero allowances if you want more taxes withheld (for example, if you earn income on the side that does not have taxes taken out). You need to complete a W-4 form so that your employer can calculate the correct tax to withhold.

- **State and local income taxes:** Most states and some cities and counties have income taxes. You must complete withholding forms for these taxes. Your employer uses the information you provide on the state withholding form to deduct the correct amount from your pay.

- **Federal Insurance Contributions Act (FICA):** This is a Social Security tax. Your employer must withhold a set percentage of your paycheck and contribute a similar amount to your FICA account. This money funds retirement benefits and is credited to your personal account. Your account number is the same as your Social Security number.

- **Medicare contributions:** Medicare provides health-care insurance to workers who have retired or are disabled. Similar to Social Security withholding, a set percentage of your pay is deducted from each paycheck for this service.

Personal Allowances

The federal government lets you claim personal allowances for a variety of reasons. An allowance reduces the amount of money on which you pay taxes. You can claim an allowance for yourself, your spouse, and any dependents (children, elderly parents, and so on). In addition, special allowances are given if you are the head of a household, if you have child-care payments in excess of a specific amount each year, and for certain other reasons established by Congress.

Pay Information

Typically, information is provided about when and how you will be paid when you complete the payroll forms. You should check the following information:

- **Method of payment:** Many companies offer employees the choice of being paid by check or by direct deposit. Direct deposit places the money directly into your checking or savings account. You receive a form showing the amount of money your employer deposits. This saves you a trip to the bank to make the deposit yourself. The payroll department can give you details if your employer offers this service. Information about your bank account will be needed to set up direct deposit. You might still choose to receive an actual paycheck you can see and deposit yourself. But be prepared to tell your employer which method you prefer.

- **Schedule of paydays:** Find out when you will receive your first paycheck. New employees are not always eligible for a paycheck on the first payday after they start work. You should also ask about the regular payday schedule. Some organizations distribute paychecks only at specific times. If your employer has such a policy and you are not scheduled to work during that time, you need to make arrangements to pick up your paycheck.

- **Check your withholdings:** You can expect 15 percent or more of your check to be withheld for taxes and other deductions. Check the calculations for withholdings and deductions after you receive your first paycheck. If you don't understand how the calculations were made, talk to the payroll department.

How Job Savvy Are You?

Janelle, a recent college graduate, has been hired as a paralegal at a large law firm in the city. Her new position pays $35,000 per year, but her supervisor has told her that, if she is willing to work overtime, she may be able to earn an additional $3,000 to $4,000 this year. Janelle is single, has no children, and has just signed an apartment lease.

1. Look at Form W-4 on the following pages. How many personal allowances should Janelle claim?

   _____

2. Why should Janelle claim this number of personal allowances?

   _____

Jade earns $45,000 annually doing computer programming. She and her husband have two preschool-aged children. Cal, her husband, cares for the children during the day and works part-time at a retail store in the evening. Last year he earned $15,000.

1. Look at Form W-4 on the following pages. How many personal allowances should Jade claim?

   _____

2. How many personal allowances should her husband claim?

   _____

3. Why should Jade and her husband claim this number of personal allowances?

   _____

   _____

   _____

Following is the Internal Revenue Service Form W-4 for 2012. The form changes slightly from one year to the next, but this sample will be useful for practice. Complete the form with the correct information for your tax withholding.

Form W-4 (2012)

Purpose. Complete Form W-4 so that your employer can withhold the correct federal income tax from your pay. Consider completing a new Form W-4 each year and when your personal or financial situation changes.

Exemption from withholding. If you are exempt, complete **only** lines 1, 2, 3, 4, and 7 and sign the form to validate it. Your exemption for 2012 expires February 18, 2013. See Pub. 505, Tax Withholding and Estimated Tax.

Note. If another person can claim you as a dependent on his or her tax return, you cannot claim exemption from withholding if your income exceeds $950 and includes more than $300 of unearned income (for example, interest and dividends).

Basic instructions. If you are not exempt, complete the **Personal Allowances Worksheet** below. The worksheets on page 2 further adjust your withholding allowances based on itemized deductions, certain credits, adjustments to income, or two-earners/multiple jobs situations.

Complete all worksheets that apply. However, you may claim fewer (or zero) allowances. For regular wages, withholding must be based on allowances you claimed and may not be a flat amount or percentage of wages.

Head of household. Generally, you can claim head of household filing status on your tax return only if you are unmarried and pay more than 50% of the costs of keeping up a home for yourself and your dependent(s) or other qualifying individuals. See Pub. 501, Exemptions, Standard Deduction, and Filing Information, for information.

Tax credits. You can take projected tax credits into account in figuring your allowable number of withholding allowances. Credits for child or dependent care expenses and the child tax credit may be claimed using the **Personal Allowances Worksheet** below. See Pub. 505 for information on converting your other credits into withholding allowances.

Nonwage income. If you have a large amount of nonwage income, such as interest or dividends, consider making estimated tax payments using Form 1040-ES, Estimated Tax for Individuals. Otherwise, you may owe additional tax. If you have pension or annuity

income, see Pub. 505 to find out if you should adjust your withholding on Form W-4 or W-4P.

Two earners or multiple jobs. If you have a working spouse or more than one job, figure the total number of allowances you are entitled to claim on all jobs using worksheets from only one Form W-4. Your withholding usually will be most accurate when all allowances are claimed on the Form W-4 for the highest paying job and zero allowances are claimed on the others. See Pub. 505 for details.

Nonresident alien. If you are a nonresident alien, see Notice 1392, Supplemental Form W-4 Instructions for Nonresident Aliens, before completing this form.

Check your withholding. After your Form W-4 takes effect, use Pub. 505 to see how the amount you are having withheld compares to your projected total tax for 2012. See Pub. 505, especially if your earnings exceed $130,000 (Single) or $180,000 (Married).

Future developments. The IRS has created a page on IRS.gov for information about Form W-4, at *www.irs.gov/w4*. Information about any future developments affecting Form W-4 (such as legislation enacted after we release it) will be posted on that page.

Personal Allowances Worksheet (Keep for your records.)

A	Enter "1" for **yourself** if no one else can claim you as a dependent	**A** ___
B	Enter "1" if: { • You are single and have only one job; or / • You are married, have only one job, and your spouse does not work; or / • Your wages from a second job or your spouse's wages (or the total of both) are $1,500 or less. }	**B** ___
C	Enter "1" for your **spouse**. But, you may choose to enter "-0-" if you are married and have either a working spouse or more than one job. (Entering "-0-" may help you avoid having too little tax withheld.)	**C** ___
D	Enter number of **dependents** (other than your spouse or yourself) you will claim on your tax return	**D** ___
E	Enter "1" if you will file as **head of household** on your tax return (see conditions under **Head of household** above) . .	**E** ___
F	Enter "1" if you have at least $1,900 of **child or dependent care expenses** for which you plan to claim a credit . . .	**F** ___
	(**Note.** Do **not** include child support payments. See Pub. 503, Child and Dependent Care Expenses, for details.)	
G	**Child Tax Credit** (including additional child tax credit). See Pub. 972, Child Tax Credit, for more information.	
	• If your total income will be less than $61,000 ($90,000 if married), enter "2" for each eligible child; then **less** "1" if you have three to seven eligible children or **less** "2" if you have eight or more eligible children.	
	• If your total income will be between $61,000 and $84,000 ($90,000 and $119,000 if married), enter "1" for each eligible child . . .	**G** ___
H	Add lines A through G and enter total here. (**Note.** This may be different from the number of exemptions you claim on your tax return.) ▶ **H** ___

For accuracy, complete all worksheets that apply.	• If you plan to **itemize** or **claim adjustments to income** and want to reduce your withholding, see the **Deductions and Adjustments Worksheet** on page 2.
	• If you are **single and have more than one job** or are **married and you and your spouse both work** and the combined earnings from all jobs exceed $40,000 ($10,000 if married), see the **Two-Earners/Multiple Jobs Worksheet** on page 2 to avoid having too little tax withheld.
	• If **neither** of the above situations applies, **stop here** and enter the number from line H on line 5 of Form W-4 below.

— — — Separate here and give Form W-4 to your employer. Keep the top part for your records. — — —

Form W-4

Department of the Treasury
Internal Revenue Service

Employee's Withholding Allowance Certificate

OMB No. 1545-0074

2012

▶ Whether you are entitled to claim a certain number of allowances or exemption from withholding is subject to review by the IRS. Your employer may be required to send a copy of this form to the IRS.

1 Your first name and middle initial	Last name	2 Your social security number

Home address (number and street or rural route)	3 ☐ Single ☐ Married ☐ Married, but withhold at higher Single rate.
City or town, state, and ZIP code	Note. If married, but legally separated, or spouse is a nonresident alien, check the "Single" box.
	4 If your last name differs from that shown on your social security card, check here. You must call 1-800-772-1213 for a replacement card. ▶ ☐

5	Total number of allowances you are claiming (from line **H** above **or** from the applicable worksheet on page 2)	**5**
6	Additional amount, if any, you want withheld from each paycheck	**6** $
7	I claim exemption from withholding for 2012, and I certify that I meet **both** of the following conditions for exemption.	
	• Last year I had a right to a refund of **all** federal income tax withheld because I had **no** tax liability, **and**	
	• This year I expect a refund of **all** federal income tax withheld because I expect to have **no** tax liability.	
	If you meet both conditions, write "Exempt" here . . . . ▶	**7**

Under penalties of perjury, I declare that I have examined this certificate and, to the best of my knowledge and belief, it is true, correct, and complete.

Employee's signature
(This form is not valid unless you sign it.) ▶ _____ Date ▶ _____

8 Employer's name and address (Employer: Complete lines 8 and 10 only if sending to the IRS.)	9 Office code (optional)	10 Employer identification number (EIN)

For Privacy Act and Paperwork Reduction Act Notice, see page 2.   Cat. No. 10220Q   Form **W-4** (2012)

Form W-4 (2012)   Page 2

Deductions and Adjustments Worksheet

Note. Use this worksheet *only* if you plan to itemize deductions or claim certain credits or adjustments to income.

1	Enter an estimate of your 2012 itemized deductions. These include qualifying home mortgage interest, charitable contributions, state and local taxes, medical expenses in excess of 7.5% of your income, and miscellaneous deductions	1	$
2	Enter: { $11,900 if married filing jointly or qualifying widow(er) $8,700 if head of household $5,950 if single or married filing separately }	2	$
3	**Subtract** line 2 from line 1. If zero or less, enter "-0-"	3	$
4	Enter an estimate of your 2012 adjustments to income and any additional standard deduction (see Pub. 505)	4	$
5	**Add** lines 3 and 4 and enter the total. (Include any amount for credits from the *Converting Credits to Withholding Allowances for 2012 Form W-4* worksheet in Pub. 505.)	5	$
6	Enter an estimate of your 2012 nonwage income (such as dividends or interest)	6	$
7	**Subtract** line 6 from line 5. If zero or less, enter "-0-"	7	$
8	**Divide** the amount on line 7 by $3,800 and enter the result here. Drop any fraction	8	
9	Enter the number from the **Personal Allowances Worksheet,** line H, page 1	9	
10	**Add** lines 8 and 9 and enter the total here. If you plan to use the **Two-Earners/Multiple Jobs Worksheet,** also enter this total on line 1 below. Otherwise, **stop here** and enter this total on Form W-4, line 5, page 1	10	

Two-Earners/Multiple Jobs Worksheet (See *Two earners or multiple jobs* on page 1.)

Note. Use this worksheet *only* if the instructions under line H on page 1 direct you here.

1	Enter the number from line H, page 1 (or from line 10 above if you used the **Deductions and Adjustments Worksheet**)	1	
2	Find the number in **Table 1** below that applies to the **LOWEST** paying job and enter it here. **However,** if you are married filing jointly and wages from the highest paying job are $65,000 or less, do not enter more than "3"	2	
3	If line 1 is **more than or equal to** line 2, subtract line 2 from line 1. Enter the result here (if zero, enter "-0-") and on Form W-4, line 5, page 1. **Do not** use the rest of this worksheet	3	

Note. If line 1 is **less than** line 2, enter "-0-" on Form W-4, line 5, page 1. Complete lines 4 through 9 below to figure the additional withholding amount necessary to avoid a year-end tax bill.

4	Enter the number from line 2 of this worksheet	4	
5	Enter the number from line 1 of this worksheet	5	
6	**Subtract** line 5 from line 4	6	
7	Find the amount in **Table 2** below that applies to the **HIGHEST** paying job and enter it here	7	$
8	**Multiply** line 7 by line 6 and enter the result here. This is the additional annual withholding needed	8	$
9	Divide line 8 by the number of pay periods remaining in 2012. For example, divide by 26 if you are paid every two weeks and you complete this form in December 2011. Enter the result here and on Form W-4, line 6, page 1. This is the additional amount to be withheld from each paycheck	9	$

Table 1

Married Filing Jointly		All Others	
If wages from **LOWEST** paying job are—	Enter on line 2 above	If wages from **LOWEST** paying job are—	Enter on line 2 above
$0 - $5,000	0	$0 - $8,000	0
5,001 - 12,000	1	8,001 - 15,000	1
12,001 - 22,000	2	15,001 - 25,000	2
22,001 - 25,000	3	25,001 - 30,000	3
25,001 - 30,000	4	30,001 - 40,000	4
30,001 - 40,000	5	40,001 - 50,000	5
40,001 - 48,000	6	50,001 - 65,000	6
48,001 - 55,000	7	65,001 - 80,000	7
55,001 - 65,000	8	80,001 - 95,000	8
65,001 - 72,000	9	95,001 - 120,000	9
72,001 - 85,000	10	120,001 and over	10
85,001 - 97,000	11		
97,001 - 110,000	12		
110,001 - 120,000	13		
120,001 - 135,000	14		
135,001 and over	15		

Table 2

Married Filing Jointly		All Others	
If wages from **HIGHEST** paying job are—	Enter on line 7 above	If wages from **HIGHEST** paying job are—	Enter on line 7 above
$0 - $70,000	$570	$0 - $35,000	$570
70,001 - 125,000	950	35,001 - 90,000	950
125,001 - 190,000	1,060	90,001 - 170,000	1,060
190,001 - 340,000	1,250	170,001 - 375,000	1,250
340,001 and over	1,330	375,001 and over	1,330

Employee Benefits and Policies

Employers can attract workers with employee benefits. Some surveys show that benefits are a major reason people work. This section explains the common benefits employers offer.

Benefits usually are available only to full-time employees. Some employers offer no benefits at all. Your employer might make full payment for some of your benefits; however, most employers now require employees to make partial contributions to help pay for them. Some employers offer "cafeteria" plans, giving you the choice of which benefits you want (see the "Cafeteria Plans" box on the next page). The following benefits are most commonly offered:

- **Health insurance** pays a percentage of doctor and hospital expenses. Most health insurance has a standard deductible—that is, the amount of medical expense you must pay before the insurance company will pay your medical bills. Some health plans cover the cost of prescription drugs and dental work.

  Health Savings Accounts are another method of providing health coverage to workers. These accounts may be used to supplement high-deductible health insurance. You do not have to pay tax on the money in the account.

  Changes in health insurance will be instituted in stages over the next few years as the Affordable Care Act is put into effect. The law calls for changes to be implemented by 2014, but there are some doubts about whether the entire act will be carried out.

- **Disability insurance** pays part or all of your salary if you are sick or injured for several weeks or more. These payments usually begin after you have used all of your paid sick leave.

- **Life insurance** is particularly important if you have dependents because you can designate a person (the beneficiary) to receive a payment from the insurance company if you die. Some employers pay for a life insurance policy equal to one year's salary and enable you to apply for higher amounts in addition to that.

- **Dependent care** comes in several forms. Some companies run child-care centers that provide low-cost care for their employees' children. Organizations that don't run day-care facilities might reimburse employees for a portion of the employees' child-care costs. As the workforce ages, many employees need care for elderly parents. Many businesses partner with adult day-care centers to offer this benefit to employees with elderly parents.

Here are two rules of thumb for choosing which benefits to accept:

- If the employer provides the benefit free of charge, you should sign up for it.

- If the employer requires you to pay part or all of the benefit costs, sign up only for those you really need.

Cafeteria Plans

This is an increasingly popular type of benefit plan in which an employer provides a wide variety of choices and a set amount of money to cover individual employees' benefits. Employees can choose which benefits to "buy." The use of cafeteria plans saves money for both the organization and the employee.[4] Benefits are adjusted as workers move through life stages. For example, a young worker starting a family might want to use the plan for child care. Later in life, the same worker might want to put that money into a disability plan.

Paid Time Off

Your employer might offer paid time off for one or several of the following circumstances. This benefit varies greatly from one employer to another.

- **Holiday pay:** The organization designates holidays on which you are not required to work. Many organizations pay their employees for holiday time.

- **Paid sick leave:** Employers normally establish a limited number of paid days that you can use for sick days each month or year. If you exceed the limit, you won't be paid for days you can't work due to illness. There are many different methods of accumulating sick time. Make sure that you understand the one your employer uses.

- **Vacation leave:** This is time off paid for by your employer. As a general rule, the amount of vacation time increases with the number of years you work for an organization.

- **Personal leave:** The definition of a personal day differs from one employer to another. For example, you might have to use it only for medical appointments or family illnesses, or you might be able to use it like an additional vacation day. Restrictions may exist. For example, using personal days may be limited to certain months of the year when the company is least busy. Understanding any restrictions applied to personal days is important.

- **Paid-time-off bank:** A paid-time-off bank allows employees to choose how time-off days will be used. Employees are given a certain number of days that may be used as vacation, sick, or personal days.

- **Jury duty leave:** Some states require employers to pay employees for time served on a jury. Some employers do so voluntarily because they feel it is a community responsibility.

- **Funeral leave:** This leave, usually limited to one to three days, is given when a member of your immediate family dies. Various organizations define "immediate family" differently. Ask about your employer's policy.

- **Military leave:** Members of the Reserve or National Guard are required to attend active-duty training for at least two weeks each year. In a national crisis, Congress can extend that period. Although they are not required to do so, some employers pay for the time that an employee is on active military leave or pay the difference in salary. When an employee is deployed for an extended time period, an employer must guarantee that a job is available when the person returns from duty. The employee must give reasonable notice to the employer before leaving for duty and report back to work in a timely manner once the military duty assignment is completed.

- **Maternity, paternity, and adoption leave:** This is time off for your child's birth or adoption. The Family and Medical Leave Act (FMLA) requires that a company with more than 50 employees provide maternity, paternity, and adoption leave. A company does not have to pay the employee during the leave, but it does have to keep the employee's job (or a similar job) open for him or her. Smaller companies must treat maternity leave like sick leave.

BENEFITS AND DEDUCTIONS YOU WANT

In the following list, place a check mark beside the benefits or deductions you want, even if you must pay a portion of the cost. Write your reasons for selecting or not selecting each item.

❑ Health insurance

_____

_____

❑ Dental insurance

_____

_____

❑ Prescription drugs

_____

_____

❑ Life insurance

_____

_____

❑ Disability insurance

_____

_____

❑ Child care/adult day care

_____

_____

❑ Child support

_____

_____

(continued)

(continued)

❑ Retirement program

_____

_____

❑ Union dues

_____

_____

❑ Savings plan

_____

_____

❑ Charity donation

_____

_____

❑ Stock options

_____

_____

Required Benefits

Federal and state laws require some employee benefits. Some of the most important laws are the following:

- **Federal Insurance Contributions Act (FICA):** An employer must match your contribution to the Social Security fund. If you die, this fund pays benefits to your children who are under age 21. The fund pays you and your dependents if you are disabled for more than 12 months. It also pays you a pension when you reach retirement age.

- **Unemployment insurance:** Your employer must contribute to an unemployment insurance fund administered by your state or agree to pay your unemployment claims. If you are laid off or dismissed from your job, you can file a claim with your state employment agency. Eligibility requirements vary from state to state. The reasons for unemployment also are taken into consideration. A state's employment office determines eligibility, and the state establishes the amounts for unemployment benefit payments. Weekly benefits are paid for 26 weeks or until you find suitable employment, whichever comes first.

- **Worker's compensation insurance:** Most states require employers to carry this insurance, which pays for injuries that occur on the job. In addition, you receive partial payment for time off the job caused by work-related injuries.

Voluntary Deductions

In addition to benefit deductions, your employer can deduct other withholdings from your paycheck with your approval. Some deductions, such as federal and state taxes, are required. Others are voluntary, such as the following:

- **Child support:** You might want to have monthly child support payments automatically deducted from your paycheck. Check with your lawyer or court representative to find out how this is done.

- **Savings plan payments:** You might have a portion of your pay sent directly to your bank or credit union account. Use it to make automatic loan payments, to add to savings, or for some other use.

- **Charity donations:** Sometimes you can arrange for a deduction to a charity. This arrangement is most often available for contributions to the United Way.

- **Union dues:** Most unions make arrangements with employers to withhold dues directly from your paycheck. In some areas, unions have agreements with employers requiring them to withhold dues, *even if you are not a union member.*

- **Retirement fund contributions:** Sometimes an employer contributes a percentage of your wage or salary to a retirement fund, such as a pension or 401(k) plan. Usually, you must contribute a percentage of your pay to the fund, and then the employer contributes an amount equal to what you contribute (up to a certain percentage). Typically, you must work for the employer a minimum number of years to become "vested." This means that if you leave before the minimum number of years, you can take your contribution but not the employer's.

- **Stock options:** You might be able to have deductions withheld to purchase company stock. Your employer might require you to be employed for several years before you are eligible for this benefit.

Employee Services

Employers provide many different services for their employees. Many organizations feel that the more they do for their employees, the more the employees will do for them. Here is a partial listing of services your employer might provide:

- **Educational assistance plans:** Employers often reimburse college or technical school tuition for employees who are working toward a degree or taking work-related courses. They also might reimburse employees for textbooks.

- **Employee assistance programs:** Employees might receive counseling for personal or work-related problems, including treatment for drug abuse or alcoholism.

- **Credit unions:** Credit unions provide financial services for employees, usually at a lower cost than banks or savings-and-loan institutions. Frequently, interest on credit union savings accounts is higher than the interest offered by banks, and interest on loans is lower.

■ **Other employee services:** These can include legal assistance, health services, an on-site cafeteria or food service, financial planning, reimbursement of housing and moving expenses, transportation, purchase discounts, and recreational services.

The following table shows the percentage of employees in the U.S. workforce who receive typical benefits.[5]

Benefit	Recipients by Percentage of U.S. Workforce
Paid vacations	74%
Paid sick leave	67%
Paid personal leave	41%
Life insurance	62%
Medical care	73%
Retirement plan	69%

CHECK THE BENEFITS YOUR EMPLOYER PROVIDES

Check the paid time off and employee assistance benefits your employer provides. If you aren't currently employed, check those that you think are important for an employer to provide.

❑ Holiday leave

_____

_____

❑ Vacation leave

_____

_____

❑ Personal leave

_____

_____

❑ Jury duty leave

_____

_____

❑ Sick leave

_____

_____

❑ Funeral leave

_____

_____

❑ Military leave

_____

_____

❑ Family leave

_____

_____

❑ Medical leave (long-term)

_____

_____

❑ Educational assistance

_____

_____

_____

❑ Employee assistance plan

_____

_____

_____

❑ Credit union

_____

_____

_____

❑ Others (specify)

_____

_____

_____

How Job Savvy Are You?

Steve and his wife have a seven-year-old daughter and three-year-old son. Steve is a carpenter for a construction firm and is working on a construction technology degree at a local community college. During the past year, the children have been sick several times. Steve and his wife just purchased a new home.

1. List six employee benefits or services that Steve needs.

_____

_____

_____

_____

_____

_____

(continued)

2. Tell why each benefit is important to Steve.

_____

_____

_____

_____

_____

_____

Pilar is the branch manager of a bank. She is divorced and has a four-year-old daughter. Pilar is active in the Naval Reserve. During the past year, she has been mildly depressed about her divorce and has been drinking more than she would like.

1. What benefits would be the most helpful for Pilar?

_____

_____

_____

2. Explain why these benefits are important.

_____

_____

_____

_____

Introduction to the Job

After orientation, your supervisor is likely to take you on a tour of the job site or work area. He or she should provide you with the following information. Be prepared to ask about these things in case he or she does not give you the information.

Work Instructions

It's important that you understand how to do your job. Your supervisor should show and tell you how to do the tasks that make up the job. Here are a few guidelines to follow as you're learning the job:

- **Don't panic.** You won't be expected to learn everything at once. And you aren't expected to do everything right the first time.
- **Listen carefully and watch closely** as the supervisor demonstrates a task.
- **Ask questions** when you don't understand something you've been told or shown.
- **Take notes.** Review these notes as you need them.

- **Learn what is expected.** Make sure you know exactly what the supervisor expects from you.

Supplies and Equipment

You need to know how and where to get the supplies and equipment you need to do your job. Some things you might need to know are the following:

- Where supplies are kept
- Procedures for checking out supplies and equipment
- Who is in charge of supply distribution

Communication Systems

All businesses rely on communication. Even if your job doesn't involve the telephone, you'll need to know the following information:

- **How to use the phone system:** You already know how to use a phone, I'm sure. But office phone systems can be incredibly complex and intimidating, with rows of buttons and lights, dozens of features, and as much wiring as a small computer. Ask a coworker to show you how to use the most common features of the phone system.
- **Telephone policy:** Who answers your phone if you're away from your desk? What should you say when you answer the phone? Can you make and receive personal calls? Is there an access code you must enter when making long-distance calls?
- **Voice mail:** Get the instructions for setting up your voice-mail account. Find out the phone number you must dial to access your account, both when you're in your office and from remote locations. Provide a password that you can easily remember.
- **Cell phone policy:** If your job requires travel or work outside the workplace, you may be given a cell phone. How does your employer expect the cell phone to be used? Can you make or receive personal calls? What is the organization's policy concerning driving and cell phone use?
- **Pagers:** These are another method of contacting employees who are working away from the office. If you are given a pager, learn how to use it. Find out how your employer expects you to respond.

The Computer System

Many businesses have a computer for every employee. These are often used for improving communication between employees through e-mail and software for scheduling meetings. Computers are also used for common tasks that might be a part of your job. This might include entering data for customer orders, writing documents with word-processing software, or creating a spreadsheet. A supervisor should give you the following information. If he or she doesn't, ask about it.

- **System (network) user name and password:** Accessing a network that links computers together requires entering a user name and password. This information comes from your company's network administrator (some organizations might use a variation of this job title). The supervisor should get this information from the network administrator or arrange for the administrator to meet you and share it with you.

- **E-mail user name and password:** The e-mail system might require a user name and password that are different from the ones you use for the overall system. You should also get these from the network administrator.

- **Instant messaging:** If the organization uses instant messaging, get help setting up an account. For security purposes, the company might use a customized IM program.

- **System and e-mail policies:** Most organizations have policies on the use of the computer system, e-mail, and instant messaging. These policies define how you can use the system and restrictions on access to information. Common issues addressed in most organizations' policies include

  - **Privacy:** Communication that happens over e-mail is often considered to be the property of the organization. That means that managers and supervisors might be able to read e-mail that you send to another employee or outside the company.

  - **Confidentiality:** Information that you find on the system about customers, business practices, pricing, inventory, employees, and so on is considered confidential. Normally, an employee is blocked from accessing information that isn't necessary to his or her job. However, you should not share any information that you can access with other employees or any person outside the organization.

  - **Personal use:** Many computer systems are connected to the Internet. You should find out restrictions that the organization might place on accessing and using the Internet. Organizations vary on whether employees can use the Internet during breaks and before and after work. You should find out whether employees are allowed to send e-mail to friends and relatives. Keep in mind that most organizations have software that allows them to monitor the websites you visit and all e-mail communication.

Building Security

Organizations are concerned about maintaining a secure workplace. Every employee becomes an important part of the security system. It is important to follow policies and procedures to ensure the security of everyone—including yourself. Some issues to consider are the following:

- **Keys/keycards:** You might be issued a key or keycard to enter a building or restricted area. Always keep these in your possession, and don't loan them to someone else—even another employee. Keys should not be duplicated.

Always return keys or keycards to the employer when you resign from a job. Usually, the employer will require you to return them and sign a statement verifying that you have done so.

- **Entry of visitors:** Visitors to a building should always be screened in accordance with company procedures. That means you shouldn't admit a person to the building without following the procedure. For example, someone coming to a rear or side entrance should be directed to the visitors' entry. Visitors should sign in and get a visitor badge before being allowed in the building. Also, don't prop open doors that might allow someone who isn't an employee to enter the building.

- **Restricted areas:** Many offices have restricted areas. Even businesses open to the general public such as retail stores and restaurants have restricted areas. You should keep doors to restricted areas closed. When you find someone who isn't an employee in a restricted area, ask the person to leave and then notify a manager about what you observed. Access to some areas is obtained by using a coded keypad. You should never share the password to these keypads with anyone.

- **Weapon restrictions:** Most organizations prohibit employees from having knives, guns, martial-arts weapons, or other weapons in the workplace. There may even be restrictions on having these in a car parked in the organization's parking lot. You should report to your supervisor or a nearby manager any employee, visitor, or customer that you think possesses a weapon.

- **Monitoring:** Some businesses—particularly retail stores and restaurants—monitor buildings with security cameras. Keep in mind that these cameras track your actions as well as those of visitors and customers.

Breaks

Different companies have different policies for taking breaks. In one, you might be able to take your breaks whenever you want to, as long as you're responsible about it. In another, you might have to take your breaks only at specified times. In a factory, an entire line might take breaks together. Many organizations prohibit smoking on the job. Others may allow it outside buildings or off company premises. If you intend to smoke during your break, you need to know where it's allowed.

- **Restroom breaks:** In some jobs you must find a replacement to do your job before taking such a break.

- **Rest breaks:** Employers often provide two 15-minute breaks (in addition to a meal break) in an eight-hour shift. Find out when you can take a break and if there is a break room.

- **Meal breaks:** You will probably be allowed a meal break around the middle of your workday, if you work an eight-hour shift. Ask when you can take a meal break and how much time is allowed.

Some organizations have in-house cafeterias. Others provide break rooms where you can eat lunch. Find out whether your employer provides a kitchen with a refrigerator or microwave oven for employee use.

Your supervisor should explain what you need to know about work tasks, supplies, telephone systems, and breaks. If he or she forgets, don't be afraid to ask. This is important information to learn during the first few days on the job.

Off to a Good Start

After your supervisor shows you around, you'll be on your own, and you'll start your new job in the same way everyone else does. You won't know much about the job. You probably won't know anyone there. You might wonder whether you can do the job and whether you'll like it. Here are some suggestions to help you adjust during the first few weeks:

- **Be positive.** Expect good things to happen. Starting a new job gives you an opportunity to prove yourself to your supervisor and coworkers.

- **Ask for help.** Your supervisor and coworkers expect you to ask questions. They are willing to help when you ask. Listen carefully so that you don't have to ask the same question more than once.

- **Don't be a know-it-all.** You are new on the job. No matter how much you know and how skilled you are, you don't know everything about this particular job. Take the first few weeks to learn. Gain the respect of your coworkers and supervisor by demonstrating your ability to do your job well. Then you can begin making suggestions to improve the way things are done.

- **Have a sense of humor.** Other workers might test new workers. Some want to see how you respond to teasing and practical jokes. You might consider this an initiation. Try your best to accept good-natured teasing. If things get out of hand and you feel unfairly treated, harassed, or abused, talk with your supervisor about the situation.

- **Find a friend.** Look for someone who seems to know the job well and ask him or her to help you if you need it. Sometimes your supervisor will assign someone to help you during the first few days.

- **Follow instructions.** Your supervisor is the most important person in your work life. He or she decides whether you stay on the job, get promoted, and receive raises. Follow his or her instructions, be helpful, and do your best possible job.

- **Read company policies.** If your company has a booklet explaining policies and procedures, read through it carefully. Ignorance is not an excuse for doing something wrong or not knowing what to do.

- **Determine evaluation policies.** Find out what is expected of you in the first few days, weeks, and months; what standards are used to measure your success; and who does the evaluation.

The first few days on the job are important. They often determine the way you feel about the job. Staying positive, asking questions, and listening help ensure that your first few days on the job are a positive experience.

How Job Savvy Are You?

On Craig's first day as a stock clerk, his supervisor, Sharon, introduced him to the other workers. She walked him around the store and explained how the shelves should be stocked, when to stock the products, where to get new items, and how to price the items. Sharon then left Craig on his own. Everything went fine until he came to a brand that he wasn't sure how to price. Craig didn't want to appear stupid, so he went ahead and marked the prices the same as another brand.

1. What would you have done if you were Craig?

   _____

   _____

   _____

2. What problems do you think Craig might have caused?

   _____

   _____

   _____

Vicky is a new administrative assistant for a law firm. Her supervisor gave her a tour of the office, introduced her to other workers, and told her what tasks she would be doing. She then told Vicky to contact her if she had questions. List five questions Vicky should ask her supervisor.

1. _____

2. _____

3. _____

4. _____

5. _____

A Useful Skill: Active Listening

From your first day on the job to the last, active listening is a useful job skill. Active listening will make adjusting to your new work environment less stressful. Practice active listening every workday to increase your value as an employee.

Begin by consciously being an active listener at your new job orientation. This means

- **Your full attention is focused on what your trainer is saying.** Look at the trainer. Make eye contact. Do more listening than speaking.

- **You take time to understand the points being made.** Listen to learn. Recognize that you need to learn. Take notes to help you remember.

- **You ask questions as appropriate.** Make sure you understand what has been said. Summarize what you have learned.

- **You do not interrupt others at inappropriate times.** Avoid finishing someone's sentences for him or her. Listen for clues like "Are there any questions?" or wait for a pause before you ask questions. Do react to what is being said: smile, nod your head, verbally agree, and answer questions.[6]

As an active listener, you will be rewarded. When you start really working, you will remember more of your training. You will have laid the foundation of a positive relationship with your trainer.

Summing Up

Preparation is the key to creating a positive first impression on a new job. Of course, you can't prepare for every situation, but the more issues you're aware of and the more questions you ask before you start work, the better you'll do on the job.

Approach your job in a businesslike manner. Be willing to learn. Expect to succeed. Remember that your supervisor and all of your coworkers once experienced their first day on the job, too.

CHAPTER 3

Making a Good Impression

Our impressions about people affect the way we treat them. This is a natural human reaction. So it should come as no surprise that the impressions other people have about you affect the way they treat you. People form impressions based on looks and actions. Your physical appearance often determines what kind of first impression you make. It's important that you look as good as possible to make a positive impression. Hygiene (personal body care) also influences your impression on people. Messy hair, bad breath, and body odor make a poor impression. In this chapter, we'll look at dressing for success and good hygiene. Dress and hygiene might seem basic, but it's often the basics that are important for success at work.

"You smell good, Mr. Fenster. We appreciate that in our profession."

Some behavioral experts have found that the way you dress affects the attitudes and behavior of other people toward you. Employees who dress neatly and appropriately are perceived in a positive way. The implication is that you care for your job in the same way you care for yourself.[1]

Your actions will influence the impression others have of you. The best-dressed, sweetest-smelling grouch in the workplace is still the grouch whom everyone avoids. If you are upbeat, your boss and coworkers will view you positively. Smiling, being friendly, and showing interest in your work will let others know that you want to be a part of the team.

I Haven't a Thing to Wear

Dress for work has changed dramatically in the last decade, becoming much more casual. A 2007 Gallup poll demonstrates the percentage of employees that dress in various work attire.[2]

Work Attire Most Days	Percentage of Participating Employers
Formal business clothes	9%
Casual business	43%
Casual street clothes	28%
Uniform	19%

It is useful to know what the descriptions in the chart mean because they have become commonly used to describe business dress codes. A search on the Web using the term "business attire" will provide examples of dress styles matching each type of dress code.

Business formal includes a suit, dress shirt, and tie for men (usually a sports coat, dress pants, and a shirt with tie would be suitable) and for women a business suit, pants suit, or dress and jacket. Both men and women should wear dress shoes. Business formal attire is typically found in offices where highly paid professionals work, but the support staff is usually expected to follow the same dress code as the professional staff.

Business casual for women includes dress or khaki pants or skirts and dress shirts and/or sweaters or a moderate-length dress. Men should wear polo shirts, dress shirts, and/or sweaters and khakis or dress pants. Both men and women should wear dress shoes. Business casual dress is often found in other office situations, such as corporate offices and government workplaces.

Casual street clothes include what you typically wear when away from work. Examples are jeans or shorts and T-shirts or sweat shirts. Sneakers or sandals are the typical footwear. Casual street clothes are usually worn in small businesses and entrepreneurial companies where there is often little personal contact with customers.

Uniforms are provided by the employer along with instructions about how to wear the uniform. Uniforms are typically used in businesses providing health care, automotive services, grocery stores, and fast food. In addition, many franchise operations, such as restaurants, have some type of uniform.

General Dress Guidelines

Even if the dress code in your workplace is more casual, it's important to remember that clothes influence the way people perceive you. These perceptions affect how well your supervisor and coworkers accept you. Here are some general guidelines about what to wear on the job:

- **Dress codes:** The best way to know how to dress is to ask. Your supervisor and coworkers know about official and unofficial dress codes for the workplace. For example, many "casual" dress codes still don't allow workers to wear jeans or shorts to the office. Clothes worn by employees in the workplace and the attire of workers "in the field" may differ. Unofficial dress codes can affect work assignments, pay raises, and promotions.

- **Appropriate dress:** You probably have some very nice clothes that are not appropriate for the workplace. Clothes you would wear for a night on the town probably aren't appropriate for the workplace. Neither are tight-fitting clothes, low-cut dresses, unbuttoned shirts, short skirts, and neon-hued or metallic outfits. If you are unsure about wearing an article of clothing, wait. When you are more attuned to the atmosphere of the workplace, you can decide if you want to make your fashion statement. A workplace survey found that the following clothing was most often cited as inappropriate—even in workplaces where casual dress codes exist.[3] (The numbers indicate the percentage of respondents who considered this type of clothing unacceptable in the workplace.)

  - Flip-flops: 71%
  - Miniskirts: 70%
  - Strapless tops and dresses: 66%

- **Neat dress:** Make sure that the clothes you wear are neat and clean. Press them if necessary. Even casual dress must be tidy. Your clothes should be in good shape, with no tears or stains. Save that expensive pair of ripped jeans for your day off. Your shoes should be clean and in good condition, and polished if they are leather.

- **Uniforms:** Some businesses require employees to wear uniforms at work. Uniforms vary depending on the type of work being done. Hats, scrubs, aprons, and/or specially designed shirts may be required. Here are some questions you need to ask about uniforms:

  - Who is responsible for keeping uniforms clean and pressed? Some employers have a cleaning service; others expect you to keep your uniform in good shape.

  - How many uniforms do you need?

  - Who must pay for repairing or replacing uniforms that are accidentally damaged?

■ How should the uniform be worn? (Do you need special shoes or blouses with it?)

- **Safety clothing:** Some jobs present possible safety hazards, and you might be required to wear certain clothing as a result. Here are some common safety considerations:

    ■ Loose clothing or dangling jewelry can get caught and pull you into moving equipment. Avoid wearing such items if you work around moving equipment.

    ■ Hard leather shoes are a must on the job if something heavy could drop on your feet. You might be required to wear steel-toed shoes or boots for protection.

    ■ Jeans help protect you from scratches and cuts that can happen on some jobs.

Special Safety Equipment

Certain jobs require protective dress considerations.[4] Find out what safety equipment is required on the job, *and then wear it.* Safety equipment can be slightly uncomfortable, but, if you don't wear it, you could lose your job (or get hurt). An employer is responsible for your safety and will not tolerate safety infractions. The following is a list of common safety equipment:

- **Safety glasses:** Required for jobs in which small particles could strike or lodge in your eyes. For example, workers drilling on metal parts wear safety glasses.

- **Ear protectors:** Needed if your job exposes you to continuous or loud noise, which can cause hearing problems. Ground personnel who work around jet airplanes wear ear protectors.

- **Hardhats:** Necessary if you work where falling objects are a risk. A hardhat might not protect you from all injuries, but it can reduce the seriousness of an injury. Most construction workers are required to wear hardhats.

- **Masks:** A must if you work where exposure to fumes from dangerous chemicals is unavoidable. Failure to wear a mask in some jobs could result in serious injury or even death. A painter in a body and trim shop typically wears a mask.

- **Gloves:** Protect against the frostbite, blisters, or rope burns that are hazards of some jobs. A person stacking hay bales or working in the frozen-food section of a grocery store probably wears gloves.

- **Protective clothing:** Worn by those who work with or near hazardous materials. This clothing includes gloves, aprons, coveralls, boots, or an entire protective suit. If you work with hazardous materials, your employer must provide the protective clothing you need and teach you how to protect yourself from harm.

How Job Savvy Are You?

Jill is a salesperson at a life insurance company. Check the items you think would be acceptable for her to wear to work.

❑ Blouse	❑ Slacks	❑ Tie
❑ Boots	❑ Dress	❑ Jewelry
❑ Khakis	❑ Socks	❑ Sweat pants
❑ Polo shirt	❑ Dress shirt	❑ Leather shoes
❑ Shorts	❑ Sweater	❑ Running shoes
❑ Business suit	❑ Jacket	❑ Hose
❑ Skirt	❑ T-shirt	❑ Sandals
❑ Capris	❑ Jeans	❑ Other _____

Why did you select these items?

_____

_____

_____

Tyler is a counter attendant in a dry-cleaning shop. Check the items you think he could wear to work.

❑ Blouse	❑ Slacks	❑ Tie
❑ Boots	❑ Dress	❑ Jewelry
❑ Khakis	❑ Socks	❑ Sweat pants
❑ Polo shirt	❑ Dress shirt	❑ Leather shoes
❑ Shorts	❑ Sweater	❑ Running shoes
❑ Business suit	❑ Jacket	❑ Hose
❑ Skirt	❑ T-shirt	❑ Sandals
❑ Capris	❑ Jeans	❑ Other _____

Why did you select these items?

_____

_____

_____

Cal is a production worker in an automotive parts factory. Check the items you think he could wear to work.

❑ Blouse	❑ Shorts	❑ Slacks
❑ Boots	❑ Business suit	❑ Dress
❑ Khakis	❑ Skirt	❑ Socks
❑ Polo shirt	❑ Capris	❑ Dress shirt

(continued)

(continued)

❏ Sweater	❏ Tie	❏ Running shoes
❏ Jacket	❏ Jewelry	❏ Hose
❏ T-shirt	❏ Sweat pants	❏ Sandals
❏ Jeans	❏ Leather shoes	❏ Other _____

Why did you select these items?

_____

_____

_____

Brandtrell is a lab assistant at a hospital. Check the items you think he could wear to work.

❏ Blouse	❏ Slacks	❏ Tie
❏ Boots	❏ Dress	❏ Jewelry
❏ Khakis	❏ Socks	❏ Sweat pants
❏ Polo shirt	❏ Dress shirt	❏ Leather shoes
❏ Shorts	❏ Sweater	❏ Running shoes
❏ Business suit	❏ Jacket	❏ Hose
❏ Skirt	❏ T-shirt	❏ Sandals
❏ Capris	❏ Jeans	❏ Other _____

Why did you select these items?

_____

_____

_____

Personal Grooming

Grooming habits that your friends accept or that seemed adequate while you were in school might cause problems at work. Imagine a typical morning preparing for work or school as you complete the following worksheet.

GROOMING CHECKLIST
1. List the hygiene and grooming activities you practice.
_____
_____
2. What other kinds of grooming do you practice on a periodic basis? How often?
_____
_____

3. How would you rate your appearance after going through the activities listed previously? Check the item that best describes you.

____ **I look perfect.** Anyone would like to be with me.

____ **I look good.** My friends, coworkers, and supervisor would like to be with me.

____ **I look fine.** At least my friends and family would like to be with me.

____ **I could look better.** I like to be with myself, anyway.

____ **I don't look very good.** Even my dog wouldn't like to be with me.

4. How can you improve your grooming so that your appearance would be acceptable to anyone?

_____

_____

_____

The following is a checklist of grooming activities you should practice on a regular basis. Place a plus (+) next to those you do regularly and a minus (−) next to those you could improve.

❑ **Shower or bathe regularly.** It's not pleasant to work with someone who has body odor.

❑ **Use deodorant daily.** This helps control body odor that results from sweating.

❑ **Brush your teeth.** Brush at least once a day and when possible after each meal. Bad breath won't win you any points at work.

❑ **Gargle with mouthwash.** If you have a problem with bad breath, use mouthwash once or twice a day.

❑ **Shave.** Facial hair can be a distraction in the work setting. Some courts have ruled a policy against facial hair unconstitutional.[5] However, at many jobs, you're expected to remain clean-shaven. This means shaving regularly, typically whenever stubble appears. A mustache is acceptable in most jobs; a beard might not be. Being beardless may be a safety issue rather than a grooming issue for fire fighters, who must wear face masks. And food-preparation or serving jobs might require you to wear a hairnet over your beard. If you want to wear a beard or mustache, remember to groom it on a daily basis and keep it neatly trimmed.

❑ **Wash your hair.** Do so every one to three days. The oiliness of your hair determines how often you need to shampoo.

❑ **Style your hair neatly.** Your hair will always look better if you keep it trimmed and take time to style it. Talk with a hairstylist about keeping your hair looking good every day. At the least, comb your hair several times a day. Wear hairstyles that are appropriate for the workplace and your lifestyle. Hair dyed in unnatural colors, such as purple or green, is not appropriate.

❑ **Counter-cultural hairstyles can cause problems.** Counter-cultural hairstyles can cause problems for you in the workplace.[6] Spikes, dreadlocks, mullets, and other styles that are more free and expressive are often unwelcome in the workplace. This might not be fair, but it is a reality.

(continued)

(continued)

❑ **Trim your hair on a regular basis.** Extremely long hair for either gender might be considered unconventional in some organizations. Long hair worn loose can be a safety problem in certain jobs. It's also a hygiene problem in jobs such as food preparation and serving, for which you might have to wear a hairnet.

❑ **Trim and clean your fingernails.** Women who wear fingernail polish should use conservative colors for work. Avoid extremely bright or unnatural colors (such as blue or black).

❑ **Use makeup sparingly.** Makeup can help you look your best, but not when it's applied wrong. Natural colors that complement your skin tone are appropriate. Bold colors, such as hot pinks and bright blues, are rarely appropriate in the workplace. If you're not sure how to apply makeup to enhance your looks, ask the consultant at a cosmetics counter.

❑ **Pierce sparingly.** Pierced earrings for women are almost the norm these days, and in some organizations they have become more acceptable for men. However, if you are a man with a pierced ear, it might be a good idea to remove your earring for interviews and for the first few days on the job. Many people are still uncomfortable with pierced ears for men. Women should not wear long, dangly, flashy earrings to work.

Other types of piercing—for example, in the lips, eyebrows, and nose—are less acceptable. Body piercing might hinder you in some workplaces, but it's considered reasonable in others. Use your own best judgment for your workplace. Exceptions might be made if piercing represents an employee's cultural or religious beliefs.[7]

❑ **Keep body art out of sight.** Tattoos and piercing have become more common among the general population. However, managers still frown on them. They particularly don't like tattoos that could be considered offensive. In most cases, wearing clothes that cover any tattoos solves the problem. Several communities have nonprofit organizations where doctors volunteer to remove what might be considered offensive tattoos free of charge.

In some jobs, your own health—as well as that of customers or patients—depends on your good hygienic practices. For example, the law requires health-care organizations and food-preparation facilities to enforce certain sanitary practices. Here is a list of the most commonly required hygienic practices:

- **Hairnets:** Sometimes required for jobs in food service or preparation.

- **Washing hands:** You must wash your hands with soap and water after using the restroom. This helps protect you from disease or from spreading germs and is particularly important in jobs where you prepare or serve food. Use soap and lather your hands for 10 to 15 seconds. Regulations require workers in health occupations to wash their hands each time they work with a patient.

- **Gloves:** Help control exposure to germs in food-preparation and health occupations.

- **Aprons:** Might be required in food-preparation jobs to prevent germs, dirt, or other foreign particles on your clothes from getting into the food.

Additional precautions are taken in many occupations. You should become familiar with the hygiene practices required for your job. In some cases (such as food-preparation jobs), state and local laws govern the hygiene standards.

Special Personal Considerations

There are three specific issues regarding appearance that justify special attention here: physical condition, weight, and acne. Let's examine these one at a time.

Physical Condition

This applies to everyone. You should exercise regularly to be in good physical condition. Exercise improves your stamina and allows you to work harder and longer.

This pays off when you are rewarded with higher pay or promotions because of your productivity. Being in good shape applies to workers in both physically and mentally demanding jobs.

Weight

People who are overweight often encounter negative reactions from other people. Yes, it's discriminatory, but many in our society think overweight people are less attractive. Some even perceive overweight people as lazy. This is quite an obstacle for an employee to overcome.

If you are overweight, you should do as much as possible to improve your appearance. This might mean going on a diet and exercising more. (Consult your physician before starting any weight-reduction program.) It also means wearing clothes that fit well and look good on you.

Do your best to overcome any weight problem.

Acne

If you have a serious acne problem (as many people do), consult a dermatologist. A better diet, improved skin care, and medication might help improve this condition.

While physical attractiveness might be a factor in getting ahead at work, a positive self-image and good mental attitude are more important. If you have a problem with your appearance, do your best to look as good as you can. Then concentrate on other things. No one can do more than his or her best.

Mannerisms and Habits

Mannerisms and habits can have as powerful an influence on people as appearance. Look at other people and determine what mannerisms they exhibit that negatively affect the way you feel about them. Examine yourself for any such behavior. Ask friends and family to tell you whether they observe undesirable traits in your conduct. (Family members will be especially willing to do this.) This list describes some common problems:

- **Using tobacco products:** Many organizations have banned smoking on the job. In some cases, smoking is restricted to certain areas outside buildings or even off the premises. People often are looked down on because of smoking.[8] Chewing tobacco or using snuff also might be prohibited and creates a negative image.

- **Wearing earphones or earbuds:** Many people use portable radios and MP3 players on the job. Be aware that this can reduce communication and create safety hazards. Your employer might also interpret it to mean you are disinterested in your job.[9]

- **Chewing gum:** It's hard to speak clearly when you've got a wad of gum in your mouth. You also run the risk of looking like a cow chewing its cud. Be smart—leave the gum at home.

- **Using slang or profanity:** Many people will think you are ignorant or uneducated if you use slang. You should use a commonly understood vocabulary. A person who uses profanity is viewed in an even worse light, appearing not only ignorant but also rude and uncouth.

- **Picking and pulling:** Sometimes people unconsciously develop a habit of picking at a certain part of their body—maybe their ears, nose, hair, chin, or fingers. This can be a real turnoff to other people.

- **Texting and talking on cell phones:** Imagine that you are talking to a friend at a party when your friend stops talking and walks away. What would your reaction be? Constantly texting or talking on your cell phone in social situations causes others to believe they are being ignored. Texting and talking on a cell phone while walking or driving is also dangerous. Studies have shown multitasking causes not only vehicle accidents but pedestrian accidents as well.[10] You can avoid offending others and be safer if you limit your mobile communications.

How Job Savvy Are You?

Sasha started work as a secretary in a large office about four weeks ago. Today, she came into work wearing a short skirt that is quite revealing when she sits down. She has on so much perfume that you can smell it 20 feet away. Her nails are very long and painted purple, to match her eye shadow and her dress. Her lipstick is also purple. She is wearing spiked heels and black mesh stockings.

1. What is your first reaction when you see Sasha?

   _____

   _____

---

2. Your supervisor just told you that Sasha will be helping you complete a proposal for a potential client. Do you think Sasha will be a good worker? Explain the reason for your answer.

_____

_____

Dan is a maintenance worker at a hospital. He is required to wear a uniform to work. His hair is shaggy and unkempt. Some employees avoid him, saying that he smells bad. Once in a while he comes to work with a three-day growth of stubble on his face.

1. What should Dan do to properly groom himself for this job?_____

_____

_____

2. Are there any on-the-job hygienic issues Dan should keep in mind?_____

_____

_____

Have a Positive Attitude

During your first months of work, your superiors and coworkers will form opinions of you based on your actions and attitudes. These first impressions are important to your success on the job. They may affect the work that you are assigned and even future promotions. Once they are formed, first impressions are difficult to change. Here are a few tips to create a positive impression:

- **Be a learner.** Pay attention to directions. Listen to others. Ask questions when you need help. Learn about the organization by observing the interaction of others.

- **Be a part of the work team.** Do your share of the work. Be friendly. Talk with your coworkers about their interests. Be helpful. If your boss asks for extra help for work assignments, volunteer.

- **Be businesslike.** Speak and conduct yourself in a professional manner. Be aware that the language you would use with your friends at a weekend gathering is different than the language used in the workplace. Be organized. Know your work schedule. Be at work on time. Avoid leaving work early.

- **Be positive.** No doubt you will experience some stressful days. All workers do. Remember that others will judge you on how you deal with difficult situations as well as the everyday times. Develop a "can-do" attitude and use it when you experience a hard day.

A Useful Skill: Speaking

When you speak, you make an impression on others. If you speak with a clear, confident voice, others will view you as confident. However, speaking in an inaudible voice or not looking at the listener when you're speaking gives the impression that you lack confidence. Use correct grammar. Asking questions makes you appear interested in the topic.

But speaking is more than talking. Organizing the thoughts you want to convey is also a part of this skill. To effectively communicate in the workplace, you must listen, process what you hear, and then speak. Your coworkers and supervisors will be doing the same. This type of communication helps you get the information you need to complete your work tasks.

Another type of conversation that happens in the workplace is small talk. Although small talk is not directly involved with work tasks, research has shown that it plays an important role in developing teamwork. Participating in small talk as you begin your new job will help you become a part of the team.

Here are a few helpful hints for communicating with coworkers and supervisors:

- **Listen before you speak.** Listening will allow you to learn more about other team members. Knowing about their interests and concerns will provide information for conversations.

- **Think before you speak.** Consider what you want to convey and how you want to make the statement.

- **Avoid controversial subjects.** Don't participate in conversations that involve gossip and rumors. Controversial topics are best avoided in the workplace.

- **Be respectful of your coworkers.** Avoid asking extremely personal questions. Listen to their ideas, feelings, and beliefs. Accept their diversity.[11]

Summing Up

Proper dress and good hygiene are crucial for two important reasons. First, they affect your appearance, and your appearance has an effect on supervisors, coworkers, and customers—either good or bad. Second, proper dress and hygiene might be important to your health and safety. Wearing clothes that protect you from injury or disease is important. Find out what the safety and health requirements are for your job, and follow them closely. Remember, how you dress and how you take care of yourself tell others a lot about you.

Your mannerisms and habits play a role in others' impression of you. Become aware of any irritating behavior or habit you have, and try to eliminate it. When you get rid of objectionable behavior, you reflect an upbeat impression.

Remember, first impressions are made only once. Make sure what you're conveying about yourself is positive.

CHAPTER 4

Being There... On Time!

An organization can't operate without dependable workers. A supervisor must be able to rely on employees coming to work on time every day. A late or absent worker causes many problems. On the average, absenteeism costs an employer $422 per worker each year. Some large companies estimate losing $764,000 per year in direct payroll costs because of absenteeism, which employers cite as their biggest complaint about workers.[1]

"The El-Cheapo 2600 is preferred by people who are looking for an excuse to be late."

The Cost of Absenteeism

When you don't show up for work, you can cause problems for everyone. Here are some examples of problems that happen when employees are absent:

- **Problems for the employer:** Employee absenteeism can cost organizations money in two ways:
  - **Reduced productivity:** Fewer workers means the organization produces fewer goods or cannot serve as many customers. In some instances, the amount of goods and services remains the same but the quality suffers.
  - **Customer dissatisfaction:** Customers won't be served as well as they should be. For instance, if a worker in a production job is absent, a customer's shipment might not be sent on time because there isn't enough help.

- **Problems for supervisors:** Worker absenteeism requires a supervisor to rearrange work schedules and plans. Another worker might have to fill in. Problems created by one absence usually continue throughout the day. Supervisors pick up the slack, which might make them angry. How the supervisor reacts depends largely on the reason and frequency of the absence.

- **Problems for coworkers:** Everyone must work harder when another worker is absent. A person who had the day off might be called into work. Someone who just finished a shift might be asked to stay and work a double shift. These people, too, might be angry with the absent employee.

- **Problems for the employee:** Being absent or late often results in "docked" pay. This means that you get no pay for the time off work. The organization's policy about days off will affect how much your paycheck is reduced. Repeated incidents could result in termination.

How Job Savvy Are You?

George supervises the morning shift at a fast-food restaurant. The phone rings at 6 a.m. "George," says the caller, "this is Lee. My car won't start, so I won't be at work today." The breakfast crowd has started to arrive in the dining room. Several cars are lined up at the drive-through window.

1. What problems did Lee create by not coming to work?

   _____

   _____

   _____

2. How does Lee's absence affect his coworkers?

_____

_____

_____

3. How many times do you think George will allow Lee to be absent from work before taking some kind of action?

_____

_____

Schedule, Attendance, and Tardiness

Work hours differ. Some companies have set hours—such as Monday to Friday from 8 till 5. In some job situations the employees may choose their work hours as long as they work a certain number of hours each week. Flexible hours are more common in salaried jobs. Irregular work schedules change weekly or even monthly. Salaried workers may normally work eight hours in a day, but during the "busy" season of the year may be required to work extra hours without additional pay.

Systems to record attendance include "clocking in" using a time card and mechanical clock. Automated systems record an employee's attendance, arrival, and leaving during the work period using badges encoded with a special chip or cards that are swiped.[2] Employee information is stored in a computer. A salaried employee may complete an attendance sheet at the end of each pay period.

One company recently initiated a new policy using an automated system and an 800 phone number. Employees calling in sick or reporting to work late are required to call the 800 number. These unauthorized absences are recorded in the system. Employees who have seven such absences within six months are fired.[3]

Defining tardiness varies from company to company. Normally a grace period, for example 10 minutes after the set hour, applies before an employee is recorded as tardy. Automated systems record the number of times a worker is tardy. Excessive tardiness can result in an individual losing the job.

What's Your Excuse?

Sometimes, being absent or late is unavoidable; more often, it's not. Read the following list of excuses. Place a check mark in the Absent column if that reason has caused you to be absent from work in the past year. Check Late if it made you late, and Both if it caused you to be both late and absent on different occasions. If you aren't currently employed, check the reasons you were late or absent from a former job or from school.

Excuse	Absent	Late	Both
Overslept			
Missed the bus			
Personal illness			
Alarm didn't ring			
Children were sick			
Car wouldn't start			
Couldn't find a baby-sitter			
Someone borrowed my car			
Wanted to sleep in			
Traffic was bad			
Didn't feel like going			
Family problems			
Wanted to do other things			
Weather was bad			
Forgot the work schedule			
No clean clothes			
Had a hangover			
Took a trip instead			
Needed a day off			

As you look over this list, consider what you should do to reduce the number of days you are absent from or late for work. You might find it interesting to compare your answers with the following reasons for absenteeism that workers gave in a study.[4]

Reason for Absenteeism	Percentage of Workers Citing Reason
Illness	34%
Dealing with family issues	22%
Taking care of personal business	18%
Escaping stress	13%
Felt entitled to the time	13%

These absences cost employers more than $400 a year per employee.[5] The next section reviews ways that you can avoid the problems that happen when you miss work.

Your Lifestyle Affects Your Work

A lifestyle is made up of the habits and activities you develop for day-to-day living. Your lifestyle includes what you eat, when and how long you sleep, and how you spend your time.

Studies show that your lifestyle can affect the amount of stress in your daily life. "Stress in America 2010," a report conducted by the American Psychological Association, found that one in five adult Americans rated their health as poor or average. Symptoms of stress—headaches, fatigue, depression, lack of motivation, and irritability—were experienced by these individuals, who admitted failing to maintain healthy lifestyles.[6]

Many of the reasons people miss work are directly related to their lifestyles. Here are some ways you can shape your lifestyle to increase your success at work:

- **Get a good night's sleep.** Most people need six to eight hours of sleep each night. According to the National Center on Sleep Disorders Research, cutting back on your sleep time just one hour can result in making bad decisions and taking greater risks. Skimping on sleep can affect your job performance.[7] Your body rests better when you sleep on a regular schedule. Many young people make the mistake of partying on work nights. They get less sleep and then skip work the next morning or are late.

- **Eat well.** Eat well-balanced meals on a regular schedule and avoid too much junk food. Consume plenty of fruits and vegetables. You are less likely to be ill when you have good eating habits.

- **Exercise regularly.** Most jobs in the United States are service and information related; they don't enable you to get much exercise. Regular exercise keeps you in top physical and mental condition and helps you release job-related stress.

- **Don't smoke.** According to plentiful medical evidence, smoking is hazardous to both smokers and nonsmokers. A Gallup poll found that 96 percent of U.S. adults want all smoking in the workplace banned or confined to a set-aside area.[8] Many organizations offer incentives and help for employees who want to quit smoking.

- **Don't drink too much.** Alcohol can cause health problems when it is abused. The more alcohol you drink, the more you can damage your body. Drinking too much will hurt your performance on the job the next day. Drinking during or before work is often considered cause for dismissal.

- **Don't do drugs.** Illegal drugs harm the body and mind. You should not take any drugs unless a physician prescribes them. Policies on illegal drug use vary among organizations. If you test positive for certain drugs, some organizations will give you a choice of entering a rehabilitation program or being fired. Other employers will simply fire you outright.

- **Keep good company.** Your relationships affect your work. For instance, if your friends don't work, they might want you to adapt to their schedule, which can leave you too tired for work the next day. If you're facing a conflict like this, you need to establish a priority for work over social activities. Avoid people who might get you into trouble with the law. Employers do not appreciate workers who miss work because they are in jail.

- **Socialize properly with coworkers.** We all need time to socialize with friends and acquaintances. Our coworkers often become our best friends because we spend so much time with them. Relationships with coworkers can be positive, or they can create problems in the workplace. These guidelines can help you avoid problems in your work relationships:

  - **Approach romances with coworkers cautiously.** Many people think work is a good place to meet people they would like to date. However, be careful not to let a romance negatively affect your relationships with coworkers. Sometimes an office romance can create awkward and unpleasant situations while you're dating and when the romance ends.

  - **Don't limit your friendships to coworkers.** When you socialize with coworkers, you spend a lot of time talking about work. To reduce stress, you need to get away from your job sometimes by not talking or even thinking about the job.

  - **Don't let friendships with coworkers interfere with your work performance.** Don't do someone else's work to cover for his or her inability or laziness. Avoid siding with a friend in a feud with another worker or supervisor. Try to be neutral in work relationships.

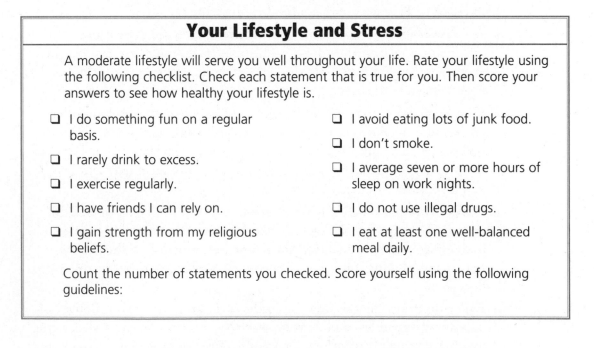

Your Lifestyle and Stress

A moderate lifestyle will serve you well throughout your life. Rate your lifestyle using the following checklist. Check each statement that is true for you. Then score your answers to see how healthy your lifestyle is.

- ❑ I do something fun on a regular basis.
- ❑ I rarely drink to excess.
- ❑ I exercise regularly.
- ❑ I have friends I can rely on.
- ❑ I gain strength from my religious beliefs.

- ❑ I avoid eating lots of junk food.
- ❑ I don't smoke.
- ❑ I average seven or more hours of sleep on work nights.
- ❑ I do not use illegal drugs.
- ❑ I eat at least one well-balanced meal daily.

Count the number of statements you checked. Score yourself using the following guidelines:

- **8 or more** checked items reflects a positive lifestyle that will help you be effective on the job.

- **6 to 7** checked reflects a moderate lifestyle that will help you on the job.

- **5 or fewer** checked reflects a vulnerable lifestyle. You might find that your lifestyle creates some job problems.

Plan for Success

Managing your life through good planning will help you avoid missing work. You can take the following five major steps to ensure a good work attendance record.

Step 1: Ensure That You Have Reliable Transportation

It's not your employer's fault that your car won't start. You are responsible for getting to work. Transportation problems can happen even if you own a new car. Try these strategies to ensure that you have reliable transportation:

- **Keep your car in good operating condition.** Maintain it regularly. If you suspect you might have car trouble, try starting the car a couple of hours before work. This will give you time to find another method of transportation if you need to. Cold or wet days can mean problems starting a car, so check the car early.

- **Know the public transportation system.** Keep a schedule of the public transportation available. Highlight the times and places that you would need to catch the bus, train, or subway to get to work.

- **Call a coworker for a ride.** Find a coworker who lives near you and has a reliable car. Make an agreement to share a ride if either of you has car trouble.

- **Carpool.** Check with coworkers and friends, or advertise in the classifieds for someone who can share a ride to work with you. This arrangement will work even when you don't work together. You just need to work in the same general area.

- **Walk or bicycle.** Think about finding housing near your workplace. Even if you live two to four miles from your job, you can still walk or ride a bike in good weather. If you don't want to move, find a job near your home. You might actually be able to work for less money at a job that doesn't cost you high transportation expenses. Your net income (wages minus work-related expenses) might be greater if you take a job close to home.

- **If all else fails, call a cab.** Riding in a taxi is costly, but it usually won't cost as much as losing a day's pay. And it's certainly less costly than losing your job. You don't want to take a taxi to work every day, but you shouldn't hesitate to do so in an emergency.

Step 2: Arrange Reliable Care for Your Dependents

Most often, your dependents are your children. However, you might be caring for an elderly parent or a disabled spouse. If you are responsible for dependents, you need reliable care.

What happens if a baby-sitter or home health aide lets you down? What if bad weather closes a day-care center? What if your dependent is ill? What if children can't get to school on the normal schedule?

You should plan ahead for substitute dependent care so that you don't get caught off guard. Here are some considerations:

- **Hire good aides.** Choose a reliable baby-sitter or home health aide. You can check this person's reliability by asking for references from people who have employed the aide in their own homes.

- **Select a good care center.** Ask for references. Learn about the center's policy for closing. What is its policy if your child, parent, or spouse is ill? There are now centers that will care for children when they are ill. You might pay more for centers with this service, but, in the long run, they might pay for themselves by reducing your absenteeism.

- **Investigate health-care programs.** In some cases, hospitals and specialized care centers will take care of your sick dependents while you are at work. Many of these programs you would use only when your child is sick. They cost more than normal child care, but they are less costly than an unpaid day off work or losing your job.

- **Have an emergency plan.** Find a friend or relative who is willing to care for your dependent for one or two days in case of an emergency. The best plan is to have at least two people willing to do this.

Step 3: Use a Calendar

Have a calendar, and use it to keep track of your work schedule. Whether you use a simple pocket-size calendar or choose to be more technical and use a cell phone calendar, record all assigned workdays and any personal appointments that might conflict with work.

Doctor and dental appointments can be noted in time to make arrangements with your employer. (Whenever possible, schedule personal appointments outside regular work hours.) You might want to note other personal business on your calendar, as well.

A calendar is one of the best tools to help you plan your workday. Use the forms that follow to plan your weekly and monthly schedules.

WEEKLY PLANNER

Monday   Date _____

Time   Appointments/Notes

_____   _____

_____   _____

_____   _____

_____   _____

_____   _____

_____   _____

Tuesday   Date _____

Time   Appointments/Notes

_____   _____

_____   _____

_____   _____

_____   _____

_____   _____

Wednesday   Date _____

Time   Appointments/Notes

_____   _____

_____   _____

_____   _____

_____   _____

_____   _____

Thursday   Date _____

Time   Appointments/Notes

_____   _____

_____   _____

_____   _____

_____   _____

_____   _____

_____   _____

(continued)

(continued)

Friday   Date _____

Time   Appointments/Notes

_____   _____

_____   _____

_____   _____

_____   _____

_____   _____

_____   _____

Saturday   Date _____

Time   Appointments/Notes

_____   _____

_____   _____

_____   _____

_____   _____

_____   _____

_____   _____

Sunday   Date _____

Time   Appointments/Notes

_____   _____

_____   _____

_____   _____

_____   _____

_____   _____

_____   _____

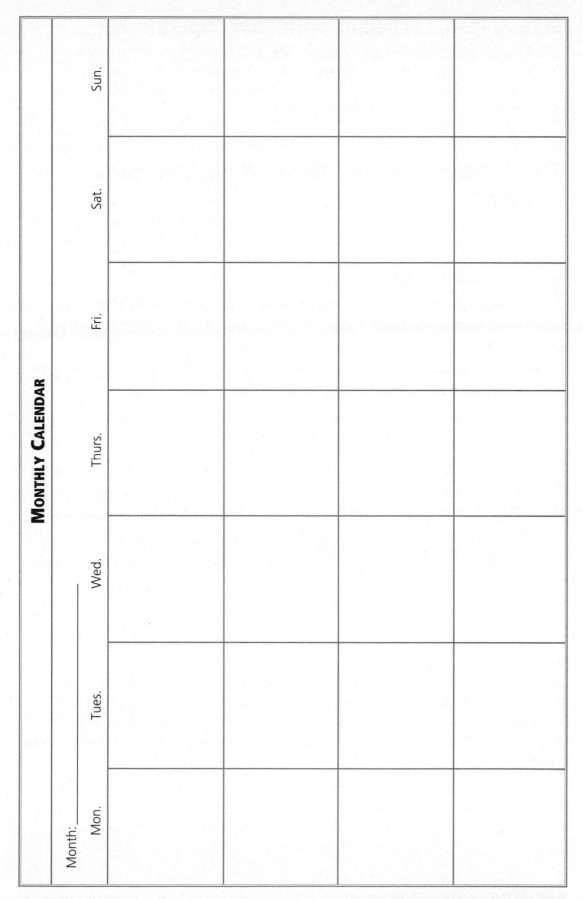

MONTHLY CALENDAR

Month: _____

Mon.	Tues.	Wed.	Thurs.	Fri.	Sat.	Sun.

Step 4: Plan a Schedule with Your Supervisor

You can plan for many events in your life, such as vacations; car maintenance; or dental, doctor, and lawyer appointments. Your supervisor usually can approve and schedule a one-day absence with only a few weeks' notice. A vacation might require several months' notice.

Ask your supervisor how much notice is needed to schedule days off.

Step 5: When You Can't Get to Work, Call Your Employer

Even the best planning won't cover all potential difficulties that can keep you from getting to work. So call your supervisor as soon as you know that you cannot get to work. An employer usually will understand if you miss work once in a while because you're sick.

To better prepare for these emergencies, ask your supervisor how many days are considered reasonable to be absent from work each year. Most organizations will take disciplinary action for

- Frequent or unexcused absences
- Absences that occur a day before or after a holiday
- Failure to call in and report an unexpected absence
- Work absence to handle nonemergency personal business

The discipline might range from a verbal warning for the first offense to immediate discharge.

When you notify your supervisor that you can't be at work, follow these steps:

- Identify yourself and say that you can't come to work.
- Explain the reason that you can't be at work. Don't lie.
- If you expect to be gone for more than a day, tell the supervisor how long you will be away from the job.
- Express your willingness to make up the hours you missed.

It may be appropriate to notify your supervisor that you are ill by using e-mail or a text message to the supervisor's cell phone. You should only use one of these methods when it is approved by the organization and your supervisor. Many supervisors still want to be contacted by phone so they can quickly communicate about how to adjust the workflow for the day. They need to know the last task you completed or how far along you were in getting the task finished.

How Job Savvy Are You?

There are good and bad reasons for being absent from work. Review the following list. Check those reasons that you think justify an absence.

- ❑ I have a headache and don't feel like coming to work.
- ❑ My child is ill, and I have to stay home.
- ❑ My car isn't working, and I don't have a ride to work.
- ❑ I have the flu.
- ❑ I have an appointment with my attorney.
- ❑ There's been a death in my family.
- ❑ My brother asked me to baby-sit his children.
- ❑ I had a fight with my spouse, and I'm too upset to work.
- ❑ I sprained my ankle and need to keep it elevated.
- ❑ I need to visit a sick friend in the hospital.
- ❑ Our house was broken into last night.
- ❑ I need to get a new pair of glasses.
- ❑ I had a car accident on the way to work.
- ❑ It was a long weekend, and I have a hangover.
- ❑ This is a religious holiday for me.

You should always tell the truth when you report to your supervisor. A lie might be discovered and cause you embarrassment. If you are caught in a lie, it will take a long time to regain your supervisor's trust.

Getting to Work on Time

Late workers cause the same problems for an employer as absent workers. There are reasonable causes for being late. However, some employers consider late arrivals excessive if they occur more than once a month or four or five times a year. These suggestions can help you plan ahead to be on time:

- **Use a reliable alarm clock.** If you have an electric clock, make sure it has a backup power source. Or use a battery-powered clock or a cell phone alarm as well, in case the electricity shuts off. You can buy battery-powered portable or travel alarms for less than an hour's wage. Don't rely on someone else to get you up. You can't afford to lose a job just because you don't get to work on time.

- **Get up early.** Allow yourself time to get ready and get to work. Plan enough time to eat breakfast and to deal with transportation delays. You should also plan to arrive at work 8 to 10 minutes early. This cushion will help you mentally prepare for the day and reduce stress. It also shows your supervisor that you are eager to work.

- **Plan for special conditions.** Some days, you'll need more time to get to work. For example, poor weather conditions usually slow traffic. Get up earlier on such days so that you will still arrive on time.
- **Call your supervisor if you will be more than 15 minutes late.** You should give the following information:
  - Tell why you will be late.
  - Explain that you are going to get to work as soon as possible.
  - Estimate when you will arrive.
  - Assure your supervisor that you will make up the time.
  - When you get to work, apologize and make it clear that it won't happen again.

How Job Savvy Are You?

Buster was absent for two days from his job as a production worker at a shoe factory. When he returned, his supervisor, Mr. Brown, was angry. "Why didn't you call to let me know you weren't coming to work?" Mr. Brown asked.

Buster was surprised and answered, "My father-in-law died, and we had to attend the funeral."

Mr. Brown replied, "I'm sorry about your father-in-law, but I'm going to issue you a written warning. If this ever happens again, you'll be fired."

1. Why did Mr. Brown react this way?

_____

_____

2. How could Buster have avoided this problem?

_____

_____

Vanessa went to a party on Thursday night, even though she had to be at work at 7:30 the next morning. She overslept on Friday morning and got to work 45 minutes late. Two weeks ago, she went to a party on Sunday and skipped work the next day. A week ago, she was 20 minutes late because she had to pick up a friend and take her to work. Her supervisor warned her then not to be late for work. When Vanessa got to the office on Friday, the receptionist told her that her supervisor wanted to see her immediately.

1. What do you think her supervisor will say?

_____

_____

2. What should Vanessa do to keep her job and avoid this situation in the future?

_____

_____

A Useful Skill: Time Management

When employees use time effectively, production within an organization improves. Employers are looking for workers who are not just busy. Employers are looking for workers who get the job done.

As an employee, you will also benefit from efficient time management, because you will be less stressed at work. Your work environment will be more pleasant.

Practicing time management involves both small and big actions. Here are a few suggestions to develop time-management skills in your work life.

- **Be on time.** Whether you are "clocking in" for your work shift, attending a staff meeting, or taking your lunch break, be aware of time.

- **Be physically and mentally ready to work.** Getting enough sleep and exercising will help you work more efficiently.

- **Focus on the tasks you are assigned.** Plan and prioritize your day. Avoid distractions. Make a to-do list.

- **Do it right the first time.** Take the time to analyze a task to find out how to do it most efficiently. Having to do a task a second time is a waste.

- **Evaluate how you spend your time.** For two or three days, write a list of how you are spending your time. Find the tasks that require the major parts of your day. Look for ways to use your time more efficiently.

- **Learn ways to be more efficient.** Do you know how to organize your e-mail? Can you break big tasks into small steps? Can you multitask during travel time?[9]

You get 24 hours each day. You can't increase or decrease this allotted time. But by learning to manage time, you can budget your time to make both your personal and work life more productive.

Summing Up

Reliable workers are essential to an effective operation. That's why good attendance and punctuality are important to employers. Many organizations encourage good attendance and punctuality through raises, bonuses, and promotions. A little planning and self-discipline will help you be a dependable and valuable worker.

CHAPTER 5

Communicating in the Workplace

Your success in the workplace depends on your ability to communicate. If you can express your ideas clearly, your coworkers, supervisors, and clients will view you positively. Employees who listen to directions are more efficient. Workers and supervisors avoid misunderstandings in the workplace when they listen to one another.

Although traditional speaking and writing skills remain important for conducting daily business, technology has brought about changes in communication. Knowing how to communicate using technology is a necessity for today's employees.

This chapter enables you to effectively communicate using both traditional and technological communication skills.

"Hey, Norman! I sent you an e-mail!"

Good Communication Skills Open Doors

Developing good communication skills will help you find a job because employers are looking for you. Check a job board on the Internet. You will find numerous job postings that list strong communication skills as a requirement for the position.

In today's business world, a change has occurred. Even professions traditionally thought to deal only with numbers (such as accounting) are hiring individuals with strong communication skills. In a recent survey of more than 2,000 business managers and other executives at U.S. companies, more than 80 percent stated that their employees' communication skills are evaluated yearly. Three out of four executives believe that these skills will become even more valued within the next three to five years.[1]

In a job interview you will have more confidence if you can speak clearly. Your positive manner will impress an employer. Looking the interviewer in the eye and expressing your ideas reflects your ability to do the job.

Just as good communication can help you get a job, poor communication skills can result in losing a job. Businesses lose millions of dollars each year due to poor communication by employees. Employers expect to make money. An employee who causes an organization to lose money will soon be unemployed.

In the workplace, good communication skills can help avoid problems. Reading an e-mail carefully will help you avoid missing a staff meeting. Listening to your supervisor's directions will help you avoid wasted time when performing your assigned duties. Taking a phone message clearly will avoid a miscommunication with a customer.

Effective communication will help you keep your job. You may have some speech habits or mannerisms that you need to eliminate. You may need to learn a new technological communication skill. Perhaps you need to improve your listening skills. Whatever you do to improve your communication skills will take time and effort, but you will be avoiding problems in the workplace.

Practicing Effective Listening

Studies consistently point out that listening is the communication skill used most frequently in our daily lives. Listening is not a natural skill. Effective listeners have developed certain abilities. You can practice active listening to be a more effective listener using the following techniques:

- **Look at the speaker.** In our culture, eye contact is important. Not looking at the speaker is an indication of not listening. Whether you are listening in a one-on-one situation or in a large group, face the speaker and maintain eye contact.

- **Use your ears and not your mouth.** Talking while another person is speaking is rude. Talking not only interferes with your listening but prevents other listeners from hearing. When another individual is speaking, be quiet.

- **Concentrate on what is being said.** Focus on the speaker's thoughts. Taking notes is an excellent method of reinforcing what is being said. Don't multitask or try to do other things while listening. Studies have shown that multitasking interferes with listening.[2]

- **Honor the other person's opinion.** Don't let your personal biases prevent you from listening. Listening doesn't mean you accept the speaker's point of view. Listening does mean you recognize the speaker's right to have an opinion.

- **Allow the speaker to complete his or her thoughts without interrupting.** This is not an easy task, especially if you disagree. But waiting and not interrupting lets all listeners understand what the speaker is saying and avoids confusion.

- **Listen with your eyes as well as your ears.** Observing a speaker's body language, such as hand gestures and body posture, gives you more insight into the speaker's message.

- **Act interested even when you may not be.** Make an effort to listen. Face the speaker. Lean forward. Concentrate on what is being said.

- **Ask questions before you respond.** Clarify the speaker's information by asking questions. You might say, "This is what I understand you said… Is that correct?" Let the speaker make any corrections to help you better understand his or her thoughts. Your response will be clearer and more intelligent if you ask questions first.

LISTENING CHECKUP

Improving your listening skills begins with learning your strengths and weaknesses. Rate your listening skills using the following checklist. Check each statement that is true for you. Then score your answers to see how you measure up in terms of listening skills.

- ❏ I face the speaker.
- ❏ I maintain comfortable eye contact.
- ❏ I am quiet while the speaker is talking.
- ❏ I concentrate on the speaker's words.
- ❏ I avoid interrupting the speaker.
- ❏ I show respect for the speaker's opinion.

- ❏ I ask questions after the speaker has finished.
- ❏ I avoid multitasking.
- ❏ I observe body language and interpret it.
- ❏ I take notes.

Count the number of statements you checked. Score yourself using the following guidelines:

(continued)

(continued)

- **8 or more** checked items reflects positive listening skills that will help you communicate effectively on the job.

- **6 to 7** checked items reflects a need to improve your listening skills to communicate effectively on the job.

- **5 or fewer** checked items reflects negative listening skills that might create some communication problems on the job.

Listening is essential in the workplace. When workers listen to directions, productivity increases. As employees and employers listen to each other, their sense of teamwork grows.

Listening to instructions to complete a task is a highly valued skill in the workplace. When you're listening to directions, pay particular attention to what your supervisor says at the beginning and the end. Often, when someone is giving instructions, he or she states the most important idea at the beginning and then repeats it at the end. Notice words that he or she stresses, and watch for anything he or she writes down. Make notes to help yourself review instructions later. Ask questions to clarify the instructions.

Customers respond positively to workers who practice active listening. When a staff member listens without interrupting and concentrates on the customer's words, active listening is taking place. Active listening shows respect for the client. You will resolve any complaint or request with less conflict when you use active listening.

Learning to listen has its rewards. Listening employees follow directions and think about their actions. When opportunities to advance are available, these workers are most often promoted. Coworkers respect good listeners. Customers react positively when employees listen.

How Job Savvy Are You?

On her first day back in the office after a week's vacation, Carmen attended the monthly staff meeting. Her supervisor, Mrs. Wyatt, began the meeting by reviewing the sales records for the month. Because she had already reviewed her sales for the month, Carmen decided to text message a client to schedule a lunch meeting. When Mrs. Wyatt asked her a question about the sales report, Carmen needed to have the question repeated. Mrs. Wyatt frowned, folded her arms, and repeated the question. She asked Carmen to see her following the meeting.

1. Why did Mrs. Wyatt react in this way?

   _____

   _____

2. What should Carmen do to solve this problem?

   _____

   _____

Jackson has a certificate in small engine repair and has been working at the Mower Shop for five years. Mr. Howard, the business owner, and Jackson are attending a workshop to learn to repair a new line of lawn care equipment. Mr. Howard paid the workshop fees and is quite excited about the workshop.

The instructor's presentation is very basic. Jackson already knows much of what is being taught. In fact, the instructor doesn't really seem to be well informed. Jackson even disagrees with some information being provided. Jackson's mind is beginning to wander.

1. What listening skills can Jackson apply in this situation?

_____

_____

2. How could Jackson use these listening skills to impress Mr. Howard?

_____

_____

Verbal Communication Skills

Your voice is the primary tool that you use to communicate. The way you speak influences the listener's opinion of you. If you speak clearly, at an even rate, and loud enough, you appear confident and capable. If you speak with a mumble, too quickly, or too quietly, you appear uncomfortable and incapable.

Using proper grammar and avoiding slang and offensive terms when communicating reflects a confident, educated individual. With an increased vocabulary, you have a greater chance of using just the right word to convey your message.

Whether you are speaking to a group or having a one-on-one conversation, the same methods apply. With practice you will become more at ease when you communicate verbally.

CHECK YOUR VERBAL COMMUNICATION SKILLS

Improving your verbal communication skills begins with learning your strengths and weaknesses. Rate your speaking skills using the following checklist. Check each statement that is true for you. Then score your answers to see how you measure up in terms of verbal communication.

❏ I speak clearly.

❏ I use correct grammar.

❏ I look at the listener.

❏ I speak loud enough for others to hear.

❏ I speak at an even rate.

❏ I vary the pitch of my voice.

❏ I avoid using slang when speaking.

❏ I avoid using offensive language.

❏ I have a varied vocabulary.

❏ I feel at ease when speaking.

(continued)

(continued)

> Count the number of statements you checked. Score yourself using the following guidelines:
>
> - **8 or more** checked items reflects positive speaking skills that will help you communicate effectively on the job.
>
> - **6 to 7** checked items reflects a need to improve your speaking skills to communicate effectively on the job.
>
> - **5 or fewer** checked items reflects negative speaking skills that might create some communication problems on the job.

Verbal Communication in the Workplace

In the workplace, all types of conversation take place. Business talk is the communication about work. Business talk may be structured, such as the agenda for a team meeting or the step-by-step instructions in a training situation. However, most conversations in the workplace are not this structured.

During a typical day, a mixture of business talk and small talk takes place. Small talk is informal conversation between workers. Although it has no relevance to the work being done, it plays the important role of forming a bond among workers that builds teamwork.

When you're communicating in the workplace, think about what you are saying before you speak. Don't spread rumors or gossip that could damage someone's reputation. Lying can cause problems in the workplace. Excessive bragging can cause people to avoid you. Constant swearing or using vulgar language is inappropriate.

Being sensitive to the ideas, feelings, and beliefs of the people you work with will help you succeed on the job. Bigoted or vulgar conversations are insulting. Using offensive terms when referring to races, ethnic groups, or sexual groups is called harassment, and it is illegal.

When misunderstandings occur in the workplace, assertive communication is needed. An assertive communicator listens to all viewpoints and seeks to understand each person's thoughts. Facts and issues rather than opinions or emotions are the focus of the conversation. After all points of view have been heard, the problem is summarized for clarification. The solution is stated very specifically, with the expectation that all those involved will act on it.

Assertive communication provides solutions to workplace problems instead of confusion and arguments.

Starting a Conversation

A conversation is the verbal exchange between two or more people. Initiating a conversation with a coworker or supervisor can be awkward. Here are some techniques to use when starting a conversation:

- **Focus on the other person.** Remember that the other individual is probably feeling as awkward as you. Forget yourself by concentrating on the other person.

- **Ask appropriate questions.** Avoid extremely personal questions. It's also best not to ask questions about controversial topics, such as religion or politics.

- **Ask open-ended questions.** An open-ended question allows the person being questioned to share an opinion or a story. For example, "What interested you in working with this company?"

- **Compliment the individual.** Offer a sincere compliment, such as "I was just admiring your ring. Is it a family heirloom?"

- **Share something about yourself.** Sharing something personal such as a hobby, a trip, or your family background helps the listener see you as an individual.

- **Discuss a shared interest.** Share a positive work experience with coworkers. But avoid complaints or gossip. Don't spread job-related rumors.

- **Talk about books, movies, or world events.** Reading newspapers or online news will help you know what the current popular topics are.

- **Prepare in advance.** If you know you are going to be in a meeting or social situation with people you don't know well, plan a few things to talk about.

- **Remember to listen.** You don't have to do all the talking. Be an active listener as well.

How Job Savvy Are You?

Devon has worked as a sales representative at United Medical Supplies for a month. Next week the entire staff will be celebrating the company's 25th anniversary with an evening reception at an elegant downtown restaurant. List some topics that Devon might use to start a conversation with his coworkers at the reception.

1. _____
2. _____
3. _____
4. _____
5. _____

(continued)

(continued)

> List five topics that you would use to start a conversation with your supervisor in a social situation.
>
> 1. _____
> 2. _____
> 3. _____
> 4. _____
> 5. _____

Communicating over the Phone

Because the caller can't see you, a telephone conversation is different from other types of verbal communication. Your voice is the basis for establishing communication with the listener on the other end of the line. Because the listener can't see your facial expressions and body language, he or she will rely on the tone of your voice to detect your mood and emotions.

Because the phone is a machine designed to transmit sounds, the caller may hear background sounds if you're not careful. Turn off the radio when speaking on the phone. Don't eat, drink, or chew gum when talking on the phone. Avoid trying to talk on the phone while talking to another person in the room.

Communicating with the Phone in the Workplace

Because the first contact a customer has with a business is often an employee answering the business phone, practicing good phone etiquette is necessary. To make a good impression, do the following:

- **Greet the caller in a friendly manner.** Businesses often have a special greeting that they use when answering the phone, such as "Thank you for calling Cathedral Painting. How may I help you?"
- **Use a friendly, enthusiastic voice.** Smiling while you speak will make your voice sound friendly.
- **Identify yourself.** Remember that the other person can't see you and probably doesn't know you.
- **Speak into the receiver.** Be sure that the listener hears your voice. Speak clearly and loudly enough.
- **Use voice messaging skillfully.** The caller may need to leave a voice message for an individual in your business. Learn how to transfer the caller to a person's voice mail. Inform the caller that you are transferring him or her.
- **Take accurate written phone messages.** The caller may ask to leave a written message for an individual in your business. Listen carefully. Print clearly. Record both the first and last name of the caller, the message, the

caller's phone number, and a convenient time to return the call. Repeat the information to the caller. Date and sign the message before you deliver it to the recipient.

- **End the call professionally.** End a call by summarizing it, thanking the caller, and saying "Good-bye."

When you're making a business call, remember that the receptionist may be busy with other calls. Allow the phone to ring six to eight times. If the receptionist answers, ask to speak to an individual or explain the reason for your call. Your call may be transferred to the individual or to his or her voice mail.

If you are leaving a voice-mail message, include your full name, phone number, business name, and a brief message. If needed, include the day, date, and time of day. At the end of the message, repeat your name and phone number.

Cell Phones in the Workplace

Cell phones are convenient because they allow people to be connected wherever they go. Employees who make service calls or deliveries may be issued business cell phones to keep connected to the main office. Sales representatives may use cell phones to arrange appointments with clients. Be aware that a cell phone issued in this manner is typically intended only for business use and not for personal use.

As a courtesy, when using a cell phone to conduct business, you should inform the listener that you are calling from a cell phone. If there is interference during the call and it is impossible to reconnect, the listener will understand what has happened. In addition, cell phone calls are often made in public places; the listener may not want to talk about private subjects.

So many accidents have occurred while drivers were conducting business on cell phones that some states have made it illegal. Businesses have issued policies concerning driving and cell phone usage. The bottom line is that using cell phones for work-related reasons while driving is unwise.

When an employee makes personal cell phone calls while on the job, he or she is not working. His or her productivity decreases. Others are disturbed by the call. Their productivity decreases. Ringing cell phones interrupt meetings. To prevent these disturbances, some companies ask employees to turn off their cell phones when entering the business facility or leave their cell phones at their desks during meetings. With the number of smart cell phones increasing, there are even more potential distractions during meetings, and their use may be discouraged. Check the policy of your organization.

Nonverbal Communication Skills

Nonverbal communication involves facial expressions, body movements, and hand gestures. Because a speaker is usually talking as well as using nonverbal communication, a listener must use both ears and eyes to accurately interpret the speaker's message.

One scientific study found that, during presentations, individuals unconsciously react by nodding, fidgeting, and using other nonverbal expressions. Even when a participant attempted to change what was dubbed "honest signals," the nonverbal communication still revealed what the individual truly thought.[3]

Developing people-watching skills and learning to understand nonverbal cues will be helpful as you communicate with others. Here are some essential elements of nonverbal communication:

- **Body posture:** Refers to the position of the speaker's body. Is the speaker sitting or standing? Is he leaning forward or tipping backward in his chair? Are his arms folded or by his sides?

- **Proximity:** The distance between a speaker and the listener sends a message. If a speaker "gets in your face," you feel uncomfortable and perhaps even threatened. Our natural tendency in this situation is to back away from the speaker.

- **Eye contact:** In Western culture, eye contact means that the speaker and listener are interested in what is being said. Having no eye contact is considered rude. Staring, however, is eye contact that makes someone uncomfortable.

- **Facial expressions:** Expressions such as frowning, smiling, or scowling indicate certain emotions. Biting one's lips might show tension or concentration. Bowing one's head might be a sign of defeat or tiredness.

An effective communicator considers the context, the nonverbal communication, and the verbal message when speaking or interpreting another speaker's meaning.

Culture and Nonverbal Communication

Hand gestures, facial expressions, and other body language do not have the same meaning in various cultures. Some common American hand gestures are insulting and even considered vulgar in other cultures.[4] Even a smile can have different meanings in various cultures. Smiling in America indicates friendliness and even agreement. But when a Japanese person smiles, he may be preparing you for bad news. A Thai person may smile to avoid conflict.

In France, formally shaking hands when greeting coworkers starts the business day. In the Arab world, men are more likely to greet one another by enthusiastically embracing and kissing on the cheek. Bowing in many Asian countries can have various meanings depending on the depth of the bow. However, in Singapore bowing is not the custom. The practice of bowing is a reflection of many Asian cultures regarding personal space. Bowing acts as a way to avoid physical touch. For a Middle Eastern person, who hugs and kisses as a greeting, standing extremely close to another individual when conversing is also normal.[5] In our culture, the preferred expression of personal space is somewhere between bowing and kissing.

Diversity is the blending of various racial and cultural backgrounds in a group. Even people from different parts of the United States may have different views on personal space or conversational style. You work in a diverse environment. Because you must communicate in the workplace, learn to understand and respect the cultures of your coworkers. Practice tolerance. Be a mentor to someone from a different culture.

Written Communication in the Workplace

Written communication is often used to clarify or formalize verbal communication. For example, after setting a meeting time while talking on the phone to Pia, Andrew e-mails her with the time, date, and location of their meeting. Because written communication can be saved, it is often used for reference at a later date. The written minutes of a committee meeting serve as a record of decisions made in the meeting.

Business correspondence includes letters, memos, notes, and e-mails. No matter what form of written communication you use, you need to follow some rules to be effective:

- **Use proper grammar.** Failing to use correct grammar reflects poorly on you. If you don't know the correct usage, look it up.
- **Use correct punctuation.** Punctuation makes writing clearer. Incorrect punctuation can change the meaning of your writing.
- **Capitalize correctly.** Capitalization acts as a guide as the reader interprets the writing. Lack of capitalized words can be very confusing.
- **Check the spelling.** When using spell-check, remember that some incorrect words pass through the program without being discovered. Check the spelling yourself as backup; spell-check won't know that you meant "two" instead of "to."
- **Use the proper format.** Your organization may have a preferred format for written correspondence. Be sure to follow it.
- **Write concisely.** Business correspondence should deliver the message without being lengthy. Concise writing avoids repeating facts or phrases.
- **Proofread all written correspondence.** Before you send any business correspondence, read it one more time. Make any corrections that are needed.

Communicating Electronically in the Workplace

Technology has greatly affected the way people communicate in the workplace. Legal documents can be faxed from one part of the world to another. With laptop computers and Internet connections, a virtual office can be set up in a coffee shop or a library. Conversations in hyperspace take place using instant messaging (IM) and text messaging. Checking e-mail has become a daily chore for most people.

As the communication structure has changed, both benefits and problems have developed in the workplace. Organizations have policies concerning personal e-mails, text messages, and instant messaging. Spending company time with personal electronic correspondence is no different than spending company time talking with friends and family on the phone. Most employers discourage it. Others ban it altogether.

As an employee, be aware of new electronic forms of communication. Know the regulations your company has concerning electronic communication. Learn how to effectively use new technology to do your work. Don't use it for personal communication while on the job.

Use the Internet Wisely

Each day hundreds of friends share the highlights and trials of their lives via social networks such as Facebook and Google+. Keeping in touch through social media sites is convenient and often is emotionally positive. It is also fun to share the latest news in your life with all those social connections you've acquired.

When using social networks, remember that they are not private. Many people may read your posts. If you complain about your supervisor, a coworker, a customer, or your company using a social network site, it is possible that a friend or a friend of a friend may read your post. And that friend of a friend might be your supervisor, your coworker, your customer, or even the president of your company. A good rule to follow: Always think before you post.

Creating your own Web log (or "blog") lets you convey your thoughts in an original manner. You choose the subject and can even include photos and videos for others to view. A blog is a creative way to communicate with others.

If you are a blogger, use wisdom. Postings on a blog can be viewed by anyone—your coworkers, your supervisor, or even your company's upper management. Posting critical comments about your company or work situation is unwise. Think before putting pictures (especially racy or unprofessional ones) on your blog. Employees have lost jobs or even been sued because of information posted on blogs.[6]

Likewise, potential employers may use the Internet to research job candidates. Don't put anything on your blog that might keep you from being hired in the future.

Always remember that the Internet is not secure. Whether you use e-mail or send an instant message, others have access to the information. Confidential information or a highly emotional message should be delivered using a different communication method.

E-mail in the Workplace

Because of its convenience, e-mail has become the leading communication form in the workplace.[7] Understanding how to use e-mail effectively will save work time and avoid problems on the job.

Begin by looking at the e-mail format on your computer. Most e-mail has the same basic parts:

- **The header:** Includes your e-mail address, the e-mail address of the recipient, and the subject line. The subject line is a brief, meaningful description of the message.

- **The salutation:** The greeting, such as "Dear Deanna:" or "Dear Mr. Gray:"

- **The body:** The message being sent. Use short sentences and bullet points to keep the body concise. Keep the message to one page. Double-space between paragraphs to make it easier to read. Use complete sentences as well as correct grammar, spelling, and punctuation.

- **The signature line:** The writer's name, and sometimes his or her contact information; indicates the end of the e-mail.

- **E-mail attachments:** Used when a longer document is sent with the e-mail. When you send an attachment, mention it in the message. To add an attachment to e-mail, click the "Attachment" or "Add File" button on the screen. Browse for the document you want to attach.

- **Out of office:** Creates a message that says you are gone but will return to reply to messages at a certain time or date. When you are contacted through e-mail, the sender will automatically receive this message.

- **Acknowledgment of receipt:** Available on some e-mail software programs. It allows the sender to know that the e-mail has been placed in the recipient's inbox.

- **Read receipt:** Available on some e-mail software programs. It allows the sender to know that the e-mail has been opened. Both acknowledgment of receipt and read receipt are part of e-mail tracking. Tracking is not always accurate but tends to be more so within a company's computer network.

Before sending e-mail, check the recipient's address to avoid having the e-mail "bounce back" if you have the wrong address. Deal with e-mail like all business correspondence: Always proofread it before clicking "Send."

Getting E-mail

When you click the inbox, the list of your e-mail messages appears. Because spam (junk e-mail) as well as attachments can be the source of computer viruses, think before you open e-mail messages. Check the sender and the subject line. If you have doubts about the origin of an e-mail message, don't open attachments or click a link in the e-mail because it may allow a computer virus to infect your computer. Delete it!

To open your e-mail, click the subject. After reading the message, you may choose to do one of the following:

- Move the message to a folder.
- Reply to the message.
- Forward the message to another person.
- Delete the message.
- Print the message.

In the workplace, managing e-mail can become a problem for workers who receive large numbers of e-mail messages during the day. One solution is to handle e-mail like regular "snail mail." Throw away the junk mail without reading it. Look at the important mail and reply to it within a reasonable time period. Deal with the high-priority mail the same day.[8]

Using work time to send and reply to personal e-mail prevents you from giving your full attention to your job. When coworkers spend time sending amusing anecdotes or jokes found on the Internet, work time is lost. Non-work-related e-mail, especially pictures and video, can interfere with the company's network, taking valuable space and slowing the system.

Electronic Distractions

Electronic communication distracts workers and lowers their productivity. E-mail, instant messaging, and texting—once considered timesavers for businesses—have become time wasters in the workplace. According to studies, the average worker at a computer will check e-mail 50 times, use instant messaging 77 times, and visit 40 websites during the workday. Such distractions are costly. One computer development company lost $1 billion in a year as employees failed to deal with information overload.

Strategies to deal with this problem vary. Some CEOs and employers have initiated "no e-mail" Fridays or another day to relieve the stress of heavy e-mail volume and increase productivity. Employees are encouraged to use the phone or meet in person instead of using e-mail to correspond within the organization on that day. A program offered by one e-mail service turns off the e-mail and tells the user to take a break. It does not return for 15 minutes. Other businesses encourage workers to only handle the message once. In other words, read it and answer or delete the message. Don't allow e-mail to accumulate.[9]

Practice Netiquette

As e-mail usage in the workplace has increased, some problems have evolved. Practicing e-mail etiquette, sometimes called netiquette, will help you avoid such problems. Here are a few tips that apply to e-mail and the workplace:

- Keep business e-mail professional.
- Writing words in all uppercase is called "shouting" and should be avoided.
- Follow your company's guidelines concerning e-mail.
- Check your personal e-mail on your own time.
- Venting your anger and frustrations using e-mail is called "flaming" and should be avoided.
- Don't send e-mail messages that might offend or harass another individual.
- E-mail should not be used to avoid talking to someone face-to-face or on the phone.
- Always remember that your e-mail might be forwarded or posted. The message you send could be read by many people other than the person you e-mailed.

How Job Savvy Are You?

Read each of the following situations. In each situation, a netiquette rule is being broken. Tell how the situation could be handled in a better way.

Stan's supervisor refused to grant his request for tuition reimbursement for a class Stan recently completed. Stan e-mails his supervisor to vent his anger. He calls his supervisor a liar and says he intends to file a complaint with the company.

What is the netiquette problem?

_____

_____

What is the better way?

_____

_____

Jana has missed two staff meetings this month. Mr. Garson, the office manager, sends the entire staff an e-mail message written in uppercase stating STAFF MEETING TOMORROW AT 8:00 A.M. BE THERE.

What is the netiquette problem?

_____

_____

What is the better way?

_____

_____

A Useful Skill: Writing

Learn to write and you will be valued in the workplace. According to a recent survey of human resource executives, entry-level workers lack basic writing skills.[10] Employers need staff members with the ability to spell correctly, use correct English grammar, and punctuate properly.

A business correspondence must state the point quickly because the recipient may read it in just a few seconds. Business writing must be both clear and concise. Using the accepted format for business letters, memos, and other correspondence provides uniformity within an organization.

Whether you are writing a memo, a business letter, or an e-mail, knowing how to write is a useful skill in the business world. Here are some points to remember when writing in the workplace:

- **Set the tone.** Consider why you are writing. Think about the person to whom you are writing.

- **Be concise.** Use short sentences and brief paragraphs. Make every word count. Don't repeat words or thoughts. Make lists. Use bullets and headings.

(continued)

(continued)

- **Get to the point quickly.** Begin by stating the general purpose of your correspondence and end with your request.
- **Use appropriate language.** Write in a businesslike manner. Avoid using slang terms.
- **Emphasize important facts.** Highlight key points using boldface type. Avoid using ALL CAPS, especially when you're e-mailing.

Summing Up

Businesses function as a team. When a team of workers listens and expresses their ideas clearly, productivity increases. For this reason, employers are looking for individuals with good communication skills.

You will be a valued employee if you learn to listen. Problems occur in the workplace when team members fail to listen to directions. The ability to write a short, clear e-mail is an excellent job skill. Observing body language and other nonverbal forms of communication will enable you to understand what others are telling you. With practice, you will increase your ability to communicate.

The way we communicate is changing as technology changes. For this reason, it is important to recognize new technologies and learn how to use them as you continue to develop even more communication skills.

CHAPTER 6

Learning—What It's All About

Knowing how to learn is probably the most critical skill for job success. You spend the early years of your life learning in school, which provides a structured approach to learning.

Sometimes, people think that they learn only when they go to school, but humans learn in a variety of ways. We watch other people doing something, and we learn. We ask other people how to do something, and we learn. We read books and magazines, and we learn.

This chapter explores many ways that you can learn so that you can be more effective on the job.

"Aye! I always like to see a few piracy seminars on a resume."

Learning Is the Key to Success

Lifelong learning is the key to success in the new labor market. Today, management experts emphasize that a successful business is a *learning organization*, which creates a climate that helps employees learn from their experiences, both individually and collectively.

Even in difficult economic times, firms maintain training budgets so that they can focus on developing the talents of their current employees.[1] In addition to any help your employer gives you, you must personally take charge of your own learning to remain a vital part of the learning organization. It's necessary to continually improve your skills to keep your job or to get a new job. This chapter explores how you can be an active learner on the job.

You'll have to learn many things at a new job. But learning doesn't end once you've mastered the job. In time, your job will require new abilities, or you might want a promotion that requires additional skills. It is also important to keep your skills up-to-date in case you decide to apply for a new job with another employer.

The following exercise will help you think about the many ways you can learn, by examining one of your past experiences in learning. As you are doing this exercise, consider how the same steps you took in that "learning project" could help you learn new skills at work.

A PERSONAL LEARNING PROJECT

1. Write something you learned outside of school within the last three months.

   _____

   _____

   _____

2. What was your purpose or objective? (What did you set out to learn?)

   _____

   _____

   _____

3. List the steps you went through during your learning project.

   _____

   _____

   _____

   _____

---

4. What resources—people, reading material, computer information, and so on—did you use in the learning project?

    _____

    _____

    _____

    _____

5. Did you learn everything you wanted to know about the subject or skill? Why or why not?

    _____

    _____

    _____

6. Are there other ways you could have learned the same thing? Explain how.

    _____

    _____

    _____

    _____

How Adults Learn

As people mature and move beyond high school, they share some common characteristics in how they learn. Adults prefer to learn using methods based on *andragogy*—a theory of adult learning developed by Malcolm Knowles, a pioneer in adult education. Four important characteristics of adult learners cited by Knowles are the following:[2]

- **Adults learn better when they assume responsibility and control over learning activities.** This means that, as an adult, you will learn more if you take charge of the learning. Don't wait for someone to teach you a new skill. Instead, seek out ways that you can learn new skills.

- **Adults learn more effectively by applying what they learn.** There are progressive steps in learning. You will learn the least when someone tells you how to do a task. You will learn more when someone demonstrates the task. You will learn the most when you do the task yourself.

- **As adults mature, they have a broader experience base to draw on.** This experience base can be used to help improve your learning. Compare a new task that you are trying to learn with past experiences. Determine what is the same and what is different in the situations. Linking new skills and knowledge to a past experience usually improves learning.

- **Adults learn better when it is clear to them why gaining the knowledge is necessary.** In school, you might have learned something because you were going to be tested on it. On the job, your motivation to learn will be stronger when you understand the reasons for and benefits of learning a new skill.

Tips for Learning

All learners share certain characteristics. Being aware of them should help you improve your learning:

- **The more time you spend on a learning task, the more learning takes place.** A common saying illustrates this point: *Practice makes perfect.* Spend time learning a new skill.

- **Learning patterns differ.** So don't compare yourself to someone else trying to learn the same job. Another person might excel at learning new tasks, whereas it might be more difficult for you. As you progress on a job, you might start learning faster than others. You should also recognize that some days are better than others. This is normal because people don't usually experience a straight line of improvement in their learning patterns. Don't let the more common, uneven pattern of learning discourage you.

- **You can organize your learning using association.** For example, if you need to learn a list of furniture items, group them by rooms in a house. Memorize codes by associating them with a special date on the calendar, telephone numbers, addresses, or such. Many people find that memorizing facts is easier when they associate the fact with a word and make the words rhyme.

- **When you have a more complex task to learn, use the "whole–part–whole" method.** First, review the task as a whole, doing every part in one continuous sequence. Next, break the task into small parts and concentrate on learning each part individually. Finally, practice the entire task as a whole again.

Practicing these ideas can help you become a more effective learner. You don't have to use all of them in each new learning experience. In fact, some ideas will be more useful than others, depending on what you're trying to learn. Pick out the ideas that you think will help you the most in learning a task, and then use them.

Learning to Do Your Job

To be successful in a job, you must do it correctly. This seems obvious, but it's a truth that's not always easy to follow. You must know the job's essentials:

- What tasks are assigned to the job
- How to perform them
- How your work will be evaluated

Let's look at how you can get this information.

LEARNING ON THE JOB

List some of the ways you can find out how to perform your job effectively. The items on your list could include things you would expect your supervisor to tell you.

_____

_____

_____

_____

Several proven methods of learning about your job are described in the following sections. Read and compare this material to your previous list.

Job Description

This written profile of the job should include all its tasks and responsibilities. Ask your supervisor to explain the job description to you. Make sure that you understand your responsibilities.

Supervisors

Managers should explain what they expect, but they might forget to tell you something. That's why it's important to ask for an explanation of your job if one is not given. Although a written job description explains the tasks you are to do, it doesn't give you all the details. Supervisors will help you understand exactly how the task should be done and, more importantly, how they will evaluate your performance.

Training

Businesses spend billions of dollars each year on classroom training to educate employees. You can expect to receive some sort of training when you begin a job. Also, you typically will continue to receive training while you remain with an employer. Most organizations provide three basic types of training:

- **On-the-job training:** Typically, this one-on-one instruction takes place as you do the job. Your supervisor or a coworker will explain what to do, show you how to do it, watch while you practice, and then tell you how well you did in practice.

- **Classroom instruction:** Classroom instruction involves training several employees at the same time. Classroom instruction uses many methods, including lectures, digital media, discussion, role playing, case studies, games, and learning exercises. It's important to listen carefully, ask questions when you don't understand something, and actively participate in all learning activities.

- **Computer or multimedia training:** Many organizations use computers to teach employees new job skills (these computer software programs are often called learning management systems). Discount stores, grocery stores, and banks use sophisticated multimedia computer programs to train cashiers. This is one reason why you should know how to operate a personal computer. Taking an introductory computer course in high school or community college is a good way to acquire the skills you need to learn more in the workplace.

Coworkers

Watch other workers who do the same job and note how they complete their tasks. They might have insight into how to do the job more easily and efficiently and how the supervisor expects the job to be done. If someone was promoted from the job you have, talk with that person. Find out how he or she did the job.

Friends Who Have Similar Jobs

Talk with friends and acquaintances who work at jobs similar to yours. Ask them how they do their jobs. You might get some good ideas to apply to your job. However, you should talk with your supervisor before trying out any of their suggestions.

Schools

You might be able to take classes to learn more about your job. If, for example, you work with personal computers, you probably can enroll in a local computer class. Such classes often are offered through adult-education or continuing-education programs at high schools or colleges. More than 40 percent of all adults participate in adult-education programs.[3] Some employers will help pay the cost of training because they know that they will benefit from your improved skills. The Lifetime Learning Credit allows you to deduct a percentage of the continuing-education cost as a federal tax credit.[4]

Conferences

Professional and trade associations often have conferences where you can learn from the experts. Conferences offer opportunities to meet and talk with other people who do work like yours. In addition, there are usually expositions, where vendors sell the latest equipment, programs, and services related to the work. You can learn a lot from these vendors and their products. Conference registration can cost anywhere from $200 to $2,000. Talk with your coworkers to find out about the conferences that they have found most useful.

Workshops

Private training companies offer workshops you can attend to learn new skills. These workshops can range in cost from $100 for one day to $3,000 for a three- to five-day workshop. The quality of workshops varies greatly. Check with coworkers and friends to find out what they know about any workshop that you plan to attend. Ask the training company to supply references from people who have attended. You might want to call some of these people. Look for workshops that provide money-back guarantees.

Reading

Read about your job. General publications—such as the *Dictionary of Occupational Titles,* the *Guide for Occupational Exploration,* and the *Occupational Outlook Handbook*—provide general occupational descriptions. These resources are good for workers just starting in a new occupation. Also read trade and professional magazines about your work. You should be able to find these and other occupational books and magazines in your local library.

The Web

Many resources are available on the Web that can help you learn more about your job. Using such resources is referred to as *distance learning.* You can use many sites on the Web to find the type of distance learning that will fit your needs. Go to a major search engine such as google.com or yahoo.com and enter "distance learning." You can also search for "distance education," "distance training," or some combination of these words.

Self-directed learning allows you to explore a subject in a way that you want to learn. Resources such as YouTube are available free of charge when you are available. Educational sites provide a variety of learning opportunities, from GED instruction to college classes. One source to explore and use is the Goodwill Community Foundation International Learn Free website. You will find computer-based training for computer software, such as Microsoft Word, Internet basics, Google, e-mail basics, reading, math, and several other subjects.

You want to be the best worker possible, so use all the information sources listed in this section, as well as any others you can think of. Compare the resources discussed here with the steps you listed in the previous exercise.

LEARNING TO IMPROVE JOB PERFORMANCE

1. List the resources from the preceding section that you have used to get information about your job.

   _____

   _____

   _____

   _____

(continued)

(continued)

2. What resources have you used that aren't listed in this book?

_____

_____

_____

_____

The Learning Organization

In his book *The Fifth Discipline: The Art and Practice of the Learning Organization,* Peter Senge defines learning organizations as "…organizations where people continually expand their capacity to create the results they truly desire, where new and expansive patterns of thinking are nurtured, where collective aspiration is set free, and where people are continually learning to see the whole together."

The basic rationale for such organizations is that, in situations of rapid change, only those that are flexible, adaptive, and productive will excel. For this to happen, it is argued, organizations need to "discover how to tap people's commitment and capacity to learn at all levels."[5]

A learning organization is dynamic and growing—it changes and improves based on what it learns. As more organizations strive to become learning organizations, new principles will be identified to help them achieve this goal. You need to be an active participant in this process in any company you work for.

How Job Savvy Are You?

Marc has a computer technology degree from a technical school and is about to start his first job as a computer operator with a large accounting firm. He has never worked with the computer that the company uses. At the interview, his supervisor assured him that the company will provide on-the-job training. On his first day at work, Marc's supervisor says he is too busy to work with Marc on training. Instead, he shows Marc how to back up disk drives to the network. He then tells Marc to spend the rest of the day doing backups.

1. If you were Marc, how would you feel about this?

_____

_____

_____

_____

_____

2. What would you do to find out more about the job that you were hired to do?

_____

_____

_____

_____

Paula began working as a receptionist last week. Her supervisor told her that she is to provide clerical support for several staff members in the real estate office. This morning, Susan asked her to file some house listings. While Paula was doing that, Karin asked her to type a letter. She had just started typing the letter when John told her to stop typing and immediately prepare a contract. As Paula was preparing the contract, she was interrupted by several phone calls. Karin came to get the letter and was upset because it wasn't finished. John came out of his office and began to argue with Karin, telling her to let Paula finish the contract.

1. If you were Paula, how would you feel?

_____

_____

_____

_____

2. What information does Paula need to help her in this situation? How can she get the information she needs?

_____

_____

_____

_____

Education for Life

You might think your education is complete when you finish school. That is far from true. You will need to continue learning throughout your life. Futurist John Naisbitt wrote, "There is no one education, no one skill, that lasts a lifetime now."[6]

You are responsible for your lifelong education. You can participate in company training, continuing-education classes, college classes, workshops, and conferences to improve your job skills.

You will always learn new things about your job because all businesses are subject to change. New machines might be installed. Policies and procedures might change. A new product might be manufactured and sold.

As the business changes, so will your job. To keep up, you must understand how you learn best and practice those techniques. Whenever you begin a new job or new position in the same company, you start learning all over again. You must learn how the organization operates and how to perform your job.

Many organizations provide ongoing training. If your employer does not provide training to keep your skills current, consider getting training on your own. It will help you stay competitive in today's job market. In addition, training makes you more valuable. Because she had taken computer courses through a special program, Rebecca was able to make a smooth transition to a new job when her manufacturing job became automated. She even helped train some of her coworkers.[7]

Learning Style

You will learn more when you understand your preferred method of learning. Everyone has a learning style, determined by the ways that person prefers to learn something new.

MY PREFERRED LEARNING STYLE

In the checklist below, rank from 1 (most preferred) to 8 (least preferred) the ways that you like to learn:

_____**Reading:** You learn by reading and writing.

_____**Listening:** You learn by listening to lectures, tapes, or records.

_____**Observing:** You learn by watching demonstrations, videos, films, or slides.

_____**Talking:** You learn by talking with other people or through question-and-answer sessions.

_____**Doing:** You learn best by actually doing what you are trying to learn.

_____**Interacting:** You learn best by interacting with computer programs, multimedia programs, or the Web.

_____**Participating:** You learn best by participating in games, role playing, and other activities.

_____**Smelling/tasting:** You learn best by associating what you are learning with a smell or taste.

Look at how you ranked the methods. Now list the three learning methods you like best and use most frequently.

1. _____

2. _____

3. _____

Your three top methods show your learning style. You might like reading, observing, and interacting, or you might prefer listening and talking. You might learn by doing, participating, and smelling or tasting. Or you might use all of your senses.

There are other ways to determine how you learn. Assessment instruments such as the Myers-Briggs Type Indicator or the Keirsey Temperament Sorter can help you determine more about your learning style. You can take the latter assessment at www.keirsey.com.

It's important that you understand the ways in which you learn best. This understanding can help you become a better learner. When you are faced with learning a new task, try to use your preferred learning methods. If you like *doing*, you will not learn as well if you try to learn by *reading*. However, there are times when you must use a method that you didn't choose, such as if your employer requires group employee training by video or a written handout. When this happens, do your best to use the required method and then try to use your preferred style to review what you have learned.

Steps to Learning

You can take some specific steps to improve the way that you learn.

At the beginning of this chapter, you completed an exercise in which you described recently learning something outside of school. This was called your *learning project*—which simply means *the process of learning something new*. The steps to complete a learning project are explained here. You probably listed some of them in the earlier exercise.

1. **Motivate yourself.** You must find something exciting or interesting about your learning project. If you aren't interested in the subject itself, you might be interested in something that could result from what you learn. For example, learning to fill out a new form required for your job might not excite you, but you might get excited about receiving a raise because you do such a good job of completing the form. Write down your reasons for wanting to complete a learning project before you start the process.

2. **Set objectives.** The final outcomes of learning are called *objectives*. You need to know your learning objectives. To identify them, ask yourself the following question:

   "When I am done with this learning project, what must I be able to do?"

   Write down these objectives. Be specific.

3. **Identify resources.** Find out what resources are available to help you reach your learning objectives. These resources can come from several areas, including these:

   - **In-house learning opportunities:** Ask your supervisor whether your company offers any courses that can help you meet your learning objectives. Perhaps there is another worker who can teach you what you want to learn.

   - **Outside education:** Ask someone in your organization (a training manager, human resources manager, personnel director, or supervisor) to help you learn about courses offered at vocational schools, community colleges, universities, specialized training firms in your community, or the Web.

- **Additional methods:** Discuss your learning needs with friends and coworkers. Find out what methods they have used to learn something similar. Ask what kinds of books, digital media, or other electronic media are available at your library. Also, check the Web for information.

4. **Choose the best resources.** Which resources will help you the most in completing your learning project? You might decide to use more than one resource. Another factor to consider is cost. Find out whether your employer will pay for any of these resources, and whether you will be allowed to take time from work to pursue your learning objective. Also keep in mind that other people are an important resource for any learning project.

5. **Schedule the project.** Plan the time needed for your project and decide when you want to complete it. If you need to take time from work for this, discuss it with your supervisor.

6. **Write down questions.** Decide what questions you need to answer in order to learn the task. Write the questions on a piece of paper. Check them off as you find the answers. Questions should ask who, what, where, when, why, and how.

7. **Implement the project.** Completing any learning project requires self-discipline. You must follow through with the plan you create. It might be helpful to find someone who will keep you on track by checking your progress.

8. **Evaluate progress.** As you complete the learning project, evaluate your progress. Are the resources you decided to use providing you with the knowledge and skills you need? Are you following the schedule you set? Are you meeting your objectives? Have an experienced person test your new skills and knowledge. Remember, the most important step in successful learning is accomplishing your objectives.

9. **Practice.** The most effective way to become more skilled is to practice what you've learned, even after you've finished the learning project. Periodically check on how well you can apply your new knowledge.

The following exercise will help you practice the steps needed to complete a learning project.

PERSONAL LEARNING PROJECT

1. Select a skill you want to learn and write it below.

   _____

2. What is your motivation? Why do you want to learn this skill? How do you think you will feel after you learn it?

   _____

   _____

   _____

   _____

3. Choose a learning objective. What are your expected outcomes?

   _____

   _____

   _____

   _____

4. Who can help you plan your learning project?

   _____

   _____

   _____

   _____

5. What resources can you use to complete your learning project?

   _____

   _____

   _____

   _____

6. What do you think will be your best resource? Keep in mind your learning style, the cost, the availability, and so on.

   _____

   _____

   _____

   _____

7. When would you like to complete the learning project?

   _____

   _____

   _____

   _____

(continued)

(continued)

8. How much time will you spend daily or weekly on the project?

    _____

    _____

    _____

    _____

9. How will you (or someone else) evaluate your progress?

    _____

    _____

    _____

    _____

10. How will you practice what you learn?

    _____

    _____

    _____

    _____

The ability to learn is the most important skill you can have. Successful people know how to learn new things. Read the following case studies and develop a plan for each person to learn a new skill. Be specific about the steps for each learning project. Use more paper if necessary.

How Job Savvy Are You?

Donna has spent the last four months working at the Quick Print Shop. She runs a copy machine for orders of 500 or fewer copies. Donna has decided that she would like to learn more about graphic arts. She wants to be able to run the offset press used for larger orders and those requiring more complex printing techniques.

What steps should Donna take to learn this new skill?

_____

_____

_____

_____

_____

Juan works as a bank teller. He would like to work in the accounting department, where he could earn a higher salary. If he knew more about accounting, he would have a better chance at a promotion to that area.

What steps should Juan take to learn more about accounting?

_____

_____

_____

_____

_____

A Useful Skill: Active Learning

As an adult, you must take charge of your learning. Observe what skills you want or need to learn. Explore ways or places to learn the skill. Ask questions and seek answers. Build on the experience and knowledge you already have.

Become an active learner. Find a method of learning that allows you to do and apply rather than just listen. Remember that adults learn best when they participate in their own learning.

As an active learner, approach your new learning by asking, "How can I use this new information or skill...

1. In my workplace?"
2. To improve my life?"
3. To solve a current problem?"
4. To solve future problems?"
5. To make decisions?"

Summing Up

On-the-job learning is an important skill to master. Training you receive on the job is important for retaining a job, getting promotions, and increasing earnings. Taking advantage of such training makes you more valuable to your employer.

When you take responsibility for your own learning, you learn best. To make learning easier, discover your preferred learning styles. Use those methods of learning as often as possible. Many times, you must learn on your own. The more you practice learning, the better your learning skills will be.

CHAPTER 7

Knowing Yourself

According to research, employers want employees with positive self-concepts—the understanding and regard they have for themselves.[1] Higher morale, more motivation, and greater productivity indicate a positive self-concept. Because productivity, work quality, creativity, and flexibility are based on self-concept, a positive self-concept affects your job success.

To be a good employee, you must believe you are a good employee. In other words, you must have confidence in your abilities. Your confidence comes from your self-concept, which is a mixture of your self-image (how you see yourself) and self-esteem (how you feel about your self-image). Let's look at how these affect the way you approach a job.

"My strengths involve organizational abilities.
My weaknesses involve chocolate."

Your Self-Image Can Make You or Break You

Have you ever known a woman who really wasn't a great beauty, but, because she acted as if she were beautiful, other people believed she was? A positive self-image can turn an ugly duckling into a beautiful swan. On the other hand, beautiful swans with poor self-images often go unnoticed and unappreciated their entire lives.

Many people influence your self-image. Parents influence how you view yourself. Many adults admit they still feel an urge to please their parents. Your brothers and sisters often are your most willing critics. Teachers and supervisors evaluate you. You might feel that a certain grade is a statement of your personal worth. Peers influence how you act, what you wear, and even where you go.

The good news is that the single most important influence on your self-image is *you*. How you feel about any facet of yourself makes up your self-esteem. You can't be negative about yourself unless you choose to be negative. By learning to know and value yourself, you can choose to have a positive self-image or self-concept.

Your work relationships will reflect your positive self-concept. The ability to communicate with your supervisor, coworkers, and customers is extremely important. If you do not view yourself in a positive way, these relationships will be hindered. In this chapter, we explore ways you can improve your self-awareness and create a positive self-concept.

How Job Savvy Are You?

Corey has been working after school at the Speedi-In Deli for a year, stocking shelves, keeping the drink machines filled, and performing general clean-up chores. Corey works fairly independently. He enjoys his job, but feels he would like to advance to a behind-the-counter job. Although Corey doesn't have a positive self-image, he believes he could do this job.

The deli manager is pleased with Corey's work. On Friday, he puts a note in Corey's pay envelope: "Great job! Looking forward to advancing you."

On Monday, Corey and the manager are the only people working in the stockroom. The manager doesn't say anything about the note, but seems to be expecting a response from Corey. Because Corey doesn't feel good about himself, he feels uncomfortable accepting the manager's praise. He doesn't know what to say.

1. How will Corey's manager react if Corey doesn't say anything?

   _____

   _____

   _____

2. Will this affect Corey's opportunity for promotion to a counter job? Explain your answer.

   _____

3. How would the answer to question 2 affect Corey's self-concept?

_____

_____

Dani had a speech problem as a child. She was often teased because of it. Speech therapy in elementary school helped Dani overcome her handicap. Although she no longer has the speech problem, Dani is not confident in social conversations. She doesn't look at people when she talks, and sometimes she mumbles.

Dani works as a file clerk. She spends her day in a back office, and she would like to become an administrative assistant. Dani knows that one of the administrative assistants is quitting at the end of the month to attend college. She really wants the administrative assistant's job, but she's afraid that her poor communication skills will hinder her in her quest for promotion.

Dani decides to overcome this obstacle. At first, she practices simple conversations with friends and coworkers. She even makes a special effort to talk to her neighbors and people she meets in social situations. She also takes a public-speaking course at school. When her supervisor has team meetings, Dani answers questions and even jokes with the group. Gradually, she feels better about talking in social situations.

1. How will Dani's actions affect her chances of becoming an administrative assistant?

_____

_____

_____

2. How is Dani's self-concept affected by her actions? Explain the reason for your answer.

_____

_____

_____

Difficulties in the workplace create job stress. Not only will your job be more enjoyable if you approach it in a positive way; you will also reduce your job stress. This positive approach begins with a positive self-image, which enhances your confidence to do the job. After all, your employer hired you because he or she believes you are qualified to do the work. Your employer believes in you. So you should believe in yourself.

Learn to Believe in Yourself

Sometimes it might seem like everyone at work knows what they are doing except you. That's not true. No one always feels confident. Anyone can experience a poor self-image, especially when circumstances change abruptly. Consider these examples:

- A teacher loses her job because there's no money to fund the gifted-student program for the coming year. She questions her ability to find a new teaching position. She wants to try a new area of work, but wonders whether she's really qualified to enter a new field. Her indecision is caused by a sudden lack of confidence.

- A man is laid off after working 23 years in the same manufacturing plant. Rumors spread that the plant will close soon and move to a new location. Questions run through his mind: "Should I move my family to the new plant location? Should I start that auto-repair shop I've always dreamed about? What if I can't pay all the bills?" He has trouble deciding what to do.

- A supervisor is asked to move up in her company. Currently, 10 employees report to her. She will be responsible for 50 workers if she accepts the new position. The hours will be the same, and the pay will be better. But she'll have to take a computer course at the local university to work in the new area. She begins to question her abilities: "Can I handle a college course? I haven't attended a university class in 10 years. What if I can't pass the course? Can I really supervise 50 people? Maybe I'm not ready for a promotion just yet."

Having a positive self-concept doesn't mean you won't ever question yourself. In fact, the people in the examples asked "healthy" questions. Questioning allows you to compare your self-image with the world around you. You don't want to put yourself in a position where you can't perform well because you inaccurately evaluated your skills and abilities. This is why self-awareness is so important: It allows you to make better decisions about your career and your job performance.

Take Control of Your Life

According to scientists who study personalities, people approach life in one of two ways: They either feel they control their own lives, or they feel that other people and things control them. The way you look at life greatly affects your self-concept. The following quiz will help you understand how you view your control over your life.

YOUR APPROACH TO LIFE QUIZ		
Answer the following questions. Put a **T** beside the statements that you think are true and an **F** beside those that you think are false.		
Views of Life	Answer	Score
1. Other people control my life.	_____	_____
2. I am responsible for the success in my life.	_____	_____
3. Success in life is a matter of luck.	_____	_____

4. When things go wrong, it's usually because of things that I couldn't control.

_____   _____

5. The last time I did something successful, I knew that it was because of my own efforts.

_____   _____

6. The last time I failed at some-thing, I knew that it was because I just wasn't good enough to get the job done.

_____   _____

7. Most successful people are born successful.

_____   _____

8. It seems that most things are beyond my control.

_____   _____

9. When I fail, it's usually someone else's fault.

_____   _____

10. When I succeed, it is usually because of someone else's efforts.

_____   _____

Total Score: _____   _____   _____

Scoring

- Statement 1: True = 0, False = 1
- Statement 2: True = 1, False = 0
- Statement 3: True = 0, False = 1
- Statement 4: True = 0, False = 1
- Statement 5: True = 1, False = 0
- Statement 6: True = 0, False = 1
- Statement 7: True = 0, False = 1
- Statement 8: True = 0, False = 1
- Statement 9: True = 0, False = 1
- Statement 10: True = 0, False = 1

Your Score and Your View of Life

The higher you score, the more you feel in control of your life. Compare your score to the following scale:

- **0–3 = Outside of My Control:** *I'm not responsible for my successes or my failures.* I need to work on my self-concept.

- **4–6 = Sometimes in Control:** *I'm sometimes responsible for my successes and failures.* My self-concept could be improved.

- **7–10 = In Control:** *I'm responsible for my successes.* I have confidence in myself and have a good self-concept.

Learn to View Life Positively

People with positive self-concepts look at their successes and believe that they are responsible for them. They also believe that, although they are responsible for their failures, the outcome is also affected by events, things, and people outside of their control.

People with negative self-concepts view the world in the opposite way. They credit their successes to luck and never accept the blame for their failures. Thus, they fail to accept responsibility for their own actions. Those whose score in the preceding quiz fell into the "Outside of My Control" category need to work harder to develop a positive self-concept. Those in the "In Control" category find it easier than those with lower scores to develop a positive self-concept.

Like anything else, this approach to life can be taken to extremes. There are times when your success is due to luck and failure is solely your own fault. But, by being realistic about your personal contributions to success and failure, you'll know how to improve yourself. Most importantly, *you must believe that you can improve*. In fact, you can overcome problems or difficulties given enough time, effort, and, when needed, help from other people. The important thing is to have faith in yourself.

You can teach yourself to view life more positively and to gain more control over your own life. Look at the circumstances every time you succeed. Give yourself credit for your success. Remember to look at the small successes that occur every day of your life. Similarly, when you experience failure, examine the reasons for it. Look for those outside factors that contributed to the failure and realize how they affected the outcome. In the next exercise, you will look at the successes and failures in your life and see how you personally contribute to your successes.

Selling Yourself on You

Joe Girard was the best car salesman in the world for eight years in a row, selling more than 11,200 cars. He succeeded because he believed in himself. In the book *How to Sell Yourself,* he gave these tips for improving self-image:[2]

- Tell yourself you are No. 1 every morning.
- Write "I believe in myself" on cards and place them where you'll see them frequently throughout the day.
- Associate with other winners, and avoid losers.
- Put negative thoughts—like envy, jealousy, greed, and hate—out of your life.
- Pat yourself on the back at least once a day.
- Repeat "I will" at least 10 times each day.
- Do the things you fear most to prove that you can successfully accomplish them.

PERSONAL EVALUATION EXERCISE

1. List three successes you had during the past week.

   _____

   _____

   _____

2. How were you responsible for making each success happen?

   _____

   _____

   _____

3. List three failures you had during the past week.

   _____

   _____

   _____

4. Describe outside factors that contributed to each failure.

   _____

   _____

   _____

There are some important lessons to learn from this exercise. First, we all have successes in our lives. You should take the credit and reward yourself for them. Second, we all have failures in our lives, but every failure can be overcome. Analyze the reasons for failure. Was it really your fault, or was it the result of something you couldn't anticipate? Look at failure as an opportunity to learn from mistakes and to avoid repeating them in the future. As you apply these principles in your life, you can learn to take control and develop a more positive self-concept.

LEARNING FROM LIFE'S UPS AND DOWNS

1. What can you learn from each of your successes?

   _____

   _____

   _____

2. What can you learn from each of your failures?

   _____

   _____

   _____

Self-Concept in the Workplace

A positive self-image helps you overcome doubt about your abilities. You face unique challenges in the work world. Many job-related situations are totally new to you and might make you doubt yourself. For instance, if you're starting a new job, you might question your ability to complete your assigned tasks. Remember that your self-confidence will increase as you gain experience. To protect your positive self-image as you begin a new job, try to remember these two simple truths:

- **You will make mistakes.** When you make mistakes, acknowledge them. Accept any criticism or advice from your supervisor, and correct the mistake. For each mistake, examine the situation and note the contributing factors. Decide how you can avoid the same mistake in the future. This way, you learn from your mistakes. You're capable of improving your self-image by learning from past mistakes—and not blaming yourself.

- **Your employer wants you to succeed.** Employers don't hire people in order to fire them. Your employer hired you because of your skills, because he or she believes that you have the ability to do the job successfully. Give yourself credit for your accomplishments. Learn to accept compliments gracefully. When you are complimented on your work, simply say, "Thank you." If your supervisor or coworkers neglect to compliment you, compliment yourself by inwardly recognizing your own abilities.

Self-Confidence

Self-confidence is a belief in yourself and in your abilities. It is vital for your success. All great leaders have this quality. Being self-confident doesn't mean that you won't have periods of doubt—particularly when you experience a failure. It does mean that you must look within yourself to discover how to overcome failures. Keep in mind that you are special and unique. No one else is quite like you. No one can bring the same qualities to a job that you can. Learn to appreciate who you are.

Identify Your Skills

Take an honest look at yourself. You might be surprised at the variety of skills you have to offer an employer. You develop skills from all your life experiences. They're designed to help you become aware of your skills, which are divided into three categories:

- Self-management or adaptive skills
- Transferable skills
- Job-related skills

Self-Management Skills

Self-management skills reflect the control you have over your life: how you plan, implement, change, and evaluate the activities in your life. Some self-management skills are necessary to please your employer. You probably have some of these skills already. Your employer expects you to use these skills most of the time. Although not all employers look for the same skills, all employers highly value the key self-management skills listed here.

SELF-MANAGEMENT SKILLS CHECKLIST

Check the most appropriate column for all the following skills that apply to you. All employers value these skills highly. Employers often will not hire a person who does not have many of these skills.

Key Self-Management Skills	Usually	Sometimes	Never
Get to work every day	_____	_____	_____
Arrive on time	_____	_____	_____
Work well with supervisors	_____	_____	_____
Get things done	_____	_____	_____
Get along well with coworkers	_____	_____	_____
Follow directions	_____	_____	_____
Work hard	_____	_____	_____
Am able to ask questions	_____	_____	_____
Am responsible	_____	_____	_____
Am willing to learn	_____	_____	_____
Am ambitious	_____	_____	_____
Am assertive	_____	_____	_____
Am creative	_____	_____	_____
Demonstrate pride in my work	_____	_____	_____
Am enthusiastic	_____	_____	_____
Am flexible	_____	_____	_____
Am friendly	_____	_____	_____
Have a good sense of humor	_____	_____	_____
Am highly motivated	_____	_____	_____
Produce quality work	_____	_____	_____
Display leadership	_____	_____	_____
Am self-directed	_____	_____	_____
Am patient	_____	_____	_____

(continued)

(continued)

Key Self-Management Skills	Usually	Sometimes	Never
Demonstrate positive self-esteem	_____	_____	_____
Conduct self in a businesslike manner	_____	_____	_____
Have a positive attitude	_____	_____	_____

Other Self-Management Skills	Usually	Sometimes	Never
Have problem-solving ability	_____	_____	_____
Demonstrate a results-oriented approach	_____	_____	_____
Am self-motivated	_____	_____	_____
Am sincere	_____	_____	_____
Am willing to learn new things	_____	_____	_____
Others: _____	_____	_____	_____
_____	_____	_____	_____
_____	_____	_____	_____
_____	_____	_____	_____
_____	_____	_____	_____
_____	_____	_____	_____

Review the charts you just filled out. Count the number of times you checked Usually and Sometimes. Record the numbers below.

Self-Management Skills Record

Usually: _____

Sometimes: _____

Total Skill Points: _____

Transferable Skills

Transferable skills can be used in many different jobs. A grocery store cashier needs to understand numbers, but so do bank tellers and accounting clerks. A nurse needs good people skills, as does a receptionist or a salesperson. Employers value some transferable skills over others. The key transferable skills listed here can help you get a higher-paying job or a more responsible position, or both.

TRANSFERABLE SKILLS CHECKLIST

Key Transferable Skills	Usually	Sometimes	Never
Accept responsibility	_____	_____	_____
Increase sales or efficiency	_____	_____	_____
Manage money, budgets	_____	_____	_____
Manage people	_____	_____	_____
Meet deadlines	_____	_____	_____
Meet the public	_____	_____	_____
Organize and manage projects	_____	_____	_____
Plan	_____	_____	_____
Solve problems	_____	_____	_____
Speak in public	_____	_____	_____
Supervise others	_____	_____	_____
Understand and control budgets	_____	_____	_____

Tactile Skills	Usually	Sometimes	Never
Assemble	_____	_____	_____
Build	_____	_____	_____
Construct/repair things	_____	_____	_____
Drive/operate vehicles	_____	_____	_____
Am good with hands	_____	_____	_____
Make things	_____	_____	_____
Observe/inspect	_____	_____	_____
Operate tools, machines	_____	_____	_____
Repair	_____	_____	_____
Use complex equipment	_____	_____	_____

Data Skills	Usually	Sometimes	Never
Analyze data	_____	_____	_____
Audit records	_____	_____	_____
Budget	_____	_____	_____
Calculate/compute	_____	_____	_____
Check for accuracy	_____	_____	_____
Classify data	_____	_____	_____
Compare	_____	_____	_____
Compile	_____	_____	_____

(continued)

(continued)

Data Skills	Usually	Sometimes	Never
Count			
Evaluate			
Investigate			
Keep financial records			
Keep track of details			
Locate answers or information			
Manage money			
Negotiate			
Observe/inspect			
Record facts			
Research			
Synthesize			
Take inventory			

People Skills	Usually	Sometimes	Never
Administer			
Am diplomatic			
Am insightful			
Am kind			
Am outgoing			
Am patient			
Am pleasant			
Am sensitive			
Am tactful			
Am tolerant			
Am tough			
Care for others			
Confront others			
Counsel people			
Demonstrate			
Help others			
Instruct			

People Skills	Usually	Sometimes	Never
Interview people			
Listen			
Mentor			
Persuade			
Socialize			
Supervise			
Teach			
Trust			
Understand			

Using Words and Ideas Skills	Usually	Sometimes	Never
Am articulate			
Am inventive			
Am logical			
Communicate verbally			
Conduct library and Internet research			
Correspond with others			
Create new ideas			
Demonstrate ingenuity			
Design			
Edit			
Remember information			
Speak publicly			
Write clearly			

Leadership Skills	Usually	Sometimes	Never
Arrange social functions			
Am self-confident			
Am self-motivated			
Compete			
Decide			
Delegate			
Direct others			
Explain things to others			

(continued)

Leadership Skills	Usually	Sometimes	Never
Get results	_____	_____	_____
Mediate problems	_____	_____	_____
Motivate people	_____	_____	_____
Negotiate agreements	_____	_____	_____
Plan	_____	_____	_____
Run meetings	_____	_____	_____
Solve problems	_____	_____	_____
Take risks	_____	_____	_____

Creative/Artistic Skills	Usually	Sometimes	Never
Am artistic	_____	_____	_____
Dance, move my body	_____	_____	_____
Draw, create art	_____	_____	_____
Express	_____	_____	_____
Perform, act	_____	_____	_____
Present artistic ideas	_____	_____	_____

Office/Technical Skills	Usually	Sometimes	Never
Access and retrieve data from the Internet	_____	_____	_____
Arm/disarm a security system	_____	_____	_____
Create electronic databases	_____	_____	_____
Create electronic spreadsheets	_____	_____	_____
Create PowerPoint presentations	_____	_____	_____
Create multimedia presentations	_____	_____	_____
Create programs using a computer language	_____	_____	_____
Maintain and design websites	_____	_____	_____
Operate DVD players	_____	_____	_____
Operate copy machines	_____	_____	_____
Operate fax machines	_____	_____	_____
Operate laminators	_____	_____	_____

Office/Technical Skills	Usually	Sometimes	Never
Operate multiline telephone systems	_____	_____	_____
Operate paper shredders	_____	_____	_____
Operate postage meters	_____	_____	_____
Operate video recorders/players	_____	_____	_____
Use database software	_____	_____	_____
Use e-mail	_____	_____	_____
Use large-screen projectors	_____	_____	_____
Use overhead projectors	_____	_____	_____
Use presentation software	_____	_____	_____
Use spreadsheet software	_____	_____	_____
Use word-processing software	_____	_____	_____
Others: _____	_____	_____	_____
_____	_____	_____	_____
_____	_____	_____	_____
_____	_____	_____	_____
_____	_____	_____	_____
_____	_____	_____	_____

Review the charts you filled out. Count the number of times you checked "Usually" and "Sometimes." Record the numbers below.

Transferable Skills Record

Usually: _____

Sometimes: _____

Total Skill Points: _____

Job-Related Skills

You use job-related skills to complete the tasks required for a particular job. For example, a semi driver must know how to drive a large truck and shift gears. A paramedic must be able to take blood pressure and use a stethoscope. Some job-related skills are the result of years of training. Others can be learned in a short time.

If you are interested in a particular job, you probably have some skills necessary to do that job. These skills come from a variety of experiences including education, other jobs, volunteer work, hobbies, extracurricular activities, and even family activities. Do the following exercise to see what skills you have that you could use in your current job or a job you want.

JOB-RELATED SKILLS CHECKLIST

1. List the skills related to your current job that you gained through school courses or vocational training.

    _____

    _____

    _____

2. List the skills related to your job that you gained through other jobs or from volunteer work.

    _____

    _____

    _____

3. List the skills related to your job that you gained through hobbies, family activities, extracurricular activities, and other experiences outside of school or work.

    _____

    _____

    _____

    Give yourself one point for each job-related skill that you listed. Record the total below.

Job-Related Skills Record

    Total Skill Points: _____

A Review of Your Skills

Add your total points for each skill area, and write them in the appropriate spaces below. This shows you the variety of skills you have to offer an employer. You are a valuable member of your employer's team!

- Total Self-Management Skills: _____
- Total Transferable Skills: _____
- Total Job-Related Skills: _____

Identifying your skills shows your strengths and weaknesses as an employee. Now that you know your skills, you can use them to improve your position in the work world. Is there a skill you aren't using? Should you start practicing a new skill? Do you have a skill that is weak? How could you improve this skill?

Write a short statement describing how you feel about yourself now that you've identified specific skills that you possess.

_____

_____

_____

_____

_____

_____

_____

_____

How Job Savvy Are You?

Darren works in a formal-wear store. Last week, a wedding party of 10 came in to be measured for tuxedoes. Darren carefully measured each person and recorded the measurements on the proper form. When the groom became impatient with the long wait, Darren joked with him about the wedding. By the time the group left, the groom was smiling. Then Darren discovered that he had undercharged the group by $50.

1. What are Darren's stronger skills?

_____

_____

_____

2. What are Darren's weaker skills?

_____

_____

_____

3. How can Darren improve his weaker skills?

_____

_____

_____

Sheila works in the university research library. A professor sent a list of research articles to be reserved for his classes. Sheila went through the stacks and pulled all but one of the requested articles. Although she was unable to find the one article, she packaged the rest and sent them to the professor. Her supervisor did not okay the order. Later, the professor complained to Sheila's supervisor that his order was incomplete. The supervisor called Sheila into the office and explained the mistake. Sheila became angry and left the office.

(continued)

(continued)

1. What are Sheila's stronger skills?

    _____

    _____

    _____

2. What are Sheila's weaker skills?

    _____

    _____

    _____

3. How can Sheila improve her weaker skills?

    _____

    _____

    _____

A Useful Skill: Monitoring

The ability to assess performance is a useful tool in the workplace. Whether you're assessing your personal job performance or that of a project team, you can solve problems by using monitoring skills. If you want to gain the respect of your employer and coworkers, learn to evaluate your job performance.

When evaluating yourself, acknowledge your strengths. Comparing your strongest abilities with the needs of your employer allows you to understand how you can best function in your particular job. If you are not using your strong skills, explore ways you can use them.

Seek to understand your weak areas. This will enable you to make improvements and take corrective action if needed. Find ways to overcome your weaknesses. Your supervisor and coworkers may advise you. Or you can take a course to learn more about this skill.

Learning from Others

A good way to learn about yourself is to ask others how they see you. Listen to the performance reviews from your supervisor at work. Work to make progress on developing your skills based on feedback from your supervisor.

There is a simple way to get more information from people who know you so you can build on strengths and try to improve your weaknesses. Follow these steps:

1. **Send an e-mail to about 10 friends, coworkers, and your supervisor.** The e-mail should state the following:

    I am working on a self-improvement plan. Please help me with this task. Please answer two questions for me. When you've seen me at my best doing a task or project, what were my greatest strengths? When you've seen me not succeed in a task or project, what suggestions would you have made to help me do better? Thank you for helping me.

2. **Make a list of all the strengths people tell you about.** Consider how you can build on these strengths to do your job better.

3. **Make a list of all the weaknesses people identify in their e-mail messages along with their suggestions for improvement.** Consider how you can begin practicing the ideas they recommend to improve your work.

4. **Go back and review these lists a month after compiling them.** Have you been able to build on your strengths? What did you do to take advantage of your strengths? Have you implemented suggestions for improvement? Which suggestions have you followed? What other suggestions could you put into practice in the upcoming weeks?

5. **Revisit your lists every few weeks, and keep on working to improve yourself.**

Summing Up

Dietitians tell us, "You are what you eat," to encourage us to develop healthy bodies through good nutrition. To develop a healthier self-image, an appropriate saying might be "You are what you think." In truth, if you believe you can do the job, you can do it. Here are some useful tips to help you believe in yourself:

- **Think positively.** Think success, not failure. Be your own cheerleader.

- **Accept compliments.** Learn to say a simple "thank you" when you are complimented.

- **Accept responsibility.** Learn to accept responsibility for your successes as well as your failures, but recognize how other factors contribute to failure. Be proud of your successes. Strive to improve your weaker skills and correct your mistakes.

- **Identify your skills.** Use your special abilities to improve your skills and to build up your positive self-concept.

- **Reward yourself.** Treat yourself for being successful. Buy something special to remember the occasion. Celebrate!

CHAPTER 8

Getting Along with Your Supervisor

According to management expert Martin Broadwell, supervision is getting a job done through other people.[1] Your supervisor wants and needs your cooperation to get the work done. You are a key part of the organization's ability to function effectively.

Your supervisor might or might not be the person who hired you. However, the supervisor makes the decisions about your work and what you do. Supervisors frequently make recommendations about promotions, salary increases, and employee firings. It is important for you to get along with your supervisor. Cooperating will make your work experience more pleasant and help advance your career. It also helps you get a positive recommendation if you look for another job.

"We've needed someone like you around here for a long time."

The Team Leader

In today's business world, the supervisor is seen as a leader, coach, cheerleader, teacher, and counselor. This person plans, schedules, orders work materials, directs the activities of employees, checks the productivity and quality of work, and coordinates all work activities with other areas of the organization. Many organizations now use the term *team leader* instead of supervisor. A team leader sometimes shares the responsibilities of a supervisor with other members of the team. The more traditional term *supervisor* is still used frequently, and we'll use it in this book.

Consider yourself part of a team if you participate in a work group. Each worker must do his or her job correctly for the team to be successful. The supervisor delegates work to the members of the group. Your supervisor depends on you to do your job and to do it right.

Delegating

Supervisors *delegate* when they assign or distribute tasks to employees. When they do the work themselves instead of delegating it, their performance often slips.[2] A supervisor must delegate tasks to employees to ensure that all the work gets done. When a task is delegated to you, be sure to follow instructions carefully. Periodically, report back to your supervisor to let him or her know how the job is progressing. Let your supervisor know when you are finished with an assigned task.

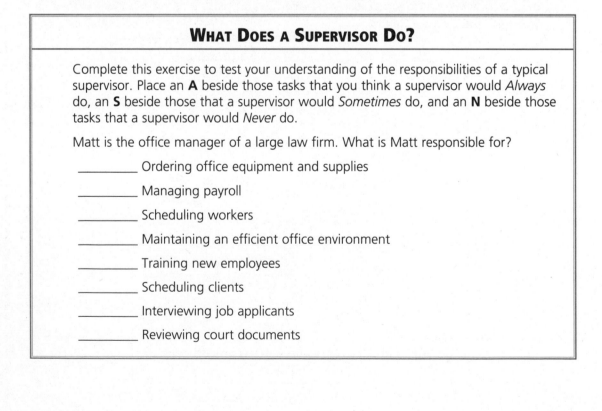

WHAT DOES A SUPERVISOR DO?

Complete this exercise to test your understanding of the responsibilities of a typical supervisor. Place an **A** beside those tasks that you think a supervisor would *Always* do, an **S** beside those that a supervisor would *Sometimes* do, and an **N** beside those tasks that a supervisor would *Never* do.

Matt is the office manager of a large law firm. What is Matt responsible for?

_____ Ordering office equipment and supplies

_____ Managing payroll

_____ Scheduling workers

_____ Maintaining an efficient office environment

_____ Training new employees

_____ Scheduling clients

_____ Interviewing job applicants

_____ Reviewing court documents

Why did you rate these tasks the way that you did?

_____

_____

_____

Krista is the supervisor of the makeup department in a local drug store. What is Krista responsible for?

_____ Ordering makeup

_____ Handling customer complaints

_____ Stocking the shelves

_____ Distributing employee paychecks

_____ Balancing the cash register

_____ Evaluating employees

_____ Demonstrating products

_____ Returning damaged products

Why did you rate these tasks the way that you did?

_____

_____

_____

Joel supervises a group of 15 telemarketing operators. What is Joel responsible for?

_____ Settling employee disagreements

_____ Scheduling vacations

_____ Listening to phone calls made by employees

_____ Tracking sales

_____ Solving problems

_____ Making phone calls

_____ Repairing electronic equipment

_____ Answering customer questions

Why did you rate these tasks the way that you did?

_____

_____

_____

(continued)

(continued)

Marta is a line supervisor at an electronic component assembly factory. What is Marta responsible for?

_____ Checking the quality of finished items

_____ Filling in for absent workers

_____ Setting personnel policies

_____ Keeping a parts inventory

_____ Signing employees' paychecks

_____ Evaluating worker performance

_____ Inspecting for safety violations

_____ Talking with union leaders

Why did you rate these tasks the way that you did?

_____

_____

_____

Jeff manages a frozen-yogurt shop. What is Jeff responsible for?

_____ Creating new yogurt flavors

_____ Taking customer orders

_____ Maintaining equipment

_____ Cleaning tables

_____ Bookkeeping

_____ Conducting health department inspections

_____ Planning advertising

_____ Making bank deposits

Why did you rate these tasks the way that you did?

_____

_____

_____

An old folk tale tells the story of a husband and wife who traded jobs for a day. Each thought he or she could do the other person's job better and more efficiently. Each planned an afternoon of leisure after a morning of efficient work.

The husband stayed home to do household chores, and his wife went off to the field. Neither did the other's job well. By the end of the day, the house was in total ruin, the dinner was burned, the cow was not milked, and the field was not plowed. Totally exhausted after a frustrating day, they shared a cold dinner and agreed that neither job was easy. The next day they returned to their own work with much relief.

Some employees think supervising is easy. It's important to realize that supervisors have responsibilities that other employees don't have. Employees are often unaware of the unseen tasks supervisors must complete. A supervisor's outlook on the workday can be affected by the stress caused by tasks that you can see as well as by unseen tasks. This chapter looks at getting along with your supervisor and helping him or her do an effective job.

Good "Followership"

Many books have been written about leadership. Workers are encouraged to become leaders. However, most of us will be followers for much of our lives. U.S. Air Force Colonel Phillip Meilinger wrote the following Ten Rules of Good Followership, which provide important and relevant advice on this topic:[3]

1. Don't blame the boss.
2. Don't fight the boss.
3. Use initiative.
4. Accept responsibility.
5. Tell the truth, and don't quibble.
6. Do your homework.
7. Be willing to implement suggestions you make.
8. Keep the boss informed.
9. Fix problems as they occur.
10. Put in an honest day's work.

Supervisors appreciate workers who follow these 10 principles. Supervisors show this appreciation in many ways, such as more flexible schedules, better assignments, and more learning opportunities. Some people think that being a good follower is "kissing up to the boss." However, it is just a good strategy for creating a pleasant work environment.

Communicate with Your Supervisor

When employees and managers communicate effectively, businesses benefit. A recent study shows that project managers' communication abilities had a significant effect on the job satisfaction and productivity of their team members.[4] Effective communication creates a domino effect, leading to positive interactions with customers, investors, and the community. Both the company and the workers benefit.

Good communication with your supervisor is important to both of you. It fosters a mutual understanding that creates a good working relationship. Let's explore four important ideas you should remember when communicating with your supervisor:

- You must be able to follow instructions.
- You need to know how to ask questions.
- You should report any problems and the results of your work.
- You need to discuss your job performance.

Following Instructions

Following instructions is important at all times, but especially during your training period. Your supervisor will be watching to see how well you do this. Use all of your senses to follow instructions correctly. Here are some tips to help you do this:

- **Concentrate.** Focus your attention on the supervisor. Don't be distracted by noise and movement.
- **Listen.** Pay attention to the words being spoken. If you hear unfamiliar words or terms, ask for clarification. Listening also means interpreting body language, voice inflections, and gestures. If this nonverbal communication is confusing, ask the supervisor to clarify what you don't understand.
- **Watch.** Sometimes a supervisor demonstrates how a task is performed. If necessary, ask the supervisor to repeat the process until you understand it completely. Sometimes a task can be too complex or time-consuming to demonstrate. In such cases, you probably will receive general instructions. If there are details you don't understand, ask for guidance to continue the task.
- **Ask.** After you have listened and observed, ask questions. A good supervisor will encourage you to ask questions. It's better to ask a question than to make a mistake because you didn't understand something.
- **Write.** Write down in a small notebook the important points to remember about the instructions you get. Don't write while your supervisor is talking or demonstrating something. Do it during a break in the instructions.
- **Practice.** With your supervisor's permission, perform the task. Make sure you have fully completed the job. This can include putting away tools or cleaning up your work area. Don't leave your work partially completed.

Jargon/Acronyms

Every organization develops its own terminology. This language is called *jargon*. Jargon might be the most difficult thing for a new employee to learn. It can be in the form of words or acronyms. For example, your supervisor might tell you that you will be "pulling" today. This could mean you'll be taking packages off a conveyor belt to be loaded onto a truck.

An *acronym* is an abbreviation of a phrase. Your supervisor might say you can't get a computer until you submit an RFP, which might refer to a "Request for Purchase." When you hear a term that is unclear, don't be afraid to ask for an explanation. Some organizations give new employees a booklet that defines terms that are unique to that business.

The following exercise will help you understand how easily instructions can be misunderstood. It illustrates why the tips suggested for communicating with your supervisor are good ideas.

How Job Savvy Are You?

1. Get a sheet of 8½ by 11–inch paper.

2. Fold the paper in half.

3. Now fold the paper in half again.

4. Fold the paper in half one more time.

Following these directions can result in at least four possible outcomes. Your folded paper could measure

- 2¾ by 4¼ inches
- 2⅛ by 5½ inches
- 1⅜ by 8½ inches
- 1¹/₁₆ by 11 inches

The results differ because the instructions are not entirely clear, just as some instructions you receive from a supervisor might not be completely clear.

1. What questions could you have asked to better understand the instructions?

   _____

   _____

   _____

2. How would you rewrite the instructions so that only one outcome is possible?

   _____

   _____

   _____

Ask Questions

If you don't understand something, ask questions. Your supervisor can't read your mind. It's better to ask a question than to make a major mistake.

Many people are reluctant to ask questions for fear of looking stupid. If this applies to you, concentrate on overcoming your reluctance. Not asking questions can result in broken equipment, angry customers, and other mistakes that will negatively affect your performance rating. It might even cost you the job.

Here are some simple guidelines for asking questions:

- **Ask immediately.** You should ask a question as soon as it arises. The longer you wait, the more irrelevant your question will seem, and then you won't ask it at all.
- **Summarize the response.** When the supervisor answers your question, repeat the answer in your own words. This lets you make sure that you clearly understand the answer.
- **Memorize or record the answer.** It's irritating to answer the same question repeatedly. Your supervisor might grow impatient with you if this happens. Record answers in a notebook if you have trouble remembering them.

Report on Results

Your supervisor needs to be kept informed of your work. Sometimes the supervisor will be close enough to observe your work at all times, but this is not always the case. It is *your* responsibility to keep the supervisor informed about your progress on a task. Contact your supervisor in the following situations:

- **When you complete a task:** The supervisor needs to know whether a job has been completed. If you don't report back, he or she will have to find you to ask whether the job is done. A busy supervisor doesn't have time to track down all employees to see whether they have completed their assigned tasks. A supervisor will appreciate knowing that you've finished a task.
- **When you aren't sure how to proceed:** At times, you won't know how to complete a task. Whenever this happens, ask your supervisor. Remember or record the answer so that you'll know how to handle a similar situation in the future.
- **When you have a problem:** Problems can develop when you are trying to complete a task. The less experience you have, the more difficult it will be to solve the problem. Equipment might not work properly. Customers might have questions you can't answer. Someone else might not have done a job right, and it keeps you from finishing your assignment. When you aren't sure how to solve a problem, contact your supervisor immediately. Doing so can keep the problem from getting worse.

Some tasks might take several hours, days, or weeks to complete. Keep your supervisor informed about ongoing assignments. This tells your supervisor that you are assuming responsibility and that he or she can trust you to complete an assignment.

Coaching Your Job Performance

Your supervisor should communicate with you frequently about your job performance. This communication, which is referred to as *coaching*, focuses on helping workers do the best job possible.[5] Just as a sports coach can help improve an athlete's performance, a good supervisor can help you improve your work performance.

Coaching techniques should include periodic encouragement and feedback about your work. Sometimes you might have negative feelings when a supervisor suggests ways to improve your work. Keep in mind that coaching is designed to be a "win-win" situation. It helps the organization because your performance is improved, but it also helps you become a more skilled worker. Coaching helps you do a better job for your organization.

Follow these simple guidelines to communicate effectively with your supervisor about your job performance:

- **Don't respond to feedback with anger.** Feedback from your supervisor is important. No one enjoys criticism, but it is sometimes necessary. If you get angry because your supervisor gives you negative feedback, get control of yourself before responding. Count to 10 if there is no other way to cool off. *Never get into a shouting match with your supervisor.*

- **Know what you have done wrong.** Your supervisor might be so upset with something you've done that you aren't sure what the problem is. Apologize if you made a mistake, and ask for an explanation of exactly what you did wrong. Don't repeat the mistake. Make the correction in the future, and move on.

- **Thank your supervisor for compliments.** You must learn to accept praise as well as criticism. Acknowledge compliments with a simple "Thank you."

- **Ask for feedback.** Some supervisors are not good about giving feedback. If you aren't sure what your supervisor thinks about the work you are doing, ask! Let him or her know that you want to succeed on the job and that you need to know how you're doing.

Performance Appraisal

A *performance appraisal* is a formal report about your job performance, based on your supervisor's evaluation of your work. You are rated on various aspects of your job for a quarterly, semiannual, or annual period, depending on your organization's policy. Performance appraisals are similar to report cards in school.

(continued)

(continued)

You usually review the appraisal form with your supervisor and have an opportunity to respond to the evaluation. Coworkers might even be asked to rate your performance. Some organizations give you a chance to rate yourself. If so, you are usually expected to explain the ratings and back them up with examples. Be honest, but don't give yourself a rating lower than you deserve. New employees usually receive performance appraisals at the end of their probation periods.

How Job Savvy Are You?

Theresa has worked for Armstrong Dry Cleaners for two months. She works behind the counter, taking customer orders. Her supervisor tells her the business is going to expand and begin cleaning leather garments. Theresa will need to fill out a special order form for leather clothing, and she is not sure that she understands all of the instructions.

1. What should Theresa do at this point?

_____

_____

_____

Bryan has just finished loading the heating and air conditioning service van when his supervisor comes up to him and starts yelling. He tells Bryan that he took too long when inspecting a furnace yesterday and is costing the company too much money. He says that Bryan had better get his act together if he expects to keep his job.

1. How should Bryan respond?

_____

_____

_____

Meet Your Supervisor's Expectations

This section reviews some of the little things you need to know to get along with your supervisor. These are important because *little things* to you can become *big things* to your supervisor when they are multiplied by all the workers he or she supervises.

Practice the following six behaviors to satisfy your supervisor's expectations.

Be Truthful

Your supervisor expects you to tell the truth at all times. If you make mistakes, don't try to cover them up by lying. Lies usually are discovered and can be grounds for disciplinary action. Supervisors need employees that they can count on to tell the truth. Without honesty between a supervisor and workers, it's impossible for either to do a good job.

What are some reasons a worker might lie to a supervisor?

_____

_____

What problems could be caused for the supervisor by these lies?

_____

_____

Don't Extend Your Breaks

Your supervisor expects you to work during your scheduled hours. Normally, a full-time worker is allowed a 15-minute break mid-morning and mid-afternoon in addition to a 30- to 60-minute lunch break. When you don't return from a break on time, it can cause problems. A customer might have to wait, another worker might not be able to take his or her break, and others might not be able to finish a task until your work is completed.

If you can't get back from break on time, explain the reason to your supervisor. Make sure you aren't extending your breaks unless there is an exceptionally good reason.

What are some acceptable reasons for extended breaks?

_____

_____

Get Your Work Done

You should complete all assigned tasks as quickly as possible while doing the best job possible. It's difficult for a supervisor to check your work all the time. You are expected to continue working productively without a supervisor present.

If circumstances prevent you from completing a job, notify your supervisor immediately. Balance your work between completing a task as quickly as possible and producing the highest quality of work you can. Ask your supervisor for feedback about how well you are meeting these priorities.

What obstacles might make it difficult or impossible for you to do your job?

_____

_____

Be Cooperative

Cooperate when your supervisor asks for your help. When someone can't work at a scheduled time, be willing to change your schedule if possible. Help with a task that's not normally your responsibility. In special situations, your supervisor might need more help from everybody.

Cooperation is a mutual thing, and most supervisors will remember your help the next time you need a day off for a special reason. Thus, cooperation benefits you and creates a more pleasant work atmosphere.

What are some reasons for cooperation?

_____

_____

Be Adaptive

Be willing to adapt to new situations. The organization you work for needs to change as the world around it changes. Employees sometimes resist change because of poor self-esteem, threats to personal security, fear of the unknown, a lack of trust, or an inability to see the larger picture. When you understand the reason for resistance, you can work to reduce it. Adjustments are difficult, but your life is more pleasant when you adjust instead of trying to resist.

Supervisors probably don't want to make changes any more than you do, but it is their responsibility to do so, and they need your cooperation. It might help to think about the positive things that result from the changes. For example, if your work schedule changes, don't focus on disruptions in your personal life but think about the new opportunities it might provide at work, such as meeting new people and learning new skills.

What are some typical reasons for change within an organization?

_____

_____

_____

_____

Take the Initiative

Find ways to help your supervisor. After your own work is completed, look around the workplace for other tasks to do. But remember, it doesn't help anyone if your work suffers because you were trying to help with something else.

How can you take the initiative to help your supervisor?

_____

_____

_____

How Job Savvy Are You?

Tonight, Jenna has a date with Brad, the quarterback at Big Moose University. Sara, her supervisor at the Bureau of Motor Vehicles, is going directly from lunch to a supervisor's meeting. Jenna knows Sara won't be back in the office until 2:30 p.m. On her lunch break, Jenna passes her favorite hair salon. A quick cut would make a great impression on Brad.

1. What should Jenna do?

   _____

   _____

   _____

2. What could happen if she stops to get her hair cut?

   _____

   _____

   _____

Ryan has three days off work this week. On his second day off, his supervisor calls. Ryan isn't home, but his sister takes a message. One of the other employees is sick, and the supervisor needs Ryan to work the next day. Ryan has already made plans for the day.

1. What should Ryan do?

   _____

   _____

   _____

2. What will be the result if he goes into work? What will happen if he doesn't?

   _____

   _____

   _____

Brandon works second shift as a lab technician at Mercy Hospital. Brandon has just finished the last lab report for the shift and is preparing to leave when the phone rings. His supervisor has just stepped out of the lab. Brandon is alone in the lab.

1. What should Brandon do?

   _____

   _____

   _____

2. Whose responsibility is it to answer the phone?

   _____

   _____

   _____

Performance Reviews

Many organizations use a performance review or appraisal to periodically evaluate employee performance. This formal process is conducted by a supervisor and includes completing a written report about your performance. Management often uses performance appraisals to determine pay increases, promotions, and training needs.

Organizations differ in how frequently they conduct performance appraisals. Some organizations do an appraisal at the end of an employee's probationary period. Most companies conduct reviews once or twice a year, and a few have quarterly appraisals. However frequently reviews happen in your organization, you should be prepared for them.[6] Here are some tips:

- **Keep a record of your accomplishments.** Once a month, write down your accomplishments. Examples include a special project you completed, customer feedback that was very positive, the amount of sales you had, or the quality of goods that you produced. You might want to compile these accomplishments and give a written report to your supervisor before the performance appraisal is conducted. It will help your supervisor remember accomplishments that he or she might have forgotten.

- **Communicate regularly with your supervisor.** Information given in a performance appraisal shouldn't be a surprise. Talk frequently with your supervisor about your performance. Ask what you can do to improve your job performance. Try to have any performance issues resolved before your review takes place.

- **Know what coworkers think.** Some organizations use a review process called 360-degree feedback. This includes reviews from yourself, coworkers, and your supervisor. Organizations that don't use 360-degree feedback appraisals often still rely on the impressions coworkers have about an employee when conducting an appraisal.

- **Listen with an open mind.** Assess the feedback from your supervisor honestly. We all have strengths and weaknesses. Encourage the supervisor to consider your strengths. Accept constructive criticism about your weaknesses. Ask for specific examples of unsatisfactory behavior or performance.

- **Develop a plan for improvement.** Ask your supervisor to give you specific recommendations about how to improve your performance. The plan might include a change in behavior, training, job restructuring, and other strategies. Work with the supervisor to develop objectives that are possible to achieve. Make sure there is a timetable established for achieving the objectives.

- **Implement the plan, and get feedback.** Determine that you will implement the plan and improve your performance. Periodically review your performance with the supervisor, and verify that your performance is improving in a satisfactory manner.

- **Be realistic.** Consider the performance review, and determine whether it is fair. It is possible to receive a poor performance review even though your work has been good or satisfactory. A supervisor might give you a poor evaluation because that person is unrealistic, unfair, or constrained by company policy to give only a certain number of excellent, good, and fair ratings. A poor performance review that you objectively consider unfair should motivate you to think about your future with the organization. You might want to consider looking for another job. However, it's not good to leave your current job until you've found a new one.

Resolving Problems

Each person looks at a situation from his or her own point of view. You might not always agree with your supervisor, and sometimes your supervisor will make mistakes. You might not do a good job at certain times. A number of problems can arise when conflicts occur. Such disagreements can be resolved by conflict resolution, through a grievance procedure, or through disciplinary actions.

Conflict Resolution

Conflicts are a part of life. You should not try to avoid them when they arise. Talk with your supervisor about any disagreements. These simple suggestions can help you keep conflicts to a minimum:

- **Don't accuse.** Everyone makes mistakes. When you make a mistake, you should do what you can to correct it. It's not a good idea to accuse your supervisor of making a mistake.

- **State your feelings.** Don't say "you" when explaining your perception of the situation. It will sound like you're accusing. Say "I feel" or "I think" or "I am" to describe your view. The supervisor will not know how you feel unless you voice your feelings.

- **Ask for feedback.** Ask your supervisor whether you understand the situation correctly and have acted appropriately. It is possible that you misunderstood what happened. You might find that you feel differently about the situation once it is clarified.

- **State what you want.** Know what you want done about a situation before you confront your supervisor. State your wishes clearly and respectfully.

- **Get a commitment.** After you state your feelings and what you want done, find out what your supervisor can do about the situation. Maybe no action is necessary. If no immediate action can be taken, your supervisor should commit to a date and time to let you know what will be done.

- **Compromise when necessary.** Not all problems are resolved the way you want. You might have failed to consider your supervisor's needs or the needs of the organization. How can your needs as well as your supervisor's be met? The ideal result of any conflict is that both parties are satisfied.

Most problems with your supervisor can be solved with these techniques. However, some problems can't be resolved in this manner. When such a situation occurs, you might be able to file a grievance.

Grievance Procedures

If your supervisor cannot resolve a conflict, you might resolve the problem by going through a grievance procedure. Some organizations have standard procedures, and you need to check this out. Be aware that filing a grievance almost always creates tension between you and the supervisor.

Organizations with unions usually have a procedure that has been negotiated between management and the union. If you are employed by such an organization, you will probably have a union representative with you at all steps in the grievance process. An arbitrator makes the final decision.

Studies show that many nonunion companies also have formal grievance procedures. Many government or government-funded organizations are required by law to have them. Some smaller organizations have no such process.

You need to know your organization's procedure before filing a grievance. In nonunion organizations, you typically have no assistance filing a grievance, and the organization's personnel director or chief executive officer probably makes the final decision. Complaints of discrimination or sexual harassment often receive special attention. Such cases might require a different procedure.

You should make every attempt to resolve a conflict with your supervisor before filing a grievance. Don't tell your supervisor that you are considering such action until you have tried every other means possible to solve the problem.

Disciplinary Action

Sometimes your work performance or behavior might be unacceptable. It is your supervisor's responsibility to address the problem and to advise you on appropriate performance. If you don't correct the problem, you could face disciplinary action. Make sure you understand your employer's disciplinary process. Such procedures usually apply only to employees past their probation period. Those still on probation might be dismissed without warning. Disciplinary procedures, like grievance procedures, vary from one employer to another. The action taken will depend on the seriousness of the violation. The five disciplinary steps explained here are common to many organizations:

1. **Oral warning:** Your supervisor warns you that your performance is not acceptable. This applies to less serious problems. Serious problems such as drinking or drug use probably will result in immediate suspension or dismissal. The oral warning goes into your personnel record but is removed later if no further problems arise.

2. **Written warning:** Repeated performance problems result in a written warning. This step takes place after an oral warning is issued. A written warning might become a permanent part of your personnel record.

3. **Suspension:** Suspension means you aren't allowed to work for a short period of time, sometimes three to five days. This is unpaid time. The disciplinary action becomes a permanent part of the personnel record.

4. **Dismissal:** The final step of any disciplinary process is dismissal. This means the organization won't tolerate your job performance any longer. Dismissal becomes a permanent part of the personnel record. It also means that any future employer who contacts your former employer might be told that you were dismissed from your job.

5. **Immediate response:** Some organizations immediately escort a terminated employee out of the building. They will stop at your desk, workstation, or locker to allow you to remove personal articles. This action is designed to protect employees, equipment, computer systems, or other assets from disgruntled employees. It is often a required security procedure, so don't take it personally.

Most organizations don't want you to fail. If you are being disciplined, follow your supervisor's instructions and you should not encounter further problems. Smaller businesses might not follow the procedure described previously. You might simply get an oral warning before suspension or dismissal.

If you think you are going to be dismissed from a job, you might want to look for another job. You might also consider looking for another job when you can't resolve a problem with your supervisor.

A Useful Skill: Social Perceptiveness

The skill of emotional intelligence (EI) is useful when you're dealing with others and is an important skill for the 21st century.[7] When you develop this skill, you have a clearer concept of how others will react to your actions. Practicing EI involves two basic steps:

1. **Being aware of the reactions of others:** Some individuals are oblivious of others' emotions and opinions, and they act with total disregard for anyone else. EI requires listening and learning to recognize nonverbal clues when communicating with others, as well as remembering to observe what an individual does.

2. **Understanding why others react as they do:** An emotionally intelligent person is conscious of factors that may play a role in the responses of individuals. Knowing the cause of reactions gives insight into how to approach individuals. For example, scheduling a meeting to discuss your recent performance review on the day your supervisor just returned from vacation and has meetings scheduled from 9 a.m. till 4:30 p.m. might result in a negative reaction. Obviously, a meeting on a less hectic day would be to your advantage.

As you advance in your career, you will find this skill useful in working with both coworkers and your supervisors.

Summing Up

Supervisors are people, too. Whether they are excellent or poor leaders, all supervisors appreciate good employees. Supervisors can't do their jobs without them. If you practice the guidelines in this chapter, you will increase the chances of establishing a positive relationship with your supervisor. If a problem does develop between you and your supervisor, try to resolve it. If a formal procedure is necessary, or your supervisor takes disciplinary action against you, make sure that you understand how your organization handles such situations. Always try to abide by your employer's rules and guidelines.

CHAPTER 9

Getting Along with Other Workers

Teamwork is important in any business operation. Most managers and supervisors use team-building principles. The use of the word *team* to refer to a work group is common in modern organizations. Teams are sometimes called *quality circles*, *self-managing teams*, *self-directed work teams*, or *work teams*. As team members learn to work together and adapt to each other's working styles, their productivity is maximized.[1] (The role of teams in problem solving is discussed in more detail in Chapter 10.)

Even if your organization does not use the word "team" to refer to the work group—also known as department, office, center, division, unit, branch, or store—managers and supervisors expect you to work as part of a team. It is important to follow instructions and cooperate with other employees to do the best job possible. That way, everyone wins—you, the supervisor, the group, and the organization.

Get to Know Your Coworkers

It's difficult to be part of the team if you don't know how to get along with the other members. Getting to know your coworkers and being accepted by them helps you succeed in your job.

GAINING COWORKER ACCEPTANCE CHECKLIST

Here are several situations describing how you might interact with coworkers. If you think the situation will help you gain acceptance from coworkers, write a **Y** in the space provided. If not, write an **N**.

_____ Greet your coworkers when you arrive at work.

_____ Join the office intramural sports league.

_____ Ask a coworker to join you for lunch.

_____ Invite your coworkers to a party at your home.

_____ Tell the group how much another worker spent on a new car.

_____ Bring Aunt Sally's handmade rugs to sell to your coworkers.

_____ Tell the latest ethnic joke during a coffee break.

_____ Loan a book you enjoyed to a fellow worker.

_____ Offer to take on additional duties when a coworker has to leave suddenly to tend to a sick child.

_____ Repeat the latest rumor about the boss's relationship with a coworker.

_____ Tell the boss when one of your coworkers leaves early.

_____ Tell the group how to do the job better.

_____ Tell the group how well the boss thinks you are doing.

_____ Offer to give a coworker a ride to the auto-repair shop.

Fitting into a team is an important skill to learn. It requires patience to become part of a team. It takes some time before you know how to work well with the other employees in your work group. Everyone likes to be respected for skills, knowledge, or other contributions to the group productivity, but that respect doesn't come right away. If you do your job well, your coworkers' respect for you will increase over time. Meanwhile, these tips can help you earn respect from other team members:

- **Know your position.** Find out what other workers expect from you. Keep in mind that these ideas should be balanced with your supervisor's expectations. Other workers might have a specific method they use to do a job. If you do it differently, you might upset their system. Other workers also might expect a newcomer to take over certain tasks, for instance, cleaning up after a project or at the end of the day. Go along with this. Eventually, another new worker will be hired and take over these tasks.

- **Accept good-natured teasing.** Other workers sometimes play jokes and tease a new worker to test what kind of person he or she is. If this happens, don't get angry. Let the others know you appreciate a good joke. If this behavior doesn't cease and makes it difficult for you to do your work, you might want to talk to coworkers about it. If this doesn't reduce the teasing, you might consider discussing it with the supervisor. However, if you think the jokes or teasing constitute racial or sexual harassment, let your supervisor know immediately.

- **Do your fair share.** Everyone in a work group is expected to do his or her best. If you don't do your fair share of the work, your coworkers have to do more. After a while, they might complain to the supervisor. The flip side is that other workers also might complain if you do too much work because that can make them look bad. Supervisors do reward good workers with salary increases and promotions. But you should try to balance your work between what the supervisor expects and what your coworkers expect. When in doubt, do what the supervisor expects.

- **Don't do other people's work.** As a team member, you should cooperate and help others when asked. However, some people try to take advantage of this cooperative spirit and push their work off on others. Remember, your supervisor will evaluate you based on how well you do *your* job. If your job suffers because you are doing someone else's work, you are likely to receive a lower evaluation. (Neither the coworker who takes advantage nor other workers will respect you for this.)

- **Know how your team functions within the organization.** How does your team relate to other teams in the organization? What are each team's responsibilities? Remember that all teams work to accomplish the employer's goals. However, conflicts sometimes occur. Discuss these problems with all people involved. Avoid letting conflicts affect your working relationships with members of other teams. Contact your supervisor when you can't resolve conflicts with other teams. You should all be working for the best interests of the organization.

Synergy

Synergy describes the extra energy and capability that results in combined group efforts to accomplish an objective. Because of synergy, a team can accomplish more than the same number of people can accomplish working individually. In this case: $1 + 1 = 3$.

That's why teamwork is so important to an organization. You should cooperate in every effort to develop synergy with your coworkers.

How Job Savvy Are You?

In the month that Rick has worked in the warehouse, he has gotten to know a couple of the other workers pretty well. In fact, he went to a baseball game with Don last weekend. When he unwrapped his sandwich at lunch today, there was no meat in it. Rick turned to the other workers and yelled that he was sick and tired of their jokes and then stomped out of the lunchroom, slamming the door behind him.

1. How do you think the other workers will react to Rick's outburst?

   _____

   _____

   _____

2. What should Rick have done in this situation to create a more positive relationship with other workers?

   _____

   _____

   _____

Lynette has worked at Hoover's Pharmacy for four days. Yesterday, a customer broke a bottle of perfume. Mika, a worker who has worked at Hoover's slightly longer than Lynette, told Lynette to clean up the mess. Lynette cleaned up the mess. Today, a small child knocked over a display of cough medicine. Tim told Lynette to restack the boxes. Lynette got upset and told Tim to do it himself.

1. How do you think this will make the other workers feel about Lynette?

   _____

   _____

   _____

2. What do you think Lynette should have done in this situation?

   _____

   _____

   _____

The Value of Diversity

You will work with many people who are different from you. The growing diversity of the U.S. workforce described in Chapter 1 affects most organizations. Diversity in an organization can be good. In a team, the strengths of one worker can overcome the weaknesses of another. The balance created by such variety makes a team stronger.

Many organizations promote diversity, believing that it results in more productivity. These organizations often provide training to help people understand how to work together.[2]

People differ from one another in three ways: in preferences, temperament, and individual characteristics (such as gender, ethnicity, and age).

Preferences

Preferences are the values we give to ideas, things, or people. Parents, friends, teachers, religious and political leaders, significant events in our lives, the media, and our community all influence the development of our preferences.

Sometimes these preferences are referred to as values. These values are not the same as moral or ethical values. Rather, they are situations, behavior, structure, personal interactions, or other things on which we place value. Although our values can be quite different, organizational behavior expert Stephen Robbins suggested that, based on their values, people fall into one of three categories:[3]

1. **Traditionalist:** People in this category value (prefer)
   - Hard work
   - Loyalty to the organization
   - Doing things the way they've always been done
   - The authority of leaders

2. **Humanist:** People in this category value (prefer)
   - Quality of life
   - Loyalty to self
   - Autonomy (self-direction)
   - Leaders who are attentive to workers' needs

3. **Pragmatist:** People in this category value (prefer)
   - Success
   - Loyalty to career
   - Achievement
   - Leaders who reward people for hard work

Which category do you fit into? Look over the values in each of the three categories. Circle those items that you value most. Note which category has the most items circled. Then, in the space below, write the category that best describes you. Explain your reasons.

_____

_____

_____

_____

_____

_____

_____

_____

_____

_____

_____

An effective work team includes people who have values in each category. At times, the team needs the traditionalist, to make sure that the team does what is best for the organization. At other times, the team needs the humanist, who stresses the need to balance life and work. There also are times when the team needs the pragmatist, who will strive to advance the team because this also advances personal achievement. Each person's values contribute to the team.

You might not fit neatly into one category—many people don't. However, we can better understand and appreciate our differences from other people when we think about which category they might fall into. You can't think in terms of right or wrong, or good or bad, when you talk about these value differences. Each set of values is sometimes positive and sometimes negative. Learn to appreciate the differences and be tolerant of people who hold a different set of values than you do.

Temperaments

Your temperament is the distinctive way you think, feel, and react to the world. Everyone has his or her own individual temperament. However, it's easier to understand differences in temperament by classifying people into categories. Management specialists assess temperaments through tests. One of the most famous is the Myers-Briggs Type Indicator. David Keirsey has adapted the Myers-Briggs to identify the following four categories of temperament:[4]

1. **Optimists:** People with this temperament
   - Must be free and not tied down
   - Like to try new things
   - Are impulsive
   - Can survive major setbacks
   - Enjoy the immediate
   - Are generous
   - Enjoy action for action's sake
   - Are cheerful
   - Like working with things

2. **Realists:** People with this temperament
   - Like to belong to groups
   - Feel obligations strongly
   - Have a strong work ethic
   - Need order
   - Are realistic

- Find tradition important
- Are willing to do a job when asked
- Are serious
- Are committed to society's standards

3. **Futurists:** People with this temperament
   - Like to control things
   - Want to be highly competent
   - Are the most self-critical of all temperaments
   - Strive for excellence
   - Judge people on their merits
   - Cause people to feel they don't measure up
   - Live for their work
   - Are highly creative
   - Tend to focus on the future

4. **Idealists:** People with this temperament
   - Are constantly in search of their "self"
   - Want to know the meanings of things
   - Value integrity
   - Write fluently
   - Are romantics
   - Have difficulty placing limits on work
   - Are highly personable
   - Appreciate people
   - Get along well with all temperaments

What kind of temperament do you have? Go through the preceding descriptions and circle the items in each style that apply to you. The category in which you circle the most items is probably your temperament style.

1. Write down your temperament style.

   _____

2. Write down your secondary temperament style (the one with the second highest number of answers).

   _____

No temperament style is better than another. In fact, a team that includes people of varied temperaments is stronger.

People with different temperament styles often find one another difficult to deal with because of their distinct approaches to life. When differences arise between you and a person with a different temperament, follow these steps to resolve the conflict:

1. Look for positive contributions the person makes to the team.

2. Identify characteristics of your temperament that conflict with the other person's temperament.

3. Talk with the person, and explain what characteristics seem to cause conflict between you.

4. Ask the other person to describe which of your characteristics upsets him or her most.

5. Discuss a plan of action that you both can pursue to reduce conflict. Often just acknowledging the differences and being willing to discuss them will reduce the conflict.

Individual Characteristics

In Chapter 1, you saw that the U.S. workforce has become more diverse over the past 20 years. This trend will continue throughout the coming decade. While the workforce of tomorrow is projected to grow at a slower rate, the assorted groups within it will continue to differ in a number of ways:[5]

- **Gender:** Women will make up nearly one-half of the workforce. The increase in the number of women in the workforce peaked in 1999 and continues to grow at a slower rate; however, the growth rate of women in the labor force is still projected to be greater than that of men. By 2018 the growth rate of women in the labor force is projected to increase by 9 percent, while men will enter at a slightly lower rate—7.5 percent.

- **Ethnicity:** Increasing racial and ethnic diversity in the workplace will continue to be the trend. Blacks and Hispanics are expected to be nearly 30 percent of the workforce by 2018. Asians and members of other ethnic groups will make up another 8.5 percent. This means that ethnic minorities will make up more than one-third of the workforce.

- **Age:** The labor force is aging. In the 10 years between 2008 and 2018, the number of primary workers ages 25 to 54 will decline by more than 4 percent, while laborers ages 55 and above will increase more than 5 percent.

Individual diversity strengthens a team. Men and women often approach problems differently. Women often are more attentive to the needs of other people, whereas men tend to be more aggressive and ambitious. Team members can learn from one another and integrate the positive characteristics of each person into the work group.

People from different cultural and ethnic backgrounds look at problems from different points of view. Eastern cultures traditionally value cooperation, and Western cultures emphasize individualism. People from different cultures can help one another develop a better appreciation of their values.

A diversity of ages also can be positive. Younger workers typically bring enthusiasm and energy into a job. Older workers bring patience, maturity, and experience. These combined characteristics often make a team stronger.

No matter what the differences are, each person can contribute to the team. It's important for all members of a team to share their thoughts and ideas. Understanding one another's viewpoints will help you overcome many differences.

Basic Human Relations

Psychology and organizational behavior studies have helped us gain a better understanding of human relations in the workplace. To get along with workers on your team, consider some practical steps derived from these studies:

- **Get to know other workers.** Take lunch breaks with your coworkers. Join employee recreational and social activities. Listen to the things your coworkers share about their personal lives and interests.

- **Don't try to change everything.** You're "the new kid on the block" when you start a job. Know and understand the organization before you think about changing something. Listen to others. Talk to coworkers about your ideas and get some feedback before you suggest changes.

- **Be honest.** One of the most important things you own is a good reputation. Honesty with your coworkers will build up your reputation. It's one of the best ways to gain and keep respect.

- **Be direct.** Let people know when they do something that bothers you. Most people want to know when there is a problem. However, don't be a constant complainer or a whiner. Make sure that your problem is important before you discuss it with others.

- **Avoid gossip.** Don't listen to other people gossiping about coworkers. More important, never gossip about others. When you gossip, people wonder what you say about them and often avoid you.

- **Be positive and supportive.** Listen to the ideas of other people. When someone makes a mistake, don't criticize. It's irritating to have someone else point out a mistake. When you realize you've made a mistake, admit it and try to do better next time.

- **Show appreciation.** Be sure you thank a coworker who does something to make your job easier. Let coworkers know you appreciate their contributions to the team. People like to be recognized and praised.

- **Share credit when it's deserved.** Take credit for the work you do. When other coworkers assist you, make sure you credit them. People feel they have been taken advantage of if someone else takes credit for their work.

- **Return favors.** A coworker might help you out by exchanging a day off with you. Return that favor. A sure way to make people dislike you is to only take and never give.

- **Live in the present.** Avoid talking about the way things used to be. People don't want to hear about how great your old job was or how great former coworkers were.

- **Ask for help and advice when you need it.** People like to feel needed. Your coworkers can be a great resource. When you aren't sure what to do, they can give you advice and assistance.

- **Avoid battles.** Let coworkers in conflict work out their own differences. Don't take sides in their arguments. This is a sure way to develop problems with coworkers. When you take sides, other people usually resent your interference. Often both sides become unhappy with you.

- **Follow group standards.** Every group has standards—sociologists call these *mores*. For example, they might take a coffee break at 9:15 a.m. Stop work and go on break with them if you are able. These group standards help build a team. Most standards are not major and require little effort to follow.

- **Take an interest in your coworkers' jobs.** People like positive attention. Taking an interest in another worker's job gives that person positive attention. It also helps you better understand how your team works together.

How Job Savvy Are You?

Rosa's family has seven children and enjoys doing most things together. Her grandmother is celebrating her 85th birthday next Thursday, and the family has planned a surprise party for her. On Monday, when the work schedule is posted, Rosa sees she is scheduled to work Thursday evening. She is quite upset, although she knows she should have asked for the evening off before the schedule was made.

1. As a coworker, what could be your positive reaction to Rosa's problem?

   _____

   _____

   _____

2. What could be your negative reaction?

   _____

   _____

   _____

Tyler belongs to an animal-rights group. He brings literature about animal rights to work and leaves it in the break room. He refuses to eat meat because he believes killing animals for food is wrong. Tyler has invited you to join him at the next meeting of his group.

1. How could you react positively to Tyler's invitation?

   _____

   _____

   _____

2. How could you react negatively?

_____

_____

_____

Gwen is a very hard worker. She comes to work early and stays late. She has to be reminded to take breaks. Her main interest is her job. Sometimes, she seems to be trying to outdo her coworkers.

1. How could you react positively to Gwen's work habits?

_____

_____

_____

2. How could you react negatively?

_____

_____

_____

Chang doesn't work on Saturdays because it's a holy day in his church and he attends services. Last Saturday, all personnel were required to work on a special project. Chang was excused from working. The entire work group is upset with him.

1. How could you react positively to Chang's situation?

_____

_____

_____

2. How could you react negatively?

_____

_____

_____

Good Electronic Manners

Most organizations today use voice mail, fax machines, e-mail, and computers. This technology has resulted in a new electronic etiquette. Coworkers react to you based on your use of this technology. The following are guidelines for using communications technology:

- **Leave voice-mail messages that are short and concise.** It's frustrating to listen to long, rambling messages. Let the person know why you called, how urgent it is, and when you are available for a return call.

- **Make sure that voice-mail messages contain essential information.** Most important are a phone number that can be used to reach you and the date and times you can be reached.

- **When you place a voice-mail greeting on your phone, keep it short.** Callers don't want to waste time hearing a poem or cute message, and they don't need your schedule for a week. Just let them know whether you are going to be able to return their call shortly or whether it will be a while.

- **Avoid leaving voice-mail messages that convey anger or frustration.** Otherwise, your call might not be returned. If it is returned, the person might be defensive or angry. Usually, it's better to have a face-to-face discussion about a problem.

- **Avoid reading faxes sent to another person.** Reading a fax is an invasion of privacy—just like opening someone's mail.

- **Call someone before sending a fax so that he or she knows it's on the way.** Include a cover page so that others at the receiving end know who should receive the fax.

- **Find out your organization's e-mail policy, and follow it.** For example, some organizations consider all e-mail to be company property, and management may read any message. Employees have lost their jobs because of violating e-mail policies.[6]

- **Avoid sending e-mail messages on important matters when your message could result in a negative emotional reaction.** For example, sending a critical e-mail might anger the recipient much more than a direct conversation would. A personal conversation lets you observe the person's reactions. It also lets you make clear anything that could be misinterpreted.

- **Carefully consider whether other people should receive copies of a message you send to someone.** A general rule is that messages containing information can be copied to other people. A message that contains opinion, criticism, or private information should be kept private.

- **Avoid "flaming."** This is a common occurrence with e-mail and involves sending a series of messages that become increasingly negative. For example, someone might make a suggestion and your response might be negative. The person returns a negative e-mail to you. You send another e-mail that is even more negative, and the process continues until someone has the good sense to stop. When it appears that flaming is happening, talk with the person directly to avoid more conflict.

- **Don't use someone else's computer without asking.** Computers can contain confidential information. Using a computer without asking might be considered a violation of privacy—just like going through a person's desk.

- **Computer files should also be considered personal and confidential.** Files stored on the computer hard drive or any other media are private. You shouldn't take or look at any electronically filed information that doesn't belong to you.

- **Be careful when you use social media.** Posting complaints about your coworkers, supervisor, managers, or company on Facebook, Google+, or other social media is unwise. In some cases such statements might be viewed as bullying. Unless you want someone to report you for negative information you've written on the Web, it is best not to post it. Employees have been terminated when they vented online. So think before you tweet.[7]

Cubicle Etiquette

Because of the economic benefits and the flexibility of space, many companies set up offices with worker cubicles. Working in a cubicle gives people easy access to coworkers; however, it limits their individual privacy. Because workers are so close together, problems can develop if they don't practice good cubicle etiquette.

Existing in the cubicle world can be challenging. Here are a few survival tips for working in a cube:

- **Use a reasonable voice.** Cubicles are not soundproof. Others can hear what you say. Use a quiet voice when conducting business.

- **Think about your cell phone use.** Check your company's policy about personal cell phone use. Avoid disturbing your coworkers with the ringing of a cell phone. Set the ringer on "vibrate" or turn it off. Take the phone with you when you leave the cube.

- **Treat your coworkers' cubicles as offices.** Knock before entering. Wait till the person responds to you before walking in. If he or she is on the phone or busy with someone else, leave and come back later.

- **Hold conversations in the cube.** Sitting in your cube and talking to the person in the next cubicle disturbs everyone around you. Leaning over the wall for a conversation is just as distracting. When you need to speak to anyone, enter the cube for the conversation.

- **Avoid overcrowding in the cubicle.** Unless you are meeting with only one other person, a cubicle is not large enough to hold a meeting. A conference room is a more appropriate place to have a meeting.

- **Be considerate of others.** A cubicle office is shared space. Eating strong-smelling foods in your cubicle may irritate others. Using scented lotions or perfumes affects people's allergies. Coworkers who hum, chew gum loudly, or clip their fingernails annoy others.

- **Express your concern.** If you are unable to do your work because of a coworker's actions, politely discuss the problem with the individual. A direct approach is much more kind and effective than gossiping about the individual or avoiding the problem.[8]

Special Problems with Coworkers

Some problems require special attention. These include sexual harassment, racial harassment, dating conflicts, and violence. This section reviews what you should know about each topic.

Sexual Harassment

Sexual harassment is unwelcome verbal or physical conduct of a sexual nature. The following list provides examples of sexual harassment but is by no means a complete list:

- Staring at another person
- Touching another person
- Telling sexual jokes
- Making sexual comments
- Commenting on a person's sexual characteristics
- Displaying nude pictures or obscene cartoons

Employers are required by law to protect employees from sexual harassment. You could be severely disciplined or fired for harassing a coworker sexually. The safest course is to avoid doing any of the things listed previously. Even if a person doesn't object to your behavior at the time, he or she might later claim to have been intimidated. It's better to be safe than sorry.

Racial Harassment

Racial harassment is unwelcome verbal or physical actions directed at a person because of his or her race. This might include these behaviors:

- Telling racial jokes
- Using racial slurs
- Commenting on a person's racial characteristics
- Distributing racist materials
- Excluding someone from company activities because of race

This form of harassment often results from ignorance. It's sometimes tempting to participate in the bad behavior of other workers. However, when someone engages in racial harassment, point out the harm that can result. Don't participate in any of these behaviors.

Dating Conflicts

You can get to know someone well by working together, and office relationships sometimes develop into romantic relationships. Many people find that the workplace is a natural place to meet people whom they would be interested in dating.

But dating a coworker can be risky. For one thing, romantic advances might be considered sexual harassment. In fact, repeatedly asking someone for a date after being turned down *is* considered sexual harassment.

Dating a coworker also can have a negative effect on your relationships with other workers. They might think that you take advantage of your romantic relationship, that you are not doing your own work but sharing work with your romantic interest, or that you support that person's ideas or actions simply because you are dating him or her.[9]

Another problem that can result from dating a coworker is that your attention is no longer on your job. You think about the other person instead of concentrating on your work. You might engage in romantic small talk rather than work, or find yourself supporting your sweetheart's actions and ideas even when you have doubts about them.

Another concern to think about is breaking up. What effect will your breakup have on your job performance and working relationship with the person? When you must work with that person every day, you might experience a great deal of discomfort and stress.

Some organizations have a policy prohibiting coworkers from dating or limiting who can date whom (for example, they might not allow a supervisor to date a person who reports to him or her). Be sure to find out whether your employer has such a policy. If you develop a romantic interest in a coworker, be discreet. Don't talk about it in the office. Don't spend any more time with that person than is normally required. Try to separate how you behave toward the person at work and on a date.

Conflict Resolution

Conflict resolution seeks to solve a disagreement between individuals or groups within an organization. The purpose of conflict resolution is to avoid emotions, stress, and violence while dealing with the facts. Companies usually have a process in place for employees to use.

First, attempt to resolve the problem between you and the other person. Go to the other person, and calmly discuss the problem.

If this attempt fails, go to your supervisor. Calmly and concisely, explain the problem. Given time, your supervisor may be able to deal with the problem.

But if your supervisor is unable to resolve the problem, go to human resources for help. If your firm doesn't have a human resources department, go to your supervisor's manager.

Remember that if another person violates the law and no one in the organization takes action, you should report it to the legal authorities. Realize that you may lose your job, but your safety is more important.

Violence in the Workplace

You have a one-in-five chance of being involved in a violent act at work.[10] Violence ranges from being struck to being raped or killed. People who kill their coworkers make headlines, but fistfights are far more common in the workplace. So what can you do to avoid violence? Here are some tips:

- People sometimes get angry. When you get angry in return, it creates the potential for violence. Tell the person that you want to solve the problem and that anger won't help. Walk away from the person if necessary.

- If a coworker threatens you with violence, notify your supervisor. You're not in school anymore, and there is no need to tolerate a bully. Coworkers who threaten violence can be fired.

- Violence sometimes occurs because a worker has mental or emotional problems. You might notice signs of this. A person who is a "loner" and who completely withdraws from other workers is exhibiting unusual behavior. Possibly this person lets stress build up and doesn't express it. Other workers might appear to always be angry; they might verbally or physically strike out at everyone. Still others might have mental illness such as paranoia. Talk with your supervisor when you observe strange behaviors like these.

- Violence often occurs due to marital disputes that spill over into the workplace. Don't hesitate to call the police when a spouse who should not be there enters the workplace or grounds.

- Follow all security procedures to protect yourself and coworkers. Keep doors locked, don't allow strangers into a building, and report suspicious behavior.

- Working in places open to the public—such as convenience stores—requires special security guidelines. Every retail chain has security guidelines. You should take time to learn the guidelines and follow them for your own safety and that of your coworkers.

Not all violence can be prevented, but following some simple guidelines can reduce it. Carefully observe your surroundings and people in the workplace. Report unusual situations to your supervisor or security guards.

A Useful Skill: Persuasion

Persuasion is the ability to convince others to change their minds or behavior. Because workers are expected to make decisions as a team, being able to convince your coworkers to reach a point of agreement is a very useful skill. Gaining a promotion or making changes in your workplace may depend on your ability to use this skill.

Studies have shown that some people may be more gifted at convincing others; however, persuading others is not a natural talent. Learning how to persuade others is a soft skill that is being taught in business schools.

When developing this skill, you need to observe people. Study how your coworkers and superiors think when making decisions. Some people ask questions when processing information. Others make statements. Some approach decisions in a calm manner, whereas others become very emotional. Recognizing these differences in individuals will make a difference in the methods of persuasion you use.

Summing Up

Becoming part of the work team is important to your success on the job. Your relationship with other workers will affect your performance. Your contribution to the team will influence how your supervisor appraises your job performance.

Getting along with your coworkers is not difficult. It takes an understanding of yourself and an appreciation of differences between people. Finally, it takes a commonsense approach to human relations. When all else fails, treat your coworkers as you would like to be treated.

CHAPTER 10

Meeting the Customer's Expectations

Customers are very important because they buy the business's products or services, providing income that the business needs to survive and make a profit. Without customers, a business will fail. Businesses conduct studies to learn what their customers want. By providing those services, the businesses build customer loyalty.[1] Government and nonprofit agencies must also serve customers well because their customers' satisfaction affects the agencies' public support and continued funding.

In this chapter you will learn about good customer service and the skills you need to provide it.

"Would you like me to wrap him up?"

The Customer Is Always Right

Providing good customer service is a key ingredient of any organization's success. Businesses spend billions of dollars advertising and promoting products or services in an effort to get new customers. A customer's decision to buy now and in the future is affected by how your organization can satisfy his or her needs in three areas: price, quality, and customer service. Which is the most important?

According to one study, businesses lose customers primarily for the reasons listed in the following table.[2]

Reason for Not Returning	Percentage of Respondents Citing It
Died	1%
Moved away	3%
Influenced by friends	5%
Lured away by the competition	9%
Dissatisfied with product	14%
Turned away by indifference on the part of an employee	68%

This study illustrates how critical customer service is. The service you provide to customers makes a major difference in their decision to patronize your organization or instead spend their money at another.

Most of us experience customer service daily when we go to the grocery store, buy gas for the car, eat at a restaurant, call a business, or buy clothes. Our most common activities often make us customers. Use the following exercise to think about your experiences as a customer and what good customer service means.

CUSTOMER SERVICE CHECKLIST

In the following checklist, mark the items that demonstrate good customer service.

❑ Smiling at customers

❑ Greeting customers

❑ Opening doors for customers

❑ Answering phone calls in a cheerful manner

❑ Forwarding a customer's call without first asking what his or her needs are

❑ Talking with friends while a customer waits

❑ Telling the customer that you want to solve his or her problem

❑ Asking a customer whether he or she needs help

❑ Letting a customer just wander around the store looking for something

❑ Listening politely to what a customer is asking

❑ Calling back a customer who has left a phone message

❑ Doing exactly what the customer requests

❑ Putting a customer on hold and letting him or her wait a long time

❑ Not expressing anger at a customer who yells at you

❑ Telling the customer about a bad customer service experience you had at another business

What things have happened to you as a customer that made you feel good about a business?

_____

_____

_____

_____

What things have happened to you as a customer that made you upset with a business?

_____

_____

_____

_____

In one or two sentences, define good customer service.

_____

_____

_____

_____

_____

One simple definition of good customer service is treating customers the way that you would like to be treated—perhaps the way that you would want your grand-mother treated. The exercise you just completed gave you some guidelines about how to do this. In the next section, we look at some specific ways to provide good customer service.

Providing Good Customer Service

Customer service begins the moment a customer contacts your business. This contact can be a face-to-face meeting, a phone call, a letter, a fax, an e-mail, or even a visit to the organization's website. Your treatment of the customer affects several possible reactions. First, it makes a difference in how the customer treats you. Second, it determines whether the customer buys the product or service your business is selling. Third, it affects what the customer thinks about your organization and whether he or she will return. The following business behaviors help make customers feel good about the service they receive.

Have a Good Attitude

Customer service begins with you and your attitude. It's easy to get caught up in the busywork that makes up every job and to think that it's the most important thing you do. But think again. Serving customers is actually the most important thing you do. When a customer asks for assistance, don't consider responding promptly as an interruption of your work. Instead, think of it as your primary job.

Too often, workers see customers as a nuisance. Frequently, these workers might keep talking on the phone, doing paperwork, or attending to other things while the customer waits. A customer senses this attitude, and the encounter starts off on the wrong foot. The next time that you think of a customer as a disruption, remember this: This is the person who actually pays your salary. Without customers, none of us is needed for the job.

Make the Customer Feel Good

Ken Blanchard, a leading business expert, says that if you deliver a hug along with everything else the customer expects, you can create a raving fan.[3] In Blanchard's view, a "hug" is any gesture designed to make the customer feel better. You should go out of your way to help customers who seek service from your organization. Be polite and courteous, and always think about the customer's needs.

Courtesy makes a business competitive. Seventy percent of respondents in one study cited courteous/helpful service as the most important reason for buying from a particular business. A nice smile helps make people feel happy. When you encounter customers, politely ask how you may help them. Say "Please" and "Thank you." Thanking customers for their visits or purchases, holding doors open, and carrying packages are all courteous actions that help customers feel good about your service.

Greet Customers

An organization's customers should feel welcome when they enter or contact the business. Many large discount and grocery stores now employ greeters to specifically welcome shoppers. Think about times when you've gone into a business only to have an employee ignore you. You probably don't feel like going back to the business again.

Whenever a customer comes into a business, immediately acknowledge his or her presence. A greeting should be polite and make the customer feel that you're interested and ready to help. For example, saying "Hello, may I help you?" indicates this attitude to a customer. Some employees make the following mistakes at this point—mistakes that you should avoid:

- **Don't keep talking with another customer.** Balancing the needs of several customers at once can be difficult. But it's important to do this; otherwise, a customer might feel unwelcome. When a second customer comes into your work area, politely excuse yourself from the first customer. Go to the new customer, and tell the person that you'll help him or her as soon as you're done with the other customer.

- **Don't keep doing another task.** Remember, giving customer service is your first and most important task. Have you ever gone into a business and had to wait for an employee to finish a task? How did it make you feel? Most people feel that the employee considers them less important than what he or she had been working on. Put aside your task, even if it means repeating previous steps.

- **Don't keep talking on the telephone or texting.** A customer who comes in person to your business took the time to travel there. You should show an appreciation for this by immediately paying attention to his or her needs. This is particularly true if the call is personal. Even when you are talking to another employee, it should be understood that the customer comes first. If you are talking with a customer on the phone, you might want to tell this person that you have to put him or her on hold for just a few seconds. While the first customer is on hold, explain the situation to the new customer and say you'll be with him or her as soon as possible.

Listen to the Customer

Practice good listening skills when talking with customers. The customer has all the information you need to provide top-notch service.[4] However, customers can't always express their needs clearly. Your role is to make sure that the customer's needs are unmistakable and understood by both parties. The following tips can help:

- **Be attentive.** Assure the customer that you are listening. A greeting can verbally express this fact. Look the person in the eye, and display body language that shows your interest. Smiling, nodding, and similar body language indicate that you are paying attention.

- **Listen without interrupting.** Let the customer explain what he or she wants without interrupting. Getting your point across and remembering your train of thought are more difficult when someone interrupts. You might have questions as the customer speaks, but wait until the person has finished talking to ask those questions. In fact, when you take time to listen to everything that the customer has to say, many of your questions get answered.

- **Ask questions.** Once the customer has expressed a need or placed an order, ask any questions you have. Ask open-ended questions that can't be answered yes or no. When the customer uses a word or term that isn't familiar to you, ask for an explanation. Perhaps the customer has "rambled," and you aren't sure what he or she needs. In this case, ask specific questions to help the customer focus his or her answer. For example, you might ask, "Exactly what are you trying to do?" or "What do you want to have happen?"

- **Repeat the need.** When you think that you understand what the customer wants, repeat it. This ensures that you both are clear about what is expected. If the customer confirms that you are correct, then you can provide the requested service. If there is still some misunderstanding, ask more questions and then repeat what you believe the customer wants. Continue this process until everyone is in agreement about what the customer wants.

- **Negotiate the final result.** In *The Customer Is Usually Wrong!*, Fred Jandt points out that it's not always possible to give the customer exactly what he or she wants.[5] When this happens, you must negotiate. Your goal is to create a win-win outcome, in which the customer and you each get something positive out of the situation. You might be able to do this by offering an alternative to what the customer wants.

For example, suppose that a person comes into a government employment program office and asks for assistance in preparing a resume. However, the program does not provide this service. It does offer a workshop on job-seeking techniques, which would serve the person better than a single resume would. The workshop teaches how to prepare resumes, but, more importantly, it teaches job seekers everything they need to know about finding a job. This is really what the customer needs. The customer wins because he or she has a real need met, and you win because the office can serve another person.

Take Action

As soon as you know what the customer wants, you can take action to provide the service or product. This is where you can make a positive impression. Give the customer the product and service he or she wants…and more. Meeting a customer's expectations results in a satisfied customer, but going beyond what is expected creates a satisfied and loyal customer. How do you go beyond what customers expect? Do exactly what they request. Then do something special. For example, let's say a customer orders a diet cola. Get the cola as quickly as possible, because this action is expected. Then tell the customer that refills are free—if this is restaurant policy. A free-drink policy is often assumed. You might know it, and regular customers might know it, but telling the customer makes him or her feel good.

How Job Savvy Are You?

Esther works as a nursing assistant in a hospital. A patient in her assigned area just had back surgery, making it difficult for him to get out of bed without assistance. In the past hour, the patient has put on the service light three times. Esther has always been busy doing something else when he called for help.

1. If you were Esther, what would you do to create a positive customer attitude?

   _____

   _____

2. What could Esther do to show exceptional customer service to the patient?

   _____

   _____

Janet works as an auto mechanic in an independent repair shop. One afternoon, she is at the shop by herself working on an alignment job when a customer comes in. Janet is at a point where it is difficult to stop what she is doing without having to repeat some of the work.

1. What should Janet do?

   _____

   _____

2. What can she do to make the customer feel welcomed?

   _____

   _____

Iliana works for an insurance agent. A policyholder comes into the office and wants to buy insurance coverage for her new computer. The customer didn't bring the serial number for the computer with her. Iliana can't complete the necessary forms for the coverage without the serial number.

1. How do you think this situation makes the customer feel?

   _____

   _____

2. What can Iliana do to help satisfy the customer's needs?

   _____

   _____

Basic Customer Needs

Every customer has specific needs. However, all customers come to an organization with some basic needs. Karen Leland and Keith Bailey identify six basic customer needs:[6]

1. Friendliness
2. Understanding and empathy
3. Fairness
4. Control
5. Options and alternatives
6. Information

As you serve customers, keep these basic needs in mind and try to meet them. If you do, a customer usually will be satisfied, even when you can't meet a specific need.

For example, let's say you go into a sporting goods store looking for a particular brand of running shoes. The clerk smiles and greets you in a friendly way, tells you the style you want is very popular, and comments on your wise choice in running gear. Next, he checks the stockroom and tells you that your size is not in stock. When he checks the computer record, he tells you that a new shipment of shoes will be delivered the middle of next week. The clerk gives you the option of reserving the shoes in your size—making it clear that you don't have to buy the shoes if you don't want them. He also tells you that the running store in the mall might have the shoes you want.

When you leave the store, you don't have the shoes, but chances are you feel good about the service you received because the clerk met your basic needs.

Good Customer Service on the Phone

Most businesses serve customers over the phone. Some enterprises—such as carryout restaurants, catalog dealers, and computer-support hot lines—do business primarily by telephone. Consequently, knowing how to give good customer service over the phone is important.

Answer the Phone Promptly

People calling a business expect to get an answer quickly. If the phone rings too many times, the caller often hangs up. Many businesses direct employees to answer a call in no more than three rings.

You should make an attempt to answer the phone as quickly as possible. Stop whatever else you're doing, and come back to the task after answering the phone. If you're talking with someone else, excuse yourself and answer the phone.

Greet the Caller Properly

You should give the caller several points of information when you answer the phone. First, identify your business by name so that customers know right away that they have reached the right number. Second, identify yourself by your first name. Giving your last name isn't necessary at this point because the caller probably won't remember both. Third, ask how you can help the caller.

Your greeting should change slightly if a receptionist or automatic answering service has greeted customers previously. In that case, customers already know that they have reached the proper business. You need only give your name and ask how you might help.

Listen to the Customer

To find out a customer's needs over the phone, follow the previously discussed guidelines for listening to a customer who comes to your business. Listening carefully to what the person is saying in a phone conversation is even more important than it is in a face-to-face encounter because, by phone, you aren't able to observe body language. Ask questions that help you understand what the customer needs. When you are certain that you know what the customer wants, repeat the message.

Take Action

Once you have heard what the customer wants, explain exactly what you are going to do. This reassures the caller because he or she can't see what you are doing. Once the customer understands what you plan to do, you can complete the action.

Putting a Customer on Hold

While trying to satisfy a request, you might have to put a caller on hold. Being put on hold can be frustrating. To make this a more pleasant experience for the caller, follow these steps:

1. Briefly explain what you need to do and why it is necessary to put the person on hold.
2. Estimate the time it will take to complete the action. For example, you might say, "It's going to be approximately a minute before I can get back to you."
3. Ask whether you may put the caller on hold.
4. Offer to call the customer back if your actions will take more than two or three minutes.
5. It might take longer than you had anticipated to complete the task, and your caller might become anxious. Time waiting on the phone often seems longer than it actually is. You can reduce a customer's frustration by picking up the phone and explaining the situation.

6. Inform the customer of the action you have taken, and thank him or her for waiting.

Putting a customer on hold can cause a negative reaction. The person might get tired of waiting and hang up, get irritated, call back and ask for a manager, or decide not to wait and never patronize the business again. Unless it is absolutely necessary, you should avoid putting a customer on hold.

Transferring a Call

At times, a customer needs help that only one of your coworkers can provide. In this case, you'd need to transfer the phone call to the other employee. Like being put on hold, being transferred can irritate customers. From their point of view, you are passing the buck or don't know your job—keep in mind that their perception might not be reality. Following these steps will help keep the customer happy:

1. Explain why you can't satisfy the request.

2. Tell the caller the name of the person who can fulfill the request.

3. Ask the caller whether he or she understands or has any questions before being transferred.

4. Make sure that the employee to whom you are transferring the call takes it.

5. If the employee is not available, explain that you will take a message and have that person return the call.

Taking a Message

If a customer needs to talk to another employee but that person is unavailable, you should take a message. Assure the customer that the call will be returned. As you take a message, follow these steps:

1. *In a positive way*, explain that the employee isn't available. For example, say that he or she is in a meeting, currently out of the office, or with another customer.

2. Tell the caller when you expect the other employee to be available. Speak in a general time frame, such as "today," "tomorrow," "at the end of the week," or "next week." If you expect the employee to return a call the same day, you might say the person is expected to be available "before lunch," "after lunch," or "by the end of the workday."

3. Ask the caller whether he or she would like to leave a message.

4. Ask the caller for a name, a phone number, and the reason for the call. If you aren't sure how to spell a name, ask.

5. Repeat the information to make sure it's correct.

6. Assure the caller that the message will be passed on and that a return call will be made.

7. Write the message in clear and readable handwriting.

8. After the caller hangs up, be sure to place the message somewhere that the other employee will see it. Some organizations have message boxes for this purpose. If you have to leave a message on an employee's desk, call the employee to make sure that he or she received it.

Good customer service requires that messages be received and calls be returned. Make sure that you do your part by getting the message to someone else. When a message from a customer is placed on your desk, return the call as quickly as possible.

Online Customer Service

Customer service is not limited to face-to-face encounters and phone conversations. With the use of online shopping, banking, and bill paying, dealing with customers online is an important part of the business world. Customers may be unhappy with merchandise or services. They might ask billing questions. Customers might not understand how to use the business's website and need help.

Good customer service online requires understanding what the consumer wants. The ability to write a clear, concise e-mail answering questions is very important. Just as important is replying promptly to the customer's e-mail. Call centers may reply with an e-mail limiting the number of business days that may pass before the customer receives a reply. If the answer is going to take some time, send an e-mail indicating when the information will be posted.

Chatting, another form of online communication, allows customers to talk with customer service representatives as if they were face-to-face. When you are dealing with customers online, it is important to reply in a helpful and courteous manner as if the customer were actually standing in front of you.

How Job Savvy Are You?

Burton works at Marconi's Pizza Shop. The shop has a dining room and a delivery service. Burton answers the phone between making pizzas. His hectic job allows little time for breaks.

1. What problems might Burton have in giving good customer service?

   _____

   _____

   _____

2. If you were Burton, how would you answer the phone?

   _____

   _____

   _____

(continued)

(continued)

Allison is a sales clerk in a dress shop. While waiting on a customer, she hears the phone ring. She is the only employee in the shop.

1. How should Allison handle the situation?

   _____

   _____

2. What should she tell the customer before she answers the phone?

   _____

   _____

Stephen, a reference librarian in a university library, is looking up information for a patron when the phone rings. The caller asks whether the library has last Wednesday's issue of the *Wall Street Journal*. He also needs to verify some statistics for a term paper.

1. What should Stephen do with the customer he is serving?

   _____

   _____

   _____

2. How should Stephen handle the customer on the phone?

   _____

   _____

   _____

Dealing with Difficult Customers

Occasionally you have to deal with difficult customers. The difficulty can result from the customer's complaint, anger, or rudeness. You can take some simple steps to help yourself and the customer in each of these situations.

Customers with Complaints

Every business receives customer complaints. Customers might complain because of a problem your organization created. For example, a customer might have gotten a faulty product or received an order late. A customer might feel that the product doesn't do what it should or that he or she received poor service.

At other times, a "problem" with your product or service might be the customer's fault. For example, a customer who broke the product, gave the wrong address for the product to be shipped to, or didn't read a description carefully before ordering a product might still want the company to fix the problem or share the blame. Regardless of the reason for the complaint, keep in mind that resolving a customer complaint will probably result in a happy and loyal customer. Try these steps for resolving customer complaints:

1. Listen carefully as the customer explains the problem.

2. If the customer is angry, let him or her vent the anger, as long as it is kept in control and doesn't offend you or other customers.

3. Ask questions until you are sure you understand the complaint, and then repeat what you understand the complaint to be.

4. Find out what will satisfy the customer. Often, the complaint can be satisfied with a direct action. For example, a faulty product can be replaced. Other times, a complaint can't be resolved immediately. For example, late delivery of a product can't be undone. However, efforts can be made to be on time with the next delivery.

5. Compare what the customer wants with the actions you can take. You may not be authorized to do everything the customer requests. If this happens, tell the customer that you must discuss the matter with your supervisor. You should also contact the supervisor when the customer requests to speak to someone with more authority.

6. Tell the customer exactly what you plan to do to resolve the problem. Be sure that you can follow through on everything you promise, or you'll end up with a bigger complaint later.

7. Take the action you promised, and let the customer know what is going to happen. Sometimes this is clear when you simply hand over a new product. Other resolutions are more involved—such as reprimanding an employee for rudeness.

8. Contact the customer after the action is taken, and make sure that he or she is now happy.

Angry Customers

Customers sometimes become angry, and there can be many reasons for their anger. Usually, the anger is in reaction to poor service or bad products. Now and then, customers carry over their anger from another event and unload it on your business. For example, a customer who has been arguing with a spouse over a purchase might come into your store angry. Use these guidelines to respond positively to an angry customer:

1. Tell the customer that you want to help correct the situation that made him or her angry.

2. Explain to the person that his or her anger is making it difficult to understand the problem.

3. Ask the customer why he or she is angry, and use the same process for clarifying a need that was explained previously.

4. Describe what you can do to resolve the problem, and ask the customer whether the solution is satisfactory. Most of the time, your solution will satisfy the customer.

5. When a customer does not respond to your attempts to resolve the problem, tell him or her that you'll get your manager to address the situation.

Rude Customers

Rudeness can be as mild as a simple lack of courtesy or as extreme as sexual or racial harassment. Most people are rude because of ignorance. Often, when someone points out that their behavior is rude, they stop. Some rude people get satisfaction from putting down others. You will not change their behavior by returning their rudeness or getting angry.

Giving good customer service doesn't require you to tolerate customer rudeness, however. You can deal professionally with a rude customer in a number of ways:

- Express to the customer that his or her rude behavior makes you uneasy.
- Tell the customer that you can give him or her better service when you are treated with respect.
- Ask how you can help, and provide the best service possible.
- Provide service without mentioning the rude behavior again, if it doesn't continue.
- If the rude behavior continues, contact your supervisor and ask for assistance.

How Job Savvy Are You?

A man with a pile of shirts comes into the dry-cleaning business where Abby works. He says the shirts weren't properly starched and packaged. Abby looks at the shirts and doesn't see any problem.

1. How should Abby deal with this complaint?

   _____

   _____

   _____

2. What should she do to keep this customer coming back to do more business?

   _____

   _____

   _____

Roscoe works in the produce department of a grocery store. A customer comes up to him and complains that she can't find the apples featured in the sales ad. When Roscoe looks for the apples, he can't find them, either.

1. How do you think the customer will feel when Roscoe says he can't find the apples?

   _____

   _____

   _____

---

2. What should Roscoe do to satisfy the customer?

_____

_____

_____

Marlene works in a child-care center. A mother comes into the room early one morning and begins yelling that her son's teddy bear wasn't sent home with him the day before. The children in the room are becoming upset.

1. What can Marlene do to immediately help calm the situation?

_____

_____

_____

2. What can Marlene do to help resolve the mother's complaint?

_____

_____

_____

Pete works as a teller in a large bank. This morning a customer came into the bank to close a joint savings account. When Pete told the customer that the account could not be closed without the signature of the other account holder, the customer began swearing loudly. Other customers seemed anxious to complete their business and leave the bank.

1. What can Pete do to make the other customers more comfortable?

_____

_____

_____

2. What can Pete do to help resolve the customer's complaint?

_____

_____

_____

A Useful Skill: Service Orientation

Business leaders are looking for workers who are service oriented. Service orientation is the skill of actively looking for ways to help people. Workers with this skill listen to customers to learn their wants and needs. Because workers often have more direct contact with customers, business owners use this customer knowledge in providing the materials or services customers need.

When workers are service oriented, their customers develop a loyalty to that particular company. This is profitable for the business. When a business can depend on returning customers, it becomes stabilized. Service orientation is a skill that you can use in any job that causes you to interact with others.

Summing Up

Knowing that the customer is the most important person in the organization and should receive good service is the key to business success. Employees must make customer service their number-one job. You can discover and meet customer needs by following some simple but critical steps. Keep in mind this fact: Customers don't interrupt your work—they *are* your work.

CHAPTER 11

Problem-Solving Skills

Managing an organization today is complicated. Competition from other countries is increasing, technology continues to grow more complex, and government regulations are sometimes difficult to understand and follow. Faced with these complexities, employers are looking for workers who are problem solvers.

Problem solving is a highly marketable skill. Employers need people who can think on their feet. Learning to solve problems is important to your success on the job. In this chapter, you'll practice seven steps to improving your problem-solving skills.

"Back to the drawing board, team. Five out of six of us incorrectly identified the problem as me."

Management Through Teamwork

Managers in today's business world rely on employees and work teams to help solve many problems—a process called *employee involvement*. These teams are sometimes referred to as *Total Quality Management (TQM)* teams. For example, if the data your team enters into a computer has a lot of mistakes, the team will be asked to solve the problem. There are several reasons for the growth of employee involvement, including the following:

- **Reduction of management:** In the last several years, businesses have made drastic cuts in the number of managers and supervisors they employ, thus saving a great deal of money. Consequently, employees must assume some of the responsibilities that managers previously performed.

- **Complexity:** Worldwide competition, high technology, government regulations, and a diverse workforce all make businesses more complex than in the past. An organization needs help from every employee to solve problems in these complex areas.

- **Motivation:** Employees are motivated to do a better job when they are involved in solving problems related to their work.

- **Proximity:** Employees work closer to most problems than managers and supervisors. They often see solutions that escape managers.

- **Change:** Modern organizations go through a great deal of change due to business acquisitions and mergers, changes in production means, expansion of products and services offered, and entry into world markets. If employers want their employees to be willing to change, they must involve them in problem-solving and decision-making processes.

Total Quality Management Teams

Experience has shown that the most effective way to manage workers is to involve them in the problem-solving process. Employees are more motivated when they have more control over their work. Participation in problem solving gives employees that control. Employee involvement is implemented through *Total Quality Management teams* or quality circles. A *quality circle* is a group of employees who meet to identify problems and find solutions.

A *process action team* is a similar group brought together from different parts of an organization to solve problems using statistical analysis.[1] Whatever these teams are called, more organizations are using them for problem solving and improving the quality of services, products, and jobs. A popular business-management strategy called Six Sigma is used in many organizations. You may be taught Six Sigma methods to help your team improve the quality of work it performs.

Employees who develop good problem-solving skills become valuable members of the team.[2] They are seen as good workers who should be rewarded with promotions and raises. The following section examines skills you need to develop to become a good problem solver.

Problem Solving

Problem solving is essentially a social process. It involves managing your thoughts and those of the group in an orderly and systematic process.[3] Several models provide a system for problem solving. This section combines the best ideas from many of these models.

Would-be problem solvers begin by adopting some basic assumptions that provide a foundation for good problem solving:

- **Problems can be solved.** The belief that a problem can be solved has motivated some of the greatest problem solvers of history. Thomas Edison, inventor of the light bulb; Henry Ford, the creator of modern manufacturing processes; and Jonas Salk, who discovered the polio vaccine, all persisted despite many failures. Edison failed more than 900 times before he produced a light bulb that worked.

- **Everything happens for a reason.** Problems have causes. Before you can solve a problem, you must look for the causes. Often, you can find only probable causes.

- **Problem solving must be a continuous process.** In other words, after finishing the last step in the process, you must return to the first step and begin the process again. This gives you the opportunity to evaluate whether the solution is working and whether it can be improved.

The problem-solving process can develop in a number of ways, but the steps and order that you follow are important. Leaving out any of the steps or doing them in a different order will limit your problem-solving abilities. Following are seven steps to effective problem solving.

Step 1: Identify the Problem

The biggest mistake you can make in solving a problem is to work on the wrong problem. Take time to discover what the real problem is.

Here is an example of the importance of this step. A tea shop manager notices that the store is frequently out of certain flavored teas. She defines the problem this way: "How do we get employees to order these teas when they see that we have run out of a flavor?" She then begins to work on getting employees to reorder teas.

However, the real problem could be something else. Perhaps the store orders a standard number of teas for each flavor when it should order larger quantities for more popular flavors. In this case, the problem should be defined as "How can we improve inventory control?"

Step 2: Gather and Organize Data About the Problem

You should gather as much data on the problem as possible. The best way to collect data is to observe what happens. Other good methods include talking with people involved and reading reports.

Organize the data in a way that will help you arrive at a solution. Called *analysis*, this organizing requires some mathematical skills. You can analyze data with three simple methods: frequency tables, percentages, and graphs. (Ask your instructor for more information about these methods.)

Step 3: Develop Solutions

After collecting data about the problem, you can use many different ways to develop as many solutions as possible:

- **Talk to other people.** Talk about the problem with coworkers who have experienced it. Find out how they have solved it in the past. One of the best ways to learn about something is to ask questions.[4] Ask friends from other organizations whether they have had a similar problem and how they solved it. (When talking to people outside your organization, do not reveal information about your business that would be considered confidential.)

- **Hold a group discussion.** The two most popular types of group discussion are
  - **Brainstorming:** In brainstorming sessions, a group of workers tries to come up with as many ideas as possible. There are some important rules to follow when brainstorming. First, don't criticize any ideas. You want those involved to suggest as many ideas as possible without being concerned about their quality. Second, stretch for ideas. When the group thinks it has exhausted all ideas, try again. Third, write all the ideas on flip charts so that the entire group can see what's been suggested.
  - **Nominal group technique:** This is a more controlled method of discussing a problem than brainstorming.[5] First, each person thinks of as many ideas as possible and writes them on a piece of paper. Second, the group shares these ideas, taking one idea from one person at a time in a round-robin manner. Third, the group discusses the ideas. Fourth, the group ranks or rates the ideas from best to worst.

- **Change places with other employees.** Spend four to eight hours in another department. See how other employees handle problems similar to the ones in your department. A change in roles often provides a new viewpoint that can help you solve a problem. This method also allows employees in another department to ask for your ideas about their problems. This interaction can generate many creative solutions.

- **Visit other organizations with similar problems.** You can learn a lot by discovering how other organizations solve their problems. Many businesses will let you visit if you don't work for a direct competitor. Look at their solutions, and evaluate how they solved similar problems. Ask how well they think the solutions work. Decide whether the solutions could be used in your organization.

- **Read about the problem.** Trade journals provide valuable information about how organizations like yours have solved problems. Trade journals exist for computer dealers, retailers, publishers, fast-food restaurateurs—the list goes on and on. Because trade journals deal with businesses just like yours, they publish articles that give helpful ideas for resolving problems. Other business magazines, books, or related websites also can give you some good ideas.

Step 4: Evaluate Possible Solutions

You should ask a number of questions when evaluating possible solutions:

- **Is the idea logical?** Look for a direct relationship between the problem and the solution. For example, giving dissatisfied customers a discount doesn't solve a customer-service problem.

- **How much will it cost?** You might have a great idea, but if it isn't affordable, it doesn't do the organization any good. Some problems are not complicated, so the solutions are not costly. However, costs for solutions to more complex problems can vary greatly. For example, pizza delivery time might improve if a store bought a new truck, but it might not be able to afford one.

- **Does the organization have workers who know how to implement the solution?** Some solutions require specialized knowledge. Without employees who have that knowledge, the solution won't work.

- **Is the solution timely?** Some problems need immediate solutions. Some ideas are good but take too long to implement. Sometimes, you must choose two solutions: one that works immediately and another that will be a better solution in the future. For example, a new copier will improve the quality of the company's printed documents, but it can't be delivered for three months. The immediate solution might be to keep the current copier and arrange a short-term contract to outsource more complex or large copy work.

Even after applying these rules, it's often difficult to select the right solution from a large number of ideas. Two ways to help sort ideas are rating and ranking:

- **Rating:** A process in which each idea is evaluated separately. You apply all four of the preceding questions to each idea. Then you rate the idea on a scale of 1 to 5, 1 being a great idea and 5 being a terrible idea. One drawback to this method is that you might end up with several ideas that are rated equal or almost equal.

- **Ranking:** A process that involves looking at all ideas, choosing the best, and ranking it number one. Then you compare the remaining ideas and select number two. Continue this process until all ideas have been ranked. A weakness of this method is that ranking more than 10 ideas at a time can be difficult.

Probably the best way to select the number-one idea is to use both rating and ranking. First, rate all ideas. Then rank the top 10. This uses the strengths of both methods and omits their weaknesses.

Step 5: Select the Best Solution

By the time you complete the analysis, you should be able to decide the best solution. The best solution might not always be the top idea, but it will usually be among the top three to five ideas. Keep the following three principles in mind when choosing a solution:

- **The best idea might not be affordable.** This means that you should select an idea that will solve the problem without greatly increasing cost. If the top two or three ideas are basically equal, select the least costly one.

- **Problem solving always involves risk.** No solution will be foolproof. Fears of risk often keep people from making a decision. You can try to reduce the risk, but you can't eliminate it.

- **Don't worry about being wrong.** Mistakes can't be totally eliminated. Think about what to do if the solution fails. Planning ahead for errors enables you to correct them more quickly.

Step 6: Implement the Solution

A good idea can be ruined if you fail to implement it correctly. Try these tips for putting solutions to work:

- **Believe in the idea.** Never implement an idea that you don't think solves a problem. If people believe an idea will be successful, it's usually easier to overcome difficulties that would otherwise jeopardize the solution.

- **Convince others to support the idea.** When a group solves the problem, you already have this step covered. Getting your supervisor's support for any idea is critical. Reaching a group solution helps convince your supervisor to support the idea. However, if you develop a solution by yourself, you need to "sell" it to other people and convince them that it's the right idea.

- **Don't let fear hold you back.** It's normal to be afraid of failure. You need to keep in check worries about losing your job or reputation if an idea fails. People sometimes wait too long before implementing a solution. Remember, inaction can kill a good idea.

- **Follow through.** A solution shouldn't be immediately rejected because it doesn't work. It takes time for ideas to work. Continue trying the solution until you know why it isn't working before taking a new approach.

Step 7: Evaluate the Solution

Within a reasonable period of time, evaluate the effectiveness of the solution and decide whether it's working. One good way to evaluate effectiveness is to repeat the analysis step (Step 2). For example, go back and do another frequency table to find out whether customers are happier or whether production or quality has improved.

Creative Thinking

Many organizations realize that they must be innovative to compete with other businesses. So employers want workers who think creatively. *Creativity* is the ability to think of new ideas. This might mean applying old ideas to new problems or coming up with entirely new ideas. These suggestions can help you think creatively.

Don't Let the Problem Limit Your Thinking

Our thinking process sometimes limits the way we look at a problem. The following exercise illustrates a common block to creative thinking.

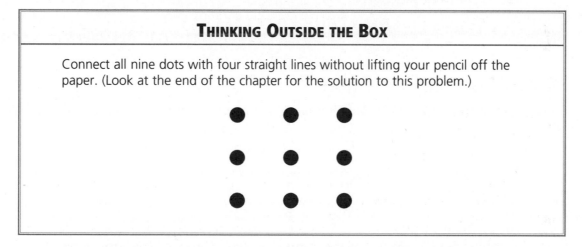

THINKING OUTSIDE THE BOX

Connect all nine dots with four straight lines without lifting your pencil off the paper. (Look at the end of the chapter for the solution to this problem.)

Look at the Problem from Different Viewpoints

Here's a simple way to do this. List ridiculous solutions to the problem. Then turn those ideas around, and ask how they might make sense. The following example illustrates this process.

Your supervisor has asked you and the other employees how to increase the number of customers who visit the shoe store where you work. Here are some "ridiculous" ideas:

- Give shoes away.
- Yell at people to come into the store.
- Carry every style of shoe made.
- Pay customers to take shoes.

Making these ideas workable would give you the following:

- Discount shoes as much as possible.
- Get people's attention through advertising.

- Have a wide variety of styles.
- Include a free pair of socks with each purchase.

Use Hazy Thinking

Other words for hazy are *unclear* or *vague*. Sometimes we're very specific and take things too literally in the problem-solving process. Maybe our thinking should be hazy and unclear. The next exercise illustrates how literal thinking can block creativity.

A DIFFERENT PERSPECTIVE

Look at the letters below. Eliminate five letters to find one familiar word in the English language. After you've tried solving the problem, look at the answer at the end of this chapter. This exercise shows that thinking in such specific ways blinds you to alternative ideas.

F H I E V L E I L C E O T P T T E E R R S

Joke About the Problem

Humor is a good way to find alternative solutions to a problem. Humor often relies on expectations. You are led to think one way and then are surprised after seeing another way. This old riddle is an example:

Question: What is black and white and read all over?

Answer: A newspaper.

When this joke is spoken, "read" is usually interpreted as "red" because "black and white" lead a person hearing it to think about colors. Humor might allow you to view the problem in an entirely different—and unexpected—way.

Give Yourself Time to Think

Take time to think about the problem and solutions. Relax, and look at the ideas you've come up with. Don't allow anything to distract you. Get away from phones, customers, coworkers, radios, televisions, and computers. Write down your thoughts during this time. Better yet, make an audio recording so that you're not distracted by writing.

Then get away from the problem. Do something entertaining. Get together with friends. Relax. Often this relaxation frees your subconscious to come up with more possible solutions.

There are other methods for being creative, such as brainstorming and researching a problem. There are many excellent books on creative thinking. Find one, and learn more about this valuable skill.

How Job Savvy Are You?

Yvonne works as a sales manager for a computer training company called Endevlo. Large companies send their employees to Endevlo for training during the day to learn the latest version of word-processing, spreadsheet, database management, and presentation software programs. The computer classrooms are seldom used at night. Yvonne's manager has asked her to assemble a team and develop a plan to use the classrooms during the evening hours.

1. Whom should Yvonne recruit for this problem-solving team?

   _____

   _____

   _____

2. Describe the characteristics that you think team members should possess.

   _____

   _____

   _____

   _____

3. What are some ideas that you would suggest to solve this problem? Why are these ideas good solutions?

   _____

   _____

   _____

Cyrus works as an assistant manager at the Clean-Up Car Wash. A customer complained to the manager that the car wash damaged her rear window wiper. The manager, Jia Li, asked Cyrus to determine whether this is a serious problem. If so, Jia expects Cyrus to come up with a solution.

1. What are some reasons that Jia Li would not automatically assume that damage to rear window wipers is a problem for the business?

   _____

   _____

   _____

2. What techniques would you suggest that Cyrus use to determine whether this is a problem?

   _____

   _____

   _____

(continued)

(continued)

3. Assume Cyrus discovers that several customers have experienced wiper damage at the car wash. How can he discover a way to solve the problem?

_____

_____

_____

4. What ideas for solving the problem would you suggest to Cyrus?

_____

_____

_____

_____

Lymon works as a cashier for a large discount retail store. The company wants more customers to sign up for a credit card. Lymon is assigned to a team that is expected to propose a solution to help increase the number of credit card applications. Reporting to the store manager, the group has suggested the following:

- Offer a bonus to the employee who signs up the most customers for credit every week.

- Offer customers a gift for signing up for the card.

- Give a gift certificate to employees every time they get a certain number of customers to apply for a credit card.

- Tell customers that every time they use a company credit card, a store employee will carry their bags to their cars.

- Give all employees a free lunch if the number of cards applied for in one month is higher than the count for the previous month.

- Offer a 10 percent discount to customers the first time they use a credit card.

1. How can Lymon's team determine which solution would be the best?

_____

_____

_____

_____

2. Are there common characteristics in these ideas that can be used to classify them into two or more groups? How can this help the team decide on the best solution?

_____

_____

_____

_____

3. Identify the idea that you think would be the best solution; explain the reason for your answer.

_____

_____

_____

_____

A Useful Skill: Complex Problem Solving

You will encounter problems on the job. Solving those problems requires individuals with complex problem-solving skills. As an employee, you will be valued if you develop these skills. As with other skills, your expertise will improve with practice.

The first step in complex problem solving is identifying the problem. Perhaps the problem seems obvious. However, it is unwise to assume that you recognize the problem without carefully reviewing the facts and observations.

One technique used to identify the basic problem is called "The Five Whys." In this instance, the obvious problem is stated, followed by the question "Why?" Each answer is followed by asking "Why?" Typically, after five whys, the real problem has been discovered.[6]

Once the problem is defined, examine different solutions. Consider each solution and its merits. After this evaluation, choose the best answer. Establish a plan to implement the solution.

Summing Up

Because they have a direct connection to the problem, workers involved with production and services at the basic level of a business are a valuable source of information to their employers. When communicating with clients, employees learn about customers' needs or dissatisfaction. In day-to-day work, they may observe ways to increase efficiency in the workplace. Their knowledge is useful in correcting problems.

Problem solving is an important skill for employees in modern business. Many organizations expect every worker to contribute solutions to problems. You should practice your problem-solving skills whenever you get the chance. These skills will improve as you apply the techniques in this chapter.

Solutions to Creative Exercises

Exercise 1: Most people see that the dots make a square. So they think they can't make their lines go outside this box. However, the instructions don't place this limit. You can't solve the problem unless you go outside the lines, as shown here.

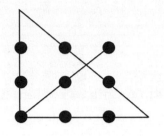

Exercise 2: You were told to cross out five letters to find one familiar word. Most people will try to follow this instruction by crossing out exactly five (5) letters. However, the way to solve the problem is to cross out the words *FIVE LETTERS*.

F H I E V L E I L C E O F P F T E E R R S

CHAPTER 12

Doing the Right Thing

Ethics are principles or standards that govern our behavior. Society usually sets many ethical principles. Communities, organizations, religions, and families establish additional ethical principles that guide people in their daily actions.

This chapter examines ethical behavior on the job. Ethical ideas govern the way that people behave toward employers, supervisors, coworkers, and customers. You'll also discover some basic principles that can guide you in making ethical decisions. To begin, let's look at how you view ethical behavior.

"Should we tell the boss that Carl is using the office copier to make his Christmas cards again?"

YOUR ETHICAL BEHAVIOR

1. List the reasons that ethical behavior is important.

   _____

   _____

   _____

2. List common ethical principles or ideals that most people observe.

   _____

   _____

   _____

3. Now list some job situations in which you would need to apply ethical principles.

   _____

   _____

   _____

Ethical Problems for Business

There are many reasons businesses are concerned about the ethical behavior of employees:

- Employee theft costs U.S. businesses billions of dollars each year. Small businesses often are the victims of their own employees' theft. According to a Small Business Administration report, approximately 30 percent of employees admit stealing from their employers.[1] A survey of top retail stores revealed that employee theft was 25 percent greater than the loss to shoplifters.[2]

- Employees who copy software illegally, sometimes referred to as softlifting, can cause an employer to be sued. Violation of copyright laws can result in fines of up to $250,000 and five years of imprisonment for each illegal use. The Business Software Alliance encourages informers to report violations.[3] An employee making illegal copies of software can be costly to an employer.

- Employees who use drugs on the job are 3.5 times more likely to have an accident.[4] Higher accident rates cost an employer more money in workers' compensation insurance payments and loss of productivity. More important, accidents harm people.

Unethical employee behavior costs businesses money and causes morale problems. Employees who behave unethically are almost always fired. In addition, bad conduct hurts those employees' reputations. Most people feel guilty about unethical behavior—even if they are not punished for it.

Common Ethical Dilemmas

At first glance, ethical behavior seems easy. All you have to do is "do the right thing." Knowing what the right thing is for every situation is the hard part. Also, what you consider "right" or "ethical" might differ from others' ideas about certain issues. Most people learn ethical behavior while growing up and use the same principles as adults.

Sometimes it's hard to know what is the right behavior. Most people face three basic dilemmas when trying to decide what is the right thing to do. The following sections describe these dilemmas.

Uncertainty About What Is Expected

At times, you face a situation and don't know what your organization considers the right or wrong response. For example, suppose that you deliver a package and the customer offers you a tip. As a new employee, you don't know whether the company allows you to accept tips. You also don't know whether you're supposed to report any tips.

What would you do in this situation?

_____

_____

_____

_____

_____

_____

_____

_____

_____

_____

Conflicts in Ethical Standards

A major problem can result when your ethical standards conflict with those of others. This kind of conflict can occur between you and your coworkers, you and your supervisor, or you and the organization itself.

Conflicts Between You and Your Coworkers

Suppose that you and two other workers are out on a repair job for a cable company. The other workers decide to report that the job took three hours, when, in fact, it took only two hours to complete. They plan to spend the extra hour drinking in a bar.

What would you do in this situation?

_____

_____

_____

_____

_____

_____

_____

_____

_____

_____

Conflicts with Your Supervisor

You might have ethical conflicts with your supervisor. Imagine that you work for a painting contractor. At the end of a day's work, your supervisor tells you to take some partially empty paint, varnish, and turpentine cans to the county landfill. You know that it's illegal to dispose of these materials in a landfill.

What would you do?

_____

_____

_____

_____

_____

_____

_____

_____

_____

_____

Conflicts with the Organization

Your ethics might conflict with those of the organization. This can happen when a company supports policies that you believe are wrong. For example, say that you work for a restaurant that regularly substitutes a lower grade of meat than is advertised on the menu.

What would you do in this situation?

_____

_____

_____

_____

_____

_____

_____

_____

Dilemmas About a Situation

Not every ethical decision is strictly right or wrong. In these situations, it can be very difficult to decide how to behave.

For instance, imagine that you are a bank teller. A coworker confides that he is working on a GED. You know that a high school diploma or GED is one of the bank's hiring requirements. The coworker apparently lied on his application. In the entire time you have known him, he has always done an excellent job as a teller. You know that he has a wife and two children who depend on his income from this job.

Should you tell your supervisor?

_____

_____

_____

_____

_____

Another example might include an overheard conversation. In the break room at an auto-parts factory, you overhear a coworker say that he would sure like to get Joe—a supervisor—alone in the parking lot one night. You know that the coworker has never done anything violent but can get very angry at times.

Should you report the person to a supervisor or some other authority?

_____

_____

_____

_____

_____

_____

Guidelines for Making Ethical Decisions

The problems illustrated in the preceding section show the difficulty in making ethical decisions. Did you have trouble trying to decide how you would act in the sample situations? Most people would have some difficulty.

However, there are some questions you can ask to help make ethical decisions and guide your behavior. You might need to answer several or all of the questions before you can make the right decision. Just because you can answer one of the following questions positively doesn't mean that the act you are considering is ethical.

- **Is it legal?** Will your decision and subsequent action violate local, state, or federal laws? Laws express the ethical behavior expected of everyone in a society. You should consider whether you could be arrested, convicted, or punished for your behavior. In the example of disposing of paint cans in a landfill, it's clear that doing what the supervisor wants is illegal. When you do something illegal, your behavior will not be excused simply because you were ordered to do it.

- **How will it make you feel about yourself?** A good self-concept is one key to doing the right thing. The book *The Power of Ethical Management* by Norman Vincent Peale and Ken Blanchard states, "People who have a healthy amount of self-esteem tend to have the strength to do what they know is right—even when there are strong pressures to do otherwise."[5] What you're really asking is this: Am I at my best? Most of us want to do our very best. We want to look at ourselves in the mirror without feeling guilt.

- **How do others feel about it?** You should discuss ethical problems with others. Sharing the problem with your supervisor might be uncomfortable or put your job at risk. In that case, talk with a coworker you trust. You can talk to friends, relatives, religious leaders, or anyone whose opinion and confidentiality you respect. Don't just talk to people you think will agree with you.[6] Listen to advice from others, but don't assume that the majority is always right.

- **How would you feel if the whole world knew about it?** What if someone made a video recording of what you did and posted it to YouTube? If you wouldn't want coworkers, supervisors, friends, relatives, the community, or everyone in the world to know what you are going to do, *don't do it*.

- **Does the behavior make sense?** Is it obvious that your proposed action could harm someone—including yourself—physically, mentally, or financially? Is it obvious that you will get caught? This last question shouldn't be the only thing you consider, but you should keep it in mind.

- **Is the behavior fair to everyone involved?** Ethical behavior should protect everyone's best interests.[7] Look at how everyone can benefit, but realize that everyone will not benefit equally by the decision that you make. No one should receive a great gain at the expense of someone else.

- **Will the people in authority at your organization approve?** How does your supervisor feel about the behavior? What would the manager of your department say? Would the organization's lawyer approve of it? Find out what those in authority think about the situation. This doesn't guarantee the right decision. Sometimes people in authority support unethical behavior. You aren't necessarily relieved of responsibility because a supervisor approves a certain act.[8] However, receiving approval indicates what behavior is thought to be right by people in authority at your organization.

- **How would you feel if someone did the same thing to you?** This is the Golden Rule: "Do to others what you would want them to do to you." When applying this principle, you should look at the situation from another person's point of view. Another way to view this issue was voiced by philosopher Immanuel Kant, who suggested that what individuals believe is right for themselves, they should believe is right for all others.[9] When you make an ethical decision, you should be willing for everyone else to do the same thing that you do. Avoid doing things you think would be unfair to you because they're probably unfair to someone else as well.

- **Will something bad happen if you don't make a decision?** Occasionally, you might decide to do nothing and it won't affect anyone. You might have good reasons for not wanting to get involved. However, you might be aware of a situation that could result in someone being hurt by your inaction. Not taking action when you think you should can result in a major problem.

Answer as many of these questions as you can when you are trying to make an ethical decision. Answering only one is not likely to result in the best ethical choice. The more principles that you can apply, the better your ethical choice will be.

How Job Savvy Are You?

Roger works at a branch office of the DMV. Recently he saw one of the driving examiners take a bribe from an elderly woman. Roger knows the woman. She lives alone and needs to drive her car to get groceries and do other business. He has never seen the examiner take a bribe before.

1. What do you think Roger should do?

   _____

   _____

   _____

2. Explain your answer.

   _____

   _____

(continued)

(continued)

Lisa works for a screw and bolt manufacturer that has a contract with the Air Force. Lisa knows that the bolts being made for the Air Force do not meet the required standards. She talked with her supervisor, and he said not to worry about it. He said it was up to management to correct the problem.

1. If you were Lisa, what would you do?

   _____

   _____

   _____

2. Explain your answer.

   _____

   _____

   _____

Jane works in a jewelry store. A customer left two rings for cleaning, but Jane accidentally gave her a receipt for just one ring. The customer didn't notice the mistake and left the store before Jane realized what she had done. One of the rings is quite beautiful. Jane thought about how nice it would look on her. She began to think about keeping the ring for herself and telling the manager the customer left only one ring. After all, the customer is very wealthy and can afford the loss.

1. What do you think Jane should do?

   _____

   _____

   _____

2. Explain your answer.

   _____

   _____

   _____

Now go back to the situations presented earlier in the chapter. Apply the ethical questions to them. What, if anything, would you do differently? Explain your reasons for each situation.

1. Taking a tip from a customer.

   _____

   _____

   _____

   _____

2. Taking an extra hour with the repair crew.

   _____

   _____

3. Dumping paint cans in the landfill.

_____

_____

_____

4. Substituting lower-grade meat.

_____

_____

_____

_____

5. Reporting a worker who lied on his application.

_____

_____

_____

_____

Common Ethical Problems

Workers often face common ethical problems on the job. This section covers seven situations in which knowing how to behave can keep you out of trouble.

Favoring Friends or Relatives

Favoritism poses a particular problem in any business that deals directly with the public. Some businesses allow employee discounts for immediate family members (father, mother, spouse, brothers, and sisters). However, friends might expect special deals and service. As a result, paying customers do not get proper service because of attention shown to friends. Know what your employer permits and expects in these situations.

List some ways that workers might show favored treatment to friends and relatives.

_____

_____

_____

_____

_____

Cheating Employers Out of Time

An employer pays employees for time spent at work. Some workers cheat the employer out of this time in a number of ways, including these:

- Breaking for longer periods than is allowed
- Talking excessively with friends and relatives while at work
- Coming to work late or leaving early
- Hiding someplace to avoid working
- Conducting personal business using office equipment
- Texting or sending personal e-mail messages
- Cyberloafing by surfing the Internet

This kind of behavior is irritating to supervisors. Less work gets done, and customer needs might not be satisfied. When employees behave this way, managers might take disciplinary action.

List some other ways workers can cheat employers out of time.

_____
_____
_____
_____
_____
_____
_____
_____
_____

Stealing from the Company

Taking money from the cash register and taking merchandise from a store are obviously stealing. However, workers often steal four other things without thinking of it as theft:

- **Supplies:** People often take pens, pencils, paper, paper clips, and other supplies from their employer. It doesn't seem like a big thing because the organization has so many supplies. However, multiplied by all the employees, this loss can cost an organization a great deal of money.
- **Photocopies:** Many employees use the copy machine for personal use without thinking of it as theft. However, it usually costs a business 2 to 5 cents per copy. Making 20 copies can cost $1. If every employee in an organization with 1,000 employees did this once a week, it would cost the employer almost $52,000 a year. Small thefts by workers can add up to major expenses for an organization.
- **Long-distance phone calls:** This is one of the more expensive crimes in business. Telephone companies charge more during business hours. Making

- **Software piracy:** Computers make it easy to copy software programs an organization owns. This is known as piracy. Global spending on counterfeit, packaged personal-computer software in 2010 was $58.8 billion according to a global software piracy study conducted by research firm IDC and the Business Software Alliance.[10] Some organizations fire employees caught pirating software.

What are other ways employees steal from their employers?

_____

_____

_____

_____

_____

_____

_____

_____

Software Piracy/Freeware/Shareware

Copying software illegally is called *piracy*. Just like books, music, and videos, software is protected by copyright laws. Commercial software is purchased, and the right to make copies is restricted.

Typically, you should follow three rules in order to avoid pirating commercial software:

1. Install the program on only one computer.
2. Make only one copy. This copy must be stored and used only if the original is damaged.
3. Never make copies for anyone else. A much more serious violation is to make a pirated copy and sell it.

Sometimes software is made available as freeware or shareware. *Freeware* means that the program developer allows anyone to freely make copies. *Shareware* means you can use the software and make copies for others. However, you are expected to pay the program developer if you continue to use the program.

Abusing Drugs and Alcohol

Drinking alcoholic beverages or using drugs on the job is wrong. Taking recreational drugs or prescription drugs (such as pain killers) without a doctor's prescription is against the law. Using them on the job can result in immediate termination. Substance abuse can generate three major job problems:

- **Lower productivity:** Employees under the influence of alcohol or illegal drugs produce fewer goods or services.
- **Lower quality:** It's impossible to perform at your best when you are under the influence. Your quality of work will be lower than your employer is paying you to provide.
- **Safety hazards:** Substance abuse can cause many safety problems. Reactions are slowed, judgment is impaired, and workers are more likely to suffer serious or fatal injuries.

List other problems that can be caused by substance abuse on the job.

_____
_____
_____
_____
_____
_____
_____
_____

Violating Confidentiality

Some employees have access to a great deal of information. If you are in a position to handle such information, don't talk to anyone about it. This includes other workers. Sharing confidential information about a company can cause great harm. Competitors can use trade secrets to duplicate proprietary products or services. With knowledge of another company's financial data, competitors can identify that business's weaknesses and strengths. Customer lists can be used to lure customers away. These and other pieces of information should be shared only with approved people.

- **Customers:** This could include private information, such as salary, credit history, or employment history. Stealing customer data—such as credit card information—can result in criminal prosecution and imprisonment. Accessing less critical information—such as the amount of money spent with your organization or a customer's address, e-mail address, and telephone number—could still cause harm to someone.
- **Employees:** This can include salary, personnel records, performance appraisals, or attendance records. Talking about any of this with others could harm the employee's reputation or cause other problems.

Many companies have policies about confidentiality. You should know your employer's policies. However, it's in everyone's best interest for you to keep all information confidential.

List other work information that should be treated as confidential.

_____

_____

_____

_____

_____

_____

_____

Knowing About the Unethical Behaviors of Others

One of the most difficult situations to face is knowing that another employee has done something wrong. There are two *reliable* ways of finding out about this type of situation:

- The other employee tells you personally.
- You see the employee do something wrong. If this happens, you should feel some obligation to report the problem to your supervisor.

Gossip is a less reliable way of finding out about another employee's misdeeds. You probably should not feel obligated to report to a supervisor any gossip you hear. In fact, when you don't have firsthand information about a situation, it's usually best not to repeat to anyone what you've heard.

List some things that you might discover about other workers, which you might need to report to your supervisor.

_____

_____

_____

_____

_____

_____

_____

Violating an Organization's Policies

Many organizations have a set of personnel policies to govern employee behavior. Policies are communicated through a policy manual, memos, or e-mail. As an employee, you are expected to follow these policies. You can be disciplined for violating them. It's important to know what the policies are and to follow them. Even if other workers get away with breaking the policies, you should not accept this as a good reason for breaking them yourself.

List some common personnel policies that an organization might establish.

_____

_____

_____

_____

_____

_____

How you deal with ethical problems determines how successful you will be on your job. The wrong behavior could cause your supervisor to be dissatisfied with your performance and could, in fact, cause you to be fired from your job.

How Job Savvy Are You?

Shane works in the payroll department. He has several friends in the computer department. One of these friends, Fran, told him that she just got a raise. Her supervisor told her that she is now the most highly paid programmer in the company. Shane knows that several other programmers have higher salaries than Fran has been promised. The supervisor has obviously lied to Fran.

1. Should Shane tell Fran what he knows?

_____

2. Explain your answer.

_____

_____

_____

Justine works in a doughnut shop. Some of her friends stop by late at night. She spends a lot of time talking with them, but there aren't any customers in the shop. A customer comes in, and Justine immediately asks whether she can help him. She then returns to her friends' table and starts talking with them.

1. Do you think Justine is doing the right thing by spending so much time talking with her friends?

_____

2. Explain your answer.

_____

_____

_____

Lance works at a fast-food restaurant. His family is very poor. The restaurant has a policy of throwing out hot sandwiches that aren't sold within 15 minutes. The policy also states that employees may not take any of the sandwiches for themselves. Lance's supervisor tells him to throw away 10 cheeseburgers. He thinks about how much his family could use the sandwiches. Instead of throwing them in the dumpster, he hides them in the back of the store and takes them home when he leaves work.

1. Should Lance have done this?

2. Explain your answer.

Demos is a project coordinator for a state health agency. The agency just upgraded the word-processing programs on everyone's computer. Demos has the discs from the older version of the program. The agency will no longer use these discs, so he decides to take them home and install that software on his personal computer.

1. Is Demos doing the right thing?

2. Explain the reasons for your answer.

A Useful Skill: Critical Thinking

Decisions made using critical thinking are based on logic and reason rather than emotions. A critical thinker identifies the strengths and weaknesses of alternative solutions to situations. Critical thinking requires a person's time and effort. After an evaluation, the individual reaches a conclusion and takes action.

Critical thinking is needed in a variety of work situations. A worker may use critical thinking when making ethical decisions or in solving a technical work-related problem. Workers who can assess problems and initiate solutions are valued in the workplace.

Summing Up

Supervisors evaluate workers based on their behavior. If they see workers doing something that they consider unethical, those workers will be disciplined. To maintain a good self-concept, you need to behave in a way that you feel is ethical. It's not always easy to know what is ethical. But if you apply the questions in this chapter, you will make the best decision when you face ethical problems.

CHAPTER 13

Getting Ahead on the Job

Two matters that usually concern workers who have been on the job for a few months are pay increases and promotions.[1] Workers in today's competitive labor market need to become valuable enough for companies to want their services, provide a raise, and promote them, because many companies quickly downsize when they face economic problems. This means that it is more important than ever to become a valuable asset to an organization. This chapter examines how you can achieve the goal of getting companies to recognize your skills and reward you for them.

"A cost of living raise is fine, as long as you realize I have an unusually expensive life."

You, Incorporated

A basic way to thrive in the workplace today is to think of yourself as a business. In Chapter 1, we looked at how you must be prepared to work as a core employee, temporary employee, or independent contractor. To be prepared, follow some basic principles:

1. **Understand that skills are the product you sell to an employer.** The strategy for selling yourself should focus on your skills. That is why you should know your strongest skills. Refer to the exercises in Chapter 7 to help identify your skills. For example, an employer pays a cashier for his or her ability to scan items, operate a cash register, and maintain good customer relations.

2. **Market your skills.** Discuss your skills with the employer during your job interview. When the opportunity comes up to use your skills within the organization, remind your supervisor about them. Apply your skills whenever you have the chance. Let coworkers know the skills that you can use to assist the team in accomplishing projects and tasks. Keep records of accomplishments that illustrate your skills. An oil-change mechanic who demonstrates an ability to use a computer may get a promotion into a customer service representative position when the opportunity occurs.

3. **Continually improve your skills.** Businesses today emphasize continuous quality improvement. This means always trying to provide customers more quality for their money. You can improve skills through experience and education by doing jobs and tasks that give you this experience—even when you are frightened by the possibility of failure. You can also improve your skills by taking advantage of educational opportunities that employers provide. An administrative assistant who attends a course to learn PowerPoint or some other software program has one more valuable asset than an assistant without this skill.

4. **Stretch out and learn new skills.** The more skills you have, the more valuable you are. You can learn new skills through continuing education, company training programs, and higher-education opportunities.[2] A computer repairer who attends classes and passes the tests for network administrator certification will become a much more valuable worker than if he or she hadn't.

5. **Monitor trends.** Keep track of changes in your occupation and the industry in which you work. Know how these trends will affect future activities and what skills you will need to keep pace with the change. For example, elevator operators were plentiful in the first half of the last century. These days, there's no such job. If operators had tracked the growing trend in automated elevators, they could have trained as elevator inspectors, retail salespeople, or some related occupation.

> ### Lifelong Learning
>
> Lifelong learning is the concept that a person's education never ends. Even after a person reaches educational goals such as high school graduation or completing a degree, the learning continues. Lifelong learning may take many different forms. Formal classroom education, online courses, seminars, and on-the-job training are examples.
>
> Companies may offer their own courses for employees through the human resources department. Some businesses have tuition-reimbursement programs, which help pay for college courses for workers returning to college. On-the-job mentoring programs use experienced employees to teach skills to other workers.[3] Industry-related conferences and seminars give employees a chance to learn about relevant topics from leaders in their field.

Getting a Raise

Organizations give pay raises for many reasons. Good pay helps businesses attract and keep good people. Raises are one way to reward good performance. The thought of earning more money can motivate employees to do a better job, but it's important to know when you can expect a raise. Unreasonable expectations can create misunderstandings between you and your employer. This could cause you to lose interest in your job and your employer to lose some respect for you.

An organization's policy on pay increases is usually discussed at the job interview. If it hasn't already been explained to you, ask your supervisor how pay raises are determined. The following list shows some common instances when employers give pay increases:

- **Completion of probation:** Probation usually lasts from one to six months. Organizations often give raises after an employee completes the probation period. Probation is considered a training period. After a worker completes training, he or she has demonstrated the ability to do the work the organization expects.

- **Incentive increases:** Organizations using this method give raises according to the quality of work during a certain time period. Typically, supervisors evaluate the work every six months or once a year. Pay increases are based on evaluations and job performance. Organizations that stress teamwork might give pay increases based on a team's evaluation.

- **Cost-of-living increases:** Companies sometimes give these raises to help employees offset inflation. Inflation is the increase in prices of things such as rent, groceries, and entertainment that lowers the value of the dollar. For example, if the cost of living rises 3 percent a year, at the end of that year it costs $1.03 to buy what cost only $1.00 the year before. In this situation, an employer might give employees a 3 percent cost-of-living increase so that the buying power of their pay doesn't decrease.

- **To keep employees:** Organizations may give highly valued workers pay increases to keep them from taking other jobs. If you receive a higher-paying job offer, it's appropriate to ask your employer for a raise. Don't use this approach unless you really have a better offer that you would realistically consider accepting. In addition to damaging your credibility, your employer may not be able to afford a raise and might tell you to take the other job.

- **Reward for special efforts:** Sometimes employees take on added job responsibilities. Employers may reward this behavior by giving raises. Some organizations reward employees for learning new skills. The more skills you learn, the more money you earn.

- **New assignments:** Companies normally give raises to workers who accept new positions in the same organization, especially if it means a promotion to a more responsible position. Some businesses give pay increases based on the number of jobs a worker learns to do. The more jobs you are trained to do, the higher your pay.

When you start a new job, make sure you understand your employer's policy on pay increases. You are less likely to be disappointed by the size of your pay raises if you know what to expect. Knowing how your employer gives raises gives you an advantage and the motivation to work hard to receive a raise.

Wage and Salary

A *wage* is a specific amount of money earned for each hour worked. A *salary* is a flat payment per week or month, regardless of hours worked. Employers are required by federal law to pay hourly workers an overtime rate for hours they work in excess of 40 hours per week. Salaried workers usually are more highly paid because they don't receive overtime pay. If the hourly workers are working a lot of overtime, it's possible for salaried employees to make less money than hourly employees in the same organization.

How Job Savvy Are You?

Keith is a grill cook at Humpty Dumpty Hamburgers. He was told he would receive a raise after working for three months and that he could be considered for another raise after six months. Keith has worked at the store for six months and still hasn't received a raise. Keith's supervisor has never talked with him about his job performance.

1. Do you think Keith deserves a raise? Why?

   _____

   _____

   _____

2. What approach should Keith take when asking for a raise?

_____

_____

_____

Roberta has worked as a clerk for Golden Auto Parts for more than three years. Each year she receives a 5 percent raise. During the past year, inflation was 6 percent. Roberta does a good job, and her supervisor frequently praises her for her work. She is concerned that if she receives the same pay increase this year as she has in past years, it will not be enough for her to live on.

1. What percentage of pay increase should Roberta ask for?

_____

_____

_____

2. How did you decide on the percentage?

_____

_____

_____

3. What approach should Roberta follow when discussing her raise?

_____

_____

_____

Barb has been a secretary at Newton Manufacturing Corporation for two years. Her performance appraisals have always been good, and she has received a good pay raise each year she's been with the company. Recently, Barb saw an ad in the newspaper for a secretary. The advertised pay was $1,000 more per year than she is currently making. Barb believes she has the qualifications needed for the advertised job, and she is upset that she isn't being paid more by Newton. She plans to go into the office on Monday and tell her supervisor she could have a job that would pay her $1,000 more than she is making.

1. Do you think Barb's plan is a good one? Why?

_____

_____

_____

2. What plan would you suggest?

_____

_____

_____

(continued)

(continued)

Wayne is a bookkeeper for Hall's Home Oil Company. A few months ago, his supervisor asked him to set up all the ledgers on a new computer system the company purchased. The new system has many advantages, and the managers now receive financial reports that help save the company thousands of dollars each month. Wayne works hard to keep the computer system working. He has begun to wonder why he has been given this new responsibility but no pay raise.

1. Do you think Wayne deserves a raise? Why?

   _____

   _____

   _____

2. What plan would you devise for Wayne to get a raise?

   _____

   _____

   _____

Getting Promoted

Many people want a more responsible position at their company, but organizations limit the number of supervisory and management jobs available. This means that promotions are harder to get. Promotions are often worth working hard for, however, because they have several advantages, including these:

- **Increased pay:** Normally, pay raises accompany promotions. However, sometimes a promotion to a salaried position is not much more money than an hourly worker earns with overtime pay.

- **More respect:** A promotion often increases your status within the organization and in society.

- **Better assignments:** A promotion usually provides more challenging work. Lower-level positions usually require less ability, and sometimes workers become bored in these jobs. A promotion offers a release from boring duties.

- **Improved self-esteem:** Your own self-esteem will improve when other people recognize you and your work. You'll feel better about yourself because of your success.

Preparing for a Promotion

Promotions typically are based on two major criteria: seniority and merit. *Seniority* refers to the amount of time on the job. Workers with more seniority often understand the organization and job better. *Merit* refers to the quality of job performance. Merit factors that most often result in promotions include leadership, communication, and technical skills. Both merit and seniority are considered when deciding which employee to promote. If specific skills or knowledge are required for the job, they are factored into the decision as well. If you want to be promoted, follow these tips:

- **Keep track of job openings.** When a job opening occurs, apply for the job. Talk to other workers. They usually know when someone is going to retire, be promoted, or leave for another job. Some companies post job openings by placing notices on a bulletin board, in the company newsletter, through memos, or by some other means.

- **Talk to your supervisor.** Tell your supervisor you are interested in a promotion. Supervisors should know where the vacancies are in the company. The supervisor can also provide guidance about the skills and experience that are normally needed to move into another job. Also, if you have a good work history, your supervisor should be willing to give you a good recommendation.

- **Notify the human resources department.** Let the human resources or personnel department know you want a promotion. They will ask your supervisor about your job performance and keep you in mind when openings occur. In some organizations, you should notify your supervisor before contacting the human resources department. Find out the proper process for your organization.

- **Create a network.** *Networking* refers to building friendships with coworkers in other departments. Secretaries and administrative assistants are excellent people to include in your network because they have access to a great deal of information. Ask people in your network to notify you when they hear of possible job openings. For a network to work well, you must be willing to share information and help others in the network.

- **Develop a good reputation.** Be a dependable, reliable employee and work hard. Get along with your coworkers. Become highly skilled in your job assignment. Supervisors and managers will notice and remember you when a promotional opportunity arises.

- **Create your own job.** It's possible to create a job for your own promotion. Look for ways to improve the organization. Make suggestions for accomplishing these improvements. Management might reward your creative thinking by placing you in a new job to carry out your suggestions.

Networking

Networking has proven to be one of the most effective job hunting techniques. You should include business acquaintances, social friends, and family in your network.[4] The network grows as you ask each member of the network to suggest others that could aid in the job search.

Networking is also a helpful technique when you are seeking a different position within your organization. To form a network, you need to build relationships with

(continued)

(continued)

> your coworkers. Don't limit yourself to those working in your department. Workers in other parts of the company may have access to information such as an upcoming retirement, an employee move, or a soon-to-be promotion that may mean a possible job for you.
>
> Not all networking is face-to-face. LinkedIn and other online professional social networks can be used to maintain contact with business associates anywhere in the world. LinkedIn has job postings as well as information about business opportunities and offers facts about other companies. Members list their work skills and interests.
>
> Remember that networking is a sharing of information. You are a source of information and support to others in your networking group. You have an obligation to them as well.
>
> One final suggestion: Keep in contact with the people in your network. Even if you move to a different department or a new company, you may need their input later in your career.

When Promotions Occur

Promotions occur only when an organization has a job vacancy or the money to create a new job. You need to be patient about getting a promotion. However, when someone with less seniority than you receives a promotion, you should ask why. Discuss with your supervisor the difference between you and the other worker. Ask for suggestions to improve your performance. Take your supervisor's advice. It will help you compete for the next promotion.

Sometimes it is important to play "office politics" to get ahead. Office politics may be the reason you are turned down for a job. For example, managers often promote people that they like. It is important to understand that being part of the "in-group" with your manager or supervisor increases the probability that you will receive a promotion. The way to become part of the in-group is to help the manager whenever there is extra work or new projects. Volunteer when a request is made. In addition, take advantage of invitations to lunch or social events that the manager provides.

1. List the skills and behaviors a worker needs to use to get a promotion.

   _____

   _____

   _____

2. Which skills or behaviors do you feel are most important? Explain your answer.

   _____

   _____

   _____

How Job Savvy Are You?

Lou has been a carpet layer at the Carpet Emporium for two years. He is dependable and gets along well with the other workers. He is very creative and often suggests timesaving methods of carpeting homes. Lou often criticizes and argues with the supervisor, but he always gets the job done.

Jan has worked at the Emporium for 16 months as a carpet layer. He also is dependable and gets along well with other workers. Jan took some classes in supervision at the local community college. He goes out of his way to help the supervisor and gets along well with him.

Business at the Carpet Emporium has been good. Management has decided to form an additional work crew to lay carpet. The department manager can't decide whether to promote Lou or Jan to supervise the new crew.

1. Who would you promote to the new supervisor's position?

   _____

2. Explain the reasons for your selection.

   _____

   _____

   _____

   _____

   _____

Jerry has been a secretary at Happy Acres Real Estate Agency for more than two years and is currently taking a real estate course at the local junior college. He will complete the course in time to take the real estate license test next month. He learned through the office grapevine that one of the agents plans to retire within three months. Jerry talked to the manager about a promotion to an agent's position.

Bobbi came to work for the agency six months ago. She has her real estate license but, because the agency wasn't hiring agents at that time, she took a position administering the deeds and titles in the office.

Jerry's information is correct. The agency is looking for another agent to replace the one who is retiring. The agency manager plans to promote from within the company rather than hire someone new. Jerry and Bobbi are the candidates.

1. Who would you promote to the agent's position?

   _____

2. Why did you choose to promote this person?

   _____

   _____

   _____

   _____

   _____

(continued)

(continued)

For the past two years, Marion has worked part-time for the Golden Years Home, a residential health-care center. Marion first started working in the home as a volunteer when she was a junior high school student. During high school, she worked as a kitchen aide. Marion is studying to be a licensed practical nurse while working weekends at the health-care center. The staff members know they can depend on Marion to be flexible. She has recently expressed an interest in working full time.

Terry has been a volunteer at the home for two years and is a recent high school gradu- ate. After graduation, she applied for a full-time position at the home and was hired as a nurse's aide. As a volunteer, Terry worked with the activities director during social times for the residents and helped plan many social events. Last summer, Terry traveled with the group to the Senior Citizens' Olympics, held in the state capital. The residents consider Terry an adopted grandchild.

Because of an increase in the number of residents, the health-care administrator has decided to create a new staff position—assistant activities director. Both Marion and Terry are being considered for the position.

1. Who would you promote or hire for this position?

   _____

2. Why did you choose this person?

   _____

   _____

   _____

   _____

   _____

Charlene has been a waitress at a French restaurant, Monsieur Jacques, for one year. Charlene is known for excellent service, and customers often ask to be seated at her tables. She receives very good tips because of her speed in serving customers, but she is impatient with the kitchen workers and those bussing tables when their work slows down her service. Charlene likes to work the business lunch crowd and usually refuses to work at other times. She knows many of the lunch customers by name and greets them as they are seated.

Alex has worked at Monsieur Jacques for two years. He is dependable and serves cus- tomers satisfactorily. Alex rarely visits with the customers, but he is always polite. He gets along well with coworkers and is willing to adjust to new work hours when needed. He even helps clear tables during rush hour. Last week the chef shared one of his secret reci- pes with Alex. No one in the restaurant has known the chef to do this before.

Due to an increase in business, the restaurant manager has decided to add a maitre d' during the lunch hour. This person would be responsible for greeting and seating cus- tomers and honoring reservations. Charlene and Alex are both being considered for the promotion.

1. Who would you choose as the maitre d'?

   _____

2. Why did you choose this person?

_____

_____

_____

_____

_____

Career Development

The term *career development* refers to the process of reaching your personal goals in work and in life. Career development may not seem important during the first few years of your work experience, but you should understand the process early in your career and use it to achieve your highest possible level of success. You can take several steps to develop your career within an organization:

1. **Explore job possibilities.** Find out what kinds of jobs are available in your organization. Most organizations have a variety of jobs. Discover the types of jobs available by asking other workers about their jobs.

2. **Identify your skills and abilities.** Get to know yourself. Identify what you do best. Match your skills with jobs in the organization that require those skills.

3. **Know your values.** Know what you want from your career. People define success in various ways. You may define success by your career achievements; or your job may be secondary to family, friends, and recreation. How much time and energy do you want to give to your job? What do you need to accomplish in your career to support your values? These are important questions to answer before setting a career goal within the company.

4. **Set a goal.** Decide on your ultimate job goal within the organization. Make sure this goal is realistic. If you want to be president of the company, are you willing to devote the time and effort required to do it? It may take months or even years before you know the organization well enough to set your career goal.

5. **Develop a career path.** What is the best way to advance to the position you want? You should ask yourself several questions about the job you want:

   - What special qualifications are needed for the job? How much experience is required? Is a license or certification necessary for the job?

   - What kind of education is needed for the job? What major area of study corresponds with the job requirements? Is a college degree necessary?

- How did other people get this job? What jobs did they have before they were promoted?
- What type of classroom or on-the-job training is needed?

6. **Write your plan.** Use the information collected in the preceding steps to create a career plan showing the progress you want to make in the organization. Put the plan in writing to motivate yourself to put forth more effort in reaching your goal. Include a timetable in your plan to show when you want to reach each job goal.

7. **Find a mentor.** A mentor is someone who takes a professional interest in you and advises you about your job. A mentor should be someone who is recognized and respected in the organization. Develop a mentor relationship by asking a person for help on a project or for advice on a situation. Another approach is to ask a person whether he or she is willing to mentor you.[5] Someone who enjoys helping you is more likely to be a good mentor.

8. **Keep a record of your accomplishments.** This is sometimes referred to as a *portfolio*. The human resources department or your supervisor probably keeps records of your work, but don't expect either of them to keep a detailed record of your accomplishments. You should do this yourself. Keep in a notebook or file any special skills you acquire, classes you attend, projects you complete, or ideas you suggest. When you apply for promotions, use these records to help prove your qualifications.

9. **Review your plan.** Look over your plan every six months, and review your progress. If you are pleased with your rate of progress, chances are you'll be motivated to continue to work hard to reach your goal. If you are unhappy about your progress, the review can help show what you need to do to make better progress.

10. **Change your plan when necessary.** Most plans aren't perfect. You will change, and so will your goals. When this happens, develop a new plan. If the organization changes, you will have to change your plan. You may even have to leave your current job and go to another organization to meet your goals.

You must take responsibility for your own career development. Companies won't do it for you, so you must take charge.

REFLECTED BEST SELF

E-mail or interview five people (family, friends, peers, subordinates, managers, professional associates, customers/clients, teachers, and so on) using this explanation:

The Work Experience course that I'm taking requires me to complete an exercise called "Reflected Best Self." I would appreciate your help in completing this activity.

Think about the times you have seen me at my best. What did I do that was meaningful to you, to people around you, or to an organization to which we belonged? What did I accomplish? What strength do you think I exhibited in achieving this accomplishment?

It isn't necessary to spend a great deal of time writing a response. Just one or two paragraphs will be sufficient. Please respond to this e-mail within the next two weeks. Thanks for your cooperation and support.

Analyze the responses. After that, reflect on the common themes that you find. Then write a self-portrait on the lines that follow. The self-portrait is a composition of what you learned about yourself. Write it in prose. The process is easier if you begin with one of the following phrases:

"I am at my best when..."

"When I am at my best..."

"People see me at my best when..."

_____

_____

_____

_____

_____

_____

_____

_____

_____

_____

_____

_____

_____

_____

_____

_____

Building a Portfolio

Artists and writers have long used portfolios to demonstrate their skills. An artist's portfolio consists of drawings, designs, paintings, and other works of art that show past accomplishments. Your portfolio should consist of examples that demonstrate your skills. The portfolio becomes a tool that you can use in an interview for a promotion or a job with a new employer. Discuss with coworkers and your supervisor what you can use to demonstrate your value to the organization. The following list shows some items that should be in everyone's portfolio:

- **Resume:** The resume should contain your name, address, phone number, and e-mail address. It should list and describe the jobs that you have held—including the dates when you worked for the employer. Also be sure to feature your most impressive accomplishments. List all schools you attended and the year you received a diploma, certificate, or degree.

- **Letters of reference:** Identify influential people in your life who would be willing to write a letter of reference. These letters should refer to specific examples of accomplishments. These letters might come from teachers, employers, volunteer service directors, community leaders, and religious leaders.

- **Transcripts:** Schools do not provide official transcripts to a graduate. However, they usually will give you an unofficial copy that you can include in the portfolio.

- **Continuing-education documents:** Include certificates from courses or training that you've completed. If you don't get a certificate, ask for a letter or some other form that documents your attendance. In addition, keep a copy of the class agenda or outline that you can use to document the skills you learned in the class.

- **Conference and association materials:** Keep a copy of all programs from conferences that you attend. Include membership certificates for professional associations, unions, and other work-related organizations.

- **Awards and honors:** Include awards and honors that you receive. These might come from schools, employers, or community organizations. Have a paper that explains how these items demonstrate skills that an employer might need.

- **Work output:** Your portfolio should include evidence that demonstrates specific skills. Examples of items that can be included in a portfolio include research papers, software programs, spreadsheets, electronic presentations, and photos of completed projects. You can also include specific products that you helped create, design, or build, such as books, clothes, mechanical items, or surveys. Be sure to obtain permission from an employer to include an item that might be considered confidential information.

You can also use a portfolio to assess your skills and plan for further education. Some colleges use portfolios to evaluate the experience and skills of potential students and to award college credit supported by the portfolio. In addition, having a portfolio to look at will help build your self-confidence.

With the increased use of electronic information storage, digital or electronic portfolios are being used to document work skills and job history. The information is basically the same, but the format is different. Software programs are available that make creating your own document simple.

Leaving a Job

Workers leave their jobs for many reasons. The reasons for resignations can be summed up in three general categories:

- **Job dissatisfaction:** Over time, you can become unhappy with a job because of personality conflicts or new management policies. Your career plans may not work out in the business. You will know you are not satisfied if you dread going to work every day.

- **New opportunities:** Even when you're happy in your job, you might be offered another job that pays more or provides more opportunities for promotion or better benefits. It can be difficult to decide what to do in these situations. In some cases you might stay at a job; however, you may very well decide to make a job change.

- **Avoiding disaster:** You may want to leave a job because something bad will happen if you don't. The business may close, leaving you unemployed. The company may lay you off, and you can't afford to wait for a recall. Maybe you know the supervisor is unhappy with your work and is going to fire you. You may decide to leave the job before one of these events happens.

The average person changes careers almost seven times in his or her working life. Chances are you will leave several jobs. You should understand how to change a career right from the start. Don't make a hasty decision to leave a job that you'll regret later. The following list offers some suggestions that can prepare you to leave a job:

- **Have another job waiting.** Normally, you should not leave a job without having another one lined up. The best time to look for a new job is when you are employed. Leaving a job to look for a job puts you at a great disadvantage. Even when you find a job, it will be harder to bargain for better pay or position if you are desperate for a paycheck.

- **Give reasonable notice.** The typical resignation notice is two weeks. Your employer may require a little more or less time than this. Find out from other workers the proper amount of time.

- **Submit a letter of resignation.** You may be asked to submit a letter of resignation. The only information required is stating that you are quitting and when you will be leaving. If you want to thank your employer and coworkers, write briefly. The *reason* for leaving is not required.[6]

Sharon Keys
435 Winding Way
Meridian, Iowa 50832

October 19, 20XX

Dr. James Hudson
Dean of Students
Bradford University
5234 North Street
Meridian, Iowa 50832

Dear Dr. Hudson,

I am officially resigning from the position of assistant dean of students. I will be vacating my position on November 1, 20XX.

During the last seven years it has been a privilege to work with you. I appreciate the knowledge I have gained through your guidance.

I am available to help in any way during this transition.

Sincerely,

Sharon Keys

Sharon Keys

- **Be tactful.** Don't resign in anger. You may be unhappy, but it isn't a good idea to tell your supervisor what you think is wrong with the organization. You need your employer for a reference and might even want to work for that person again someday. Tell the supervisor the main reason you are leaving and that you aren't angry about the situation.

- **Know the expectations.** Ask your supervisor what is expected during your remaining time on the job. There may be forms to fill out. Often the human resources department will conduct an exit interview to find out why you are leaving. Equipment, tools, uniforms, keys, or other items must be returned. Be sure to get a written receipt showing that you have returned the materials.

- **Don't be disruptive.** Coworkers will wonder why you're leaving. Don't complain about your current employer to them. Let them know you've enjoyed working with them and hope to keep in touch. Leaving a job can be sad because you often leave behind friends. If you want to be remembered as a good worker and friend, act accordingly on your last days on the job.

- **Leave immediately when asked.** Some companies require that employees leave immediately upon submitting a resignation. This occurs more frequently when an employee has access to computer-based information that the organization wants to protect. Don't take it personally.

The most important thing about leaving a job is to be fair to both your employer and yourself. Following the guidelines just discussed helps maintain a good relationship with an employer. Your employer will be happy to give you a good reference and may even rehire you in the future if you treat him or her fairly.

How Job Savvy Are You?

Tamara has been a clerk in the post office for five years. She recently completed a four-year degree in accounting and was offered a position with a public accounting firm. The firm wants her to start work in two weeks. Tamara must decide how to resign from her job at the post office.

1. What steps should Tamara follow to resign from her current job?

   _____

   _____

   _____

Eric is unhappy with his job. The supervisor has been giving him all the "dirty work." He has talked with his supervisor about the problem, but it hasn't helped. Eric found another job that pays better. The new employer wants him to start work immediately. Eric knows that his current employer expects at least two weeks' notice. However, Eric is so mad at his supervisor that he plans to call him on the phone to say he won't be at work anymore.

1. Do you think Eric should do this?

   _____

   _____

   _____

2. Explain the reasons for your answer.

   _____

   _____

   _____

A Useful Skill: Negotiation

Negotiation is the ability to bring together others and try to reconcile differences. In some instances this skill is applied to highly emotional situations that require reaching an agreement between employers and employees on a large scale.

This skill is also useful to you as an individual. When you want a raise or a promotion, you will need to negotiate with your supervisor. If your coworker disagrees with the way you are doing a task, you may need to come to a compromise. If a customer wants a refund and doesn't have the receipt, negotiation may occur.

To learn to negotiate, overcome shyness. Control your emotions. State facts, and listen to others. Mastering the skill of negotiating will make your job easier and more rewarding.

Summing Up

A job provides you with many opportunities, including pay raises, promotions, challenges, satisfaction, recognition, friendships, and a career. It's up to you to take advantage of these opportunities. By following the suggestions in this chapter, you can reach the career goals you set for yourself. Good luck on your journey!

In Closing

Y ou have an exciting future ahead. Your job is an important part of that future. It can provide you with the money you need to support a family, home, car, recreational activities, and lifestyle. To support your lifestyle, you must work hard at being successful in the job you have.

You have the ability to control your success by putting these skills into practice:

- Know what your employer expects from you and do your best to meet those expectations.
- Be a dependable employee who is punctual and works whenever scheduled.
- Dress and groom yourself to fit into the workplace.
- Learn to do your job well. Take advantage of opportunities to improve your skills whenever training is offered. Be a lifelong learner.
- Believe in yourself and in your abilities. Know your skills and apply them. Work to improve your weaknesses.
- Recognize the important role your supervisor plays in your job success. Listen, complete assigned tasks, and volunteer to help your supervisor. Make yourself an important part of the team.
- Cooperate and be friendly with coworkers. Your success can be built on the success of the work group.
- Participate in problem solving at work. Look for problems that you can help solve. Work with your supervisor and coworkers to solve problems.
- Be an honest employee. Your employer should be able to rely on your ethical behavior.
- Know what success on the job means for you. Plan your career and know how your current job fits into your career plans. If you want pay raises and promotions, know what your employer expects you to do to get them.

Follow these practical, simple guidelines. Then say to yourself, "Look out, world! Here I come!"

Sources

Chapter 1: Your Employment Relationship

1. Lucy P. Eldridge and Sabrina Wulff Pabilonia, "Bringing Work Home." *Monthly Labor Review* (December 2010), 18–35.

2. Mitra Toossi, "Labor Force Projections to 2018: Older Workers Staying More Active." *Monthly Labor Review* (November 2009), 30–51.

3. Rose A. Woods, "Employment Outlook 2008–2018: Industry Output and Employment Projections to 2018." *Monthly Labor Review* (November 2009), 52–81.

4. Alan B. Krueger and Sarah Charnes, "JOLTS as a Timely Source of Data by Establishment Size." *Monthly Labor Review* (May 2011), 16–24.

5. Bureau of Labor Statistics, Occupational Outlook Handbook, 2010–2011 edition online. Last modified date: December 3, 2010. Available at: http://bls.gov/oco/oco2003 .htm#education.

6. Bureau of Labor Statistics, Employment Projections: Education Pays.... (May 4, 2011). Available at: http://bls.gov/emp/ep_chart_001.htm.

7. U.S. Department of Labor, The Secretary's Commission on Achieving Necessary Skills, *Learning a Living: A Blueprint for High Performance—A SCANS Report for America 2000* (Washington, DC: Government Printing Office, 1992).

8. Anthony P. Carnevale, *America and the New Economy* (San Francisco, CA: Jossey-Bass Publishers, 1991).

9. American Society for Training and Development White Paper, "Bridging the Skills Gap: How the Skills Shortage Threatens Growth and Competitiveness...and What to Do About It." (Alexandria, VA: ASTD Press, 2006).

10. American Management Association, "AMA 2010 Critical Skills Survey: Executive Summary." Available at: www.amanet.org/PDF/Critical-Skills-Survey.pdf.

11. Craig A. Clagett, "Workforce Skills Needed by Today's Employers." *Market Analysis* (Washington, DC: ERIC, 1997).

12. Beverly Kaye and Sharon Jordan-Evans, "Engaging and Retaining Talent." *The Executive Guide to Integrated Talent Management*, Kevin Oakes and Pat Galagan (editors) (Alexandria, VA: ASTD Press, 2011), 121–132.

Chapter 2: Avoiding the New Job Blues

1. Steven Dunn and Dale Jasinski, "The Role of New Hire Orientation Programs." *Journal of Employment Counseling* (September 2009), 115.

2. Bureau of Labor Statistics, Employee Benefits in the United States—March 2011 (July 26, 2011). Available at: http://www.bls.gov/news.release/pdf/ebs2.pdf.

3. Michael R. Frone and Amy L. Brown, "Workplace Substance-Use Norms as Predictors of Employee Substance Use and Impairment: A Survey of U.S. Workers." *Journal of Studies on Alcohol and Drugs* (July 2010), 526–534.

4. Anonymous, "Section 125 Cafeteria Plans Must Meet Certain Criteria." *Payroll Practitioner's Monthly* (July 2011), 10.

5. Bureau of Labor Statistics, News Release: Employee Benefits in the United States—March 2010 (July 27, 2010).

6. Marsha Ludden, *Effective Workplace Communication,* 3rd Ed. (Indianapolis, IN: JIST Publishing, 2007), 23.

Chapter 3: Making a Good Impression

1. Flora Carlin, "Personal Packaging." *Psychology Today* (July/August, 2009).

2. Joseph Carroll, "'Business Casual' Most Common Work Attire: Women More Likely Than Men to Wear Formal Business Clothing on the Job." *Gallup Poll Briefing* (October 4, 2007).

3. Kate Rogers, "Summer Office Etiquette: No Flip Flops and Get Moving." FOXBusiness (July 14, 2011). Available at: www.foxbusiness.com/personal-finance/2011/07/14/summer-office-etiquette-no-flip-flops-and-get-moving/#ixzz1U5qMOz6Q.

4. U.S. Department of Labor, Occupational Safety and Health Administration, "Personal Protection Equipment 3151" (2003). Available at: www.osha.gov/Publications/osha3151.pdf.

5. U.S. Court of Appeals, District of Columbia Circuit Court of Appeals, "Potter v. District of Columbia." 558 F. 3d 542 (2009).

6. Nicolina Kamenou and Anne Fearful, "Ethnic Minority Women: A Lost Voice in HRM." *Human Resource Management Journal* (2006), 154–172.

7. Brian Elzweig and Donna K. Peeples, "Tattoos and Piercings: Issues of Body Modification and the Workplace." *SAM Advanced Management Journal* (Winter 2011, 76: 1), 13–23.

8. Cassandra Dillenberger, "Smoking in the Workplace: The Haze May Be Clearing." *Contractor's Business Management Report* (April 2010, Issue 4), 1–13.

9. Tim Alton, "Are iPods in the Workplace Music to an Employer's Ears?" *Indianapolis Business Journal* (February 26, 2011).

10. Matt Richtel, "Forget Gum. Walking and Using Phone is Risky." *The New York Times* (January 17, 2010).

11. Marsha Ludden, *Effective Workplace Communication,* 3rd Ed. (Indianapolis, IN: JIST Publishing, 2007), 25–34.

Chapter 4: Being There...On Time!

1. Anonymous, "17th Annual Unscheduled Absence Survey." *Medical Benefits* (December 15, 2007, 24: 23) 1–2.

2. Society for Human Resource Management, "Workplace Management." *HR Magazine* (May 2007, 52: 5), 124.

3. Chris Silva, "Wal-Mart Adopts Automated Absenteeism System." *Employee Benefit News* (February 1, 2007).

4. Roy Saunderson, "Absence Makes It Hard to Grow Fonder." *Employee Benefit Plan Review* (August 2009, 64: 2) 17–19.

5. Anonymous, "17th Annual Unscheduled Absence Survey." *Medical Benefits* (December 15, 2007, 24: 23) 1–2.

6. American Psychological Association, "Stress in America" (2010). Available at: www.apa.org/news/press/releases/stress/national-report.pdf.

7. National Heart, Lung, and Blood Institute, "In Brief: Your Guide to Healthy Sleep" (2006). Available at: www.nhlbi.nih.gov/health/public/sleep/healthysleepfs.htm.

8. Frank Newport, "For First Time, Majority in U.S. Supports Public Smoking Ban—Little Support for Making Smoking Illegal, However" (July 15, 2011). Available at: www.gallup.com/poll/148514/first-time-majority-supports-public-smoking-ban.aspx.

9. Jesse Wilkins, "8 Steps You Can Take to Better Manage Your Inbox." *Infonomics* (September/October 2009, 23: 5) 19.

Chapter 5: Communicating in the Workplace

1. Michael Laff, "3 Rs or 4 Cs?" *Training* (July/August 2010, 47: 4), 8.

2. Clive Shepherd, "The Multitask Assumption." *e.learning age* (December 2009/January 2010), 10.

3. Jennifer Robinson, "The Impact of Unconscious Communication." *Gallup Management Journal Online* (September 9, 2009), 1.

4. Shelley Widhalm, "What Did You Say: Body Language Often More Telling Than Words." *World & I* (December 2006, 21: 11).

5. Brian Johnston, "Body of Work: Greetings Around the World Can Take Many Forms—Should You Shake Hands, Bow, or Hug the Next Time You Do Business Abroad?" *Business Traveller Middle East* (May 1, 2007), 43.

6. John J. Kalter, "Friend Me: An Employment Law Perspective on Social Media." *On Balance* (November 2010, 6: 6), 6–9.

7. John J. Kalter, "Study Shows That Email Has to Change!" *M2PressWIRE* (April 14, 2010).

8. Peter Kenworthy, "How to Take Back Control of Email." *People Management* (November 15, 2007, 13: 23), 46–47.

9. Peter Kenworthy, "Managing Information Overload." *Trends Magazine* (October 2009, Issue 78), 32–34.

10. Randy Hines and Joseph Basso, "Do Communication Students Have the 'Write' Stuff? Practitioners Evaluate Writing Skills of Entry-Level Workers." *Journal of Promotion Management* (2008, 14: 3–4), 293–307.

Chapter 6: Learning—What It's All About

1. Joanne L. Stewart, "Train for the Future: Invest in Learning." *Training and Development* (July 20, 2011, 65: 7), 54–57.

2. Malcolm S. Knowles, Elwood F. Holton, and Richard A. Swanson, *The Adult Learner: The Definitive Classic in Adult Education and Human Resource Development*, 7th Ed. (Burlington, MA: Elsevier, Inc., 2011).

3. U.S. Department of Education, "The Condition of Education 2007." National Center for Education Statistics (Washington, DC: 2007 NCES 2007-064 Indicator 10). Available at: http://nces.ed.gov/fastfacts/display.asp?id=89.

4. National Association of Student Financial Aid Administrators, "2010 Federal Tax Benefits for Higher Education." NASFAA (Washington, DC: January 26, 2011). Available at: www.nasfaa.org/AnnualPubs/TaxBenefitsGuide.html.

5. Peter Senge, *The Fifth Discipline: The Art and Practice of the Learning Organization* (New York, NY: Doubleday, 2006).

6. John Naisbitt and Patricia Aburdene, *Reinventing the Corporation* (New York: Warner Books, 1985).

7. Mark Shoeff Jr., "Program Finds Education Can Fuel Inspiration." *Workforce Management* (January 30, 2006), 14.

Chapter 7: Knowing Yourself

1. Anthony P. Carnevale, "The Workplace Realities." *School Administrator* (February 2008, 65: 2), 34–38.

2. Joe Girard and Robert Casemore, *How to Sell Yourself* (New York: Warner Books, 2003).

Chapter 8: Getting Along with Your Supervisor

1. Martin W. Broadwell and Carol Broadwell Dietrich, *The New Supervisor: How to Thrive in Your First Year as a Manager*, 5th Ed. (Cambridge, MA: Perseus Books, 1998).

2. Anthony J. Urbaniak, "Giving Others Authority." *Supervision* (July 2010, vol. 71), 13–15.

3. Phillip S. Meilinger, "The Ten Rules of Good Followership." *A.U. Concepts for Air Force Leadership* (2001), 99–101. Available at: www.au.af.mil/au/awc/awcgate/au-4/meilinger .pdf.

4. Linda S. Henderson, "The Impact of Project Managers' Communication Competencies: Validation and Extension of a Research Model for Virtuality, Satisfaction, and Productivity on Project Teams." *Project Management Journal* (June 2008), 48–59.

5. LaVerne L. Ludden and Tom Capozzoli, *Supervisor Savvy: How to Retain and Develop Entry-Level Workers* (Indianapolis, IN: JIST Publishing, 2000).

6. The Dominon Post, "Reviews Are Just Part of the Modern Job." *The (Wellington, N.Z.) Dominion Post* (July 27, 2011), C9.

7. Richard E. Boyatzis, "Competencies in the 21st Century." *Journal of Management Development* (2008, 7: 1), 5–12.

Chapter 9: Getting Along with Other Workers

1. Gerben S. van der Vegt, Stuart Bunderson, and Ben Kuipers, "Why Turnover Matters in Self-Managing Work Teams: Learning, Social Integration, and Task Flexibility." *Journal of Management* (September 2010), 1168–1191.

2. Todd Henneman, "Making the Pieces Fit." *Workforce Management* (August 2011), 12–18.

3. Stephen Robbins and Timothy A. Judge, *Organizational Behavior*, 14th Ed. (Englewood Cliffs, NJ: Prentice Hall Higher Education, 2010).

4. David Keirsey, *Please Understand Me II* (Del Mar, CA: Prometheus Nemesis Books, 1998).

5. Mitra Toossi, "Labor Force Projections to 2018: Older Workers Stay Active Despite Their Age." *Monthly Labor Review* (November 2009), 30–51.

6. Jake Himmelspach, "Workplace E-mail: The Risky New Watercooler." *Grand Rapids Business Journal* (March 2, 2009, 27: 9), 17.

7. Kashmir Hill, "Tweets That Will Get You Fired." *Forbes.com.* (March 17, 2011). Available at: www.forbes.com/sites/kashmirhill/2011/03/17/tweets-that-will-get-you-fired/.

8. Philip Delves Broughton, "Does Your Office Have Bad Manners?" *Evening Standard* (August 10, 2009), 28.

9. Sean M. Horan and Rebecca M. Chory, "When Work and Love Mix: Perceptions of Peers in Workplace Romances." *Western Journal of Communication* (October–December 2009, 73: 4), 349–369.

10. Thomas Capozzoli and R. Steve McVey, *Managing Violence in the Workplace* (Delray Beach, FL: St. Lucie Press, 1996).

Chapter 10: Meeting the Customer's Expectations

1. John Allen, "Customer Loyalty." *Smart Business Houston* (August 2011, 6: 2), 6.

2. Betsy Sanders, *Fabled Service: Ordinary Acts, Extraordinary Outcomes* (San Diego, CA: Pfeiffer, 1995).

3. Kenneth Blanchard and Sheldon Bowles, *Raving Fans* (New York, NY: Morrow, 1993).

4. Robert Spector and Patrick D. McCarthy, *The Nordstrom Way: The Inside Story of America's #1 Customer Service Company* (New York, NY: Wiley, 1996).

5. Fred Jandt, *The Customer Is Usually Wrong!* (Indianapolis, IN: Park Avenue, 1995).

6. Karen Leland and Keith Bailey, *Customer Service For Dummies,* 3rd Ed. (Hoboken, NJ: John Wiley and Sons, Inc., 2006).

Chapter 11: Problem-Solving Skills

1. Douglas C. Montgomery and William H. Woodall, "An Overview of Six Sigma." *International Statistical Review* (December 2008, 76: 3), 329–346.

2. Wendall Williams, "Employee Competencies for the Future." *Journal of Corporate Recruiting Leadership* (May 2011, 6: 4), 15–17.

3. Joyce S. Osland, David A. Kolb, Irwin M. Rubin, and Marlene E. Turner, *Organizational Behavior: An Experiential Approach*, 8th Ed. (Upper Saddle River, NJ: Prentice Hall, 2006).

4. Ronald Gross, *Peak Learning: How to Create Your Own Lifelong Learning Education Program for Personal Enlightenment and Professional Success* (New York, NY: Putnam, 1999).

5. Gary Yukl, *Leadership in Organizations* (Upper Saddle River, NJ: Prentice Hall, 2005).

6. Randall Richard, "Ask 'Why?' Five Times to Dig Up the Real Root Cause of a Problem." *Central Penn Business Journal* (July 1, 2011, 27: 27), 11.

Chapter 12: Doing the Right Thing

1. Kevin M. Hart, "Not Wanted: Thieves," *HR Magazine* (April 2008, 53: 4), 119–123.

2. Kathy Finn, "Video Patrol." *FSB: Fortune Small Business* (November 2009, 19: 9).

3. Business Software Alliance, Eighth Annual BSA Global Software 2010 Piracy Study (Washington, DC: BSA, May 2011).

4. U.S. Department of Health and Human Services: Substance Abuse and Mental Health Services Administration Center for Substance Abuse Treatment, "What You Need to Know About the Cost of Substance Abuse: Issue Brief #7 for Employers" (2008), SMA 08-4350 – 2008. Available at: www.samhsa.gov.

5. Kenneth Blanchard and Norman Vincent Peale, *The Power of Ethical Management* (New York, NY: Morrow, 1988), 47.

6. Archie Carroll, *Business and Society: Ethics and Stakeholder Management,* 5th Ed. (Cincinnati, OH: South-Western, 2002).

7. Larue Hosmer, *The Ethics of Management,* 6th Ed. (New York, NY: McGraw-Hill Higher Education, 2007).

8. Manuel Valasquez, *Business Ethics: Concepts and Cases,* 6th Ed. (Englewood Cliffs, NJ: Prentice Hall, 2005).

9. Immanuel Kant, *The Moral Law: Groundwork of the Metaphysics of Morals* (New York, NY: Routledge, 2005).

10. Business Software Alliance, Eighth Annual BSA Global Software 2010 Piracy Study (Washington, DC: BSA, May 2011).

Chapter 13: Getting Ahead on the Job

1. Shari Bench, "Promotion: Get Ahead or Off with Your Head." *Supervision* (October 2010, 71: 10), 17–18.

2. Donna Rosato, "Three Smart Ways to Get Ahead at Work." *Money* (September 2011, 40: 8), 19.

3. Tom Camarda, "Lifelong Learning: A Necessity, Not an Option." *Manufacturing Today* (Winter 2010, 10: 1), 26–27.

4. Susan Adams, "Get a Job Using the Hidden Job Market." *Forbes.com* (July 5, 2011), 11.

5. Kenya McCullum, "Passing The Baton," *OfficePro* (July 2010, 70: 4), 16–19.

6. Marsha Ludden, *Effective Workplace Communication,* 3rd Ed. (Indianapolis, IN: JIST Publishing, 2007).

Index